Praise for *Snake Sisters and Ghost Daughters*

"In *Snake Sisters and Ghost Daughters*, Cathy Yue Wang dives into the rich repository of Chinese myths and legends and examines their adaptations in the modern and contemporary world through a feminist lens. Through extensive research and incisive reading, she makes available to the Western audience a dazzling array of Chinese sources, which are not cold gems frozen in the past but shifting dynamisms addressing current issues within and beyond China. Her critical mind and lyrical voice contribute to fairy-tale studies, genre fiction studies, and feminist scholarship in general and invite further explorations along the path she has paved for us."

—Zhange Ni, associate professor of religion
and literature, Virginia Tech

"Theoretically informed and skillfully written, this book deeply engages with a wide range of fantastic female figures in contemporary adaptations of traditional tales. Weaving cognitive narratology in close textual analyses to reveal dynamic communications between readers and writers, Wang makes excellent contributions to the interdisciplinary studies of Chinese fantasy."

—Liang Luo, author of *The Global White Snake*

"Built on a methodology that applies perspectives from feminism and cognitive narratology to adaptations of Chinese fantasy narratives, this innovative work teaches us new ways to think about intertextuality and cultural tradition. It is vital reading for anyone interested in movements in contemporary Chinese film and fiction."

—John Stephens, editor of *The Routledge Companion
to International Children's Literature*

"*Snake Sisters and Ghost Daughters* is as intriguing as its title. Having watched and waited for Chinese children's literature scholarship to explode on the international stage, this book's commitment to tracing adaptations of Chinese traditional stories is a welcome contribution to a rapidly growing body of research in this area. It will prove useful to both the scholars of children's literature wishing to consider the rich traditions and its entanglement with the fantasy genre."

— literature, Newcastle University

D1218486

SNAKE SISTERS AND
GHOST DAUGHTERS

The Donald Haase Series in Fairy-Tale Studies

Series Editor

Anne E. Duggan, Wayne State University

Founding Editor

Donald Haase, Wayne State University

Donald Haase

A complete listing of the advisory editors and the books in this series can be found online at wsupress.wayne.edu.

SNAKE SISTERS

AND

GHOST DAUGHTERS

*Feminist Adaptations of Traditional
Tales in Chinese Fantasy*

Cathy Yue Wang

Wayne State University Press
Detroit

© 2023 by Wayne State University Press, Detroit, Michigan, 48201. All rights reserved. No part of this book may be reproduced without formal permission.

ISBN 9780814348628 (paperback)
ISBN 9780814348635 (hardcover)
ISBN 9780814348642 (e-book)

Library of Congress Control Number: 2022951623

Cover design by Philip Pascuzzo / Pepco Studio.

Published with the assistance of a fund established by Thelma Gray James of Wayne State University for the publication of folklore and English studies.

Wayne State University Press rests on Waawiyaataanong, also referred to as Detroit, the ancestral and contemporary homeland of the Three Fires Confederacy. These sovereign lands were granted by the Ojibwe, Odawa, Potawatomi, and Wyandot Nations, in 1807, through the Treaty of Detroit. Wayne State University Press affirms Indigenous sovereignty and honors all tribes with a connection to Detroit. With our Native neighbors, the press works to advance educational equity and promote a better future for the earth and all people.

Wayne State University Press
Leonard N. Simons Building
4809 Woodward Avenue
Detroit, Michigan 48201-1309

Visit us online at wsupress.wayne.edu.

Contents

Acknowledgments

This book began its life as my doctoral thesis. I would like to thank my doctoral advisors John Stephens, Sung-Ae Lee, and Victoria Flanagan, who have patiently guided and helped me throughout the process. This book would not have taken shape without their support. I am also indebted to the staff of the International Youth Library at Munich. The friendly environment they created during my stay there encouraged me to work productively. Special thanks are owed to Lucia Obi. I am very grateful to the anonymous reviewers of the book for their thoughtful and thought-provoking comments. I thank Emily Gauronskas, Carrie Teefey, Marie Sweetman, Kelsey Giffin, and everyone at Wayne State University Press for making this book possible to publish. It took me eight years to complete this book—four years while doing my doctorate at Macquarie University in Australia and another four years at Shanghai Normal University in China, where I am currently a lecturer. I'm lucky to have some wonderful colleagues and friends in both the universities and the two countries. I would like to thank the members of the children's literature writing group at Macquarie University and the Innovative Team of International Comparative Literature at Shanghai Normal University. Lastly, special thanks are reserved for my family. My mother Zhixiang used to read me bedtime stories when I was young, so that's where the idea for this book came from. She never stopped encouraging me to pursue my dream. Wuyang was once a close friend and is now a wonderful life partner. I appreciate Tiancai, my cat, for keeping me company.

Portions of chapter 3 and chapter 4 appeared in "Chinese Folklore for Modern Times: Three Feminist Re-visions of The Legend of the White Snake" (*Asian Studies Review*, 2020). An earlier version of chapter 6 was first published in the article "Disappearing Fairies and Ghosts: Female and Child Characters as Others in Chinese Contemporary Children's Fantasy" (*Children's Literature in Education*, 2020).

Introduction

The modern and contemporary adaptations of traditional stories enjoy constant popularity all around the world, to the extent that every generation tends to produce their own version of the most beloved stories and tales. Among the many modern genres, fantasy may be the one that has the closest relationship with old stories. Since the beginning of the twenty-first century, especially after 2010, China's bustling film industry has experienced a boom of fantasy blockbusters based on classical literary novels and tales.[1] The classical literary works these films are based on embrace a wide range of historical periods and a diverse range of genres, from the legendary story of White Snake (*Baishe zhuan*), which originated in a Song dynasty *huaben* and circulated mainly in vernacular stories and dramas in the Ming and Qing eras, to the masterpieces of the Ming dynasty vernacular novels *Investiture of the Gods* (*Fengshen yanyi*) and *Journey to the West* (*Xiyou Ji*), to Pu Songling's *Strange Tales from Liaozhai* (*Liaozhai Zhiyi*), a tale collection dating back to the Qing dynasty written in Classical Chinese that has been influential in its time and afterward.[2]

---

1. The big screens in myriad cinemas have been occupied by these films: Gordon Chan's *Painted Skin* (*Hua pi*, 2008) and its sequel, *Painted Skin: Resurrection* (*Hua pi II zhuansheng shu*, 2012, directed by Wu Ershan); Ching Siu-Tung's *The Sorcerer and the White Snake* (*Baishe chuanshuo*, 2011); Wilson Yip's *A Chinese Ghost Story* (*Qian nü you hun*, 2011); Stephen Chow and Derek Kwok's *Journey to the West: Conquering the Demons* (*Xiyou xiangmo pian*, 2013) and its sequel, *Journey to the West: The Demons Strike Back* (*Xiyou fuyao pian*, 2017, directed by Tsui Hark); Cheang Pou-soi's *The Monkey King trilogy* (*Xiyou Ji zhi danao tiangong*, 2014, *Xiyou Ji zhi sun wukong sanda baigujing*, 2016, and *Xiyou Ji zhi nüer guo*, 2018); Koan Hui's *League of Gods* (*Fengshen chuanqi*, 2016); and the list goes on.
2. In this book, names of Asian origin are listed surname first. For works published in English, names are listed as they are published, typically in Western form. Transliteration will be used for author names that are Internet pseudonyms. If a novel or a film has been distributed internationally with an English-language title, I will use that title, with original titles following. Non-English words and phrases are italicized.

In Linda Hutcheon's seminal study *A Theory of Adaptation*, she delves into the cultural practice of adaptation by asking several empirical questions: What? Who? Why? How? When? Where? (xvi). In Qin Liyan's article on the intertwinement of Chinese film and literature, she also tries to answer two interrelated questions: what Chinese filmmakers choose to adapt during different periods, and how they adapt different kinds of literary sources (363). Combining and simplifying their questions, I chose two questions to start my book on adaptation in Chinese fantasy narratives: Why do creative artists and media producers wish to adapt these novels, instead of others, and what purpose do their story retellings wish to achieve? In which ways do they approach these pre-texts and what strategies do they employ during the process of adaptation?

The answer to the first question, apart from the apparent financial appeal and personal preference, could be handily summarized by one word: familiarity. Viewing the list in the beginning paragraph, we envisage that it is the familiar stories that are often adapted. As Hutcheon notes, they are adapted not only because they *are* familiar, but because they *should* be familiar ("Harry Potter" 173, original italics). They are stories that are worth knowing, for they are part of the cultural capital and social heritage of one culture, "transmitting many of a culture's central values and assumptions and a body of shared allusions and experiences" (Stephens and McCallum, *Retelling Stories* 3). Besides being lucrative, retold classics bear significant cultural and ideological functions.

The values and ideologies that implicitly prescribe the parameters of traditional stories are historically contingent and culturally constructed entities. In the Chinese context, traditional stories are produced and circulated under male-, adult-, and human-centered ideologies generated by Confucianism. This value system was centrally concerned with the question of "how to establish a harmonious secular order in a man-centered world" (King 65). In other words, beliefs in the superiority of male over female, of adult over child, and of human over other creatures are the three ideologies ingrained in the pre-modern stories and tales from myths to folktales to full-length genre fiction. These ideologies, when confronted with the globalized impact brought by the narratives of feminism, children's well-being, and animal studies, are under severe challenge. In the meantime, traditional stories also provide a counter voice for people who wish to formulate and propose a local identity without imported influence, in an attempt to resist the unbalanced cultural exchange brought by globalization. Therefore, adaptation becomes a battlefield where conflicting powers are engaging and contesting.

In the postsocialist Chinese context, such contestation is complicated and intensified by a social background composed of an economic capitalist system (a fiercely competitive society and corresponding high expectation of the intellectual and profit-making ability of new members in society) and a conservative culture (a largely normative society and rigid cultural censorship). The newly adopted market system and its pursuit of profit is part of the reason why so many film and other media adaptations of classical literature have appeared recently, and the political and cultural factors are responsible for the changed, or unchanged, messages conveyed by these adaptations.

This book engages with the unequal power relationships between male and female visible in the adaptation of old materials in contemporary society. The power struggle within this gendered domain is manifested in the textual transformation from ancient tradition to modern and contemporary discourse. In foregrounding the centrality of gender politics in the transformations of stories, I aim to offer a critical reflection of adaptation works in the contemporary Chinese context.

Chinese traditional literature, bringing together both classical and vernacular fiction, abounds with supernatural women, such as goddesses, celestial women, animal spirits, female ghosts, and sorceresses. Fantasy narratives produced in contemporary China innovatively rewrite and adapt alien woman in their narratives, drawing parallels between these supernatural characters and more standardly marginalized members of society: women and children. For this reason, these characters hold a paradoxical position. On the one hand, as either fairies or ghosts, witches or vampires, they enjoy such supernatural powers as flight, clairvoyance, and shape-shifting, which are unavailable to human beings in their natural state, and thus they have the potential to break normative rules and perform miraculous feats; on the other hand, they are also discriminated against for their otherness and otherworldliness. As John Stephens's analysis of witch figures in recent Western children's fiction illustrates, they represent both "the subaltern" and "the subversive" ("Witch-Figures" 195–202). In that they provide alternative scenarios and possibilities, supernatural characters, along with their fantasy narratives, are latently subversive of the dominant and conformist ideology, which is itself informed by a belief in rationality. In particular, alien women figures, representing female others, are capable of interrogating the cultural and social expectations of normative femininity in patriarchal societies.

To answer the second question, what strategies have been employed during the process of adaptation, the formal and aesthetic aspects of narrative discourses should be takin into consideration. According to John Stephens and Robyn McCallum, "the ideological effect of a retold text is generated from a three-way relationship between the already-given story, the metanarrative(s) which constitutes its top-down framing, and its bottom-up discoursal processes" (*Retelling Stories* 4). The bottom-up production of narrative discourses, ranging from the cutting and expansion of characters and plots to the shift in chronotope, focalization, and language style, has an impact on the readers' comprehension and understanding of the stories as well as the reinforcement and contestation of the grounding ideologies. In delineating the transformation of traditional stories across a wide range of genres and mediums, this book hopes to shed new light on issues such as gender and status hierarchy, marriage and family life, and in-group/out-group distinction. In combination with ideological interrogation and formal and aesthetic analysis, this book seeks to provide an empirically as well as theoretically rigorous examination of adaptation in a Chinese context. On the one hand, the cultural and historical specificity of Chinese examples is fully acknowledged, while on the other hand, the Chinese adaptations are integrated into a world history of adaptation rather than held apart as unique. This study of adaptation in Chinese fantasy, as an interactive dialogue between studies of adaptation and retelling in the West and East Asia, contributes to the academic examination of the complicated negotiation between the past and the present, tradition and the modern, the elite and the popular, the East and the West, and text and reality in a globalized and postmodern world.

Engaging Readers in Adaptation Studies

Existing studies of adaptation in the Chinese context have generally failed to emphasize the crucial role readers have played in the story-understanding process. These studies are either medium-centered or text/author-centered. Many studies of film adaptation of literature have been devoted to the specific relationship between the two mediums, and they usually tend to emphasize medium specificity even though not prioritizing one over the other. Other studies provide an extended and detailed case study of one specific story cycle. Such diachronic readings offer meticulous examinations, but are sometimes inclined to ignore the synchronic relationship between contemporary adaptations of other works. As Hutcheon remarks on various adaptations of one specific text, multiple versions exist laterally, not vertically (*A Theory of Adaptation* xv). Even though these versions are produced chronologically, readers and audiences do not necessarily experience them in the same order. Similarly, many adaptations of different works also exist laterally, and to better understand adaptation in contemporary China as a creative art as well as a cultural practice, we need more inclusive methods and more general scope. A more nuanced and balanced method is required in adaptation studies.

The interdisciplinary approach of cognitive narratology offers enormous potential for the study of adaptation. Theories about scripts and schemas help to illustrate how "the particularity of an individual work is at least in certain respects comprehensible only by reference to the ways in which it relates to a more general pattern" (Hogan 9), and cognitive narratology provides new analytic tools to rethink intertextuality to include social and political contexts. Conceptual blending is an effective way to destabilize old scripts and create new scripts. As Stephens comments, on the one hand, readers construct a mental model from the narratological elements of the text. On the other hand, readers also "inhabit a context of interpretation, and thence draw up analogous models based in the world they themselves inhabit and know." Meaning lies in the exchange ("Narratology" 52). This context of interpretation includes both social and cultural context, such as the gender, class, and culture to which an individual reader belongs, and literary context, which is the knowledge of a literary tradition, genres, and tropes. And the exchange from which meaning is born is particularly crucial for adaptations. Combining the scientific aspects of structuralist narratology and the ideological framework promoted by postclassic narratology, cognitive narratology reveals the process of the generation of meaning in readers' narrative understanding and reception of transformative works.

This interdisciplinary perspective locates this study at the intersection of China studies, adaptation studies, media and communications studies, and East Asian pop cultural studies. A broad array of materials from diverse genres and periods enables this study to traverse the divide between modern and premodern in Chinese literary studies and to bridge genre studies and ideological critics.

Chapter Overview

The structure of subsequent chapters is broadly organized around crucial genres in Chinese folk narrative and literature with fantastic elements: adaptations of myths, folktales, classic literary texts, and so on. I am not attempting to produce a comprehensive and encyclopedic research into adaptation in China. My corpus, which encompasses both highbrow literature and popular cultural products, works in various media forms, includes texts for both young and adult audiences, and provides a group of imaginative scenarios in which readers can engage and reflect their learned literary traditions and their lived experience.

The first chapter lays the theoretical background within which to understand the complicated and manifold cultural practice of adaptation, complete with discussion of common academic terms in recent adaptation studies. By mapping three predominant ideologies behind Chinese traditional stories: the subordination of wives to husbands, of children to parents, and of subjects to rulers, this chapter articulates an intersectional feminist approach to examining the contestation between old and new ideologies in the context of contemporary China. It concludes by introducing analytical frameworks that are part of the critical methodology.

Chapter 2 provides an account of the Chinese fantasy tradition and its status quo. It explains the Chinese literary tradition of the fantastic and supernatural that existed before fantasy as a modern Western genre came to China. This tradition began in ancient myths and morphed into strange tales (*zhiguai*) produced during the Six Dynasties, the Tang tales (*chuanqi*), the vernacular novels about gods and demons from the Ming and Qing dynasties, and the martial arts fiction that flourished in the Republican era. Within this Chinese fantastic tradition, I choose several seminal canonical works that have been most popular and influential among generations of readers and have thus become part of the nation's cultural capital. These stories are naturally retold and adapted endlessly, incorporated into educational curricula and upheld as cultural icons of Chinese identity. They embody significant ideological values and expectations that legitimate certain actions and attitudes, with special focus on gender norms.

The next four chapters are case studies that each deal with a separate subgenre of traditional tale alongside its contemporary adaptations. Chapter 3 focuses on the transformation of Chinese mythology. The mythology of a culture, being usually its earliest oral and/or written records, initiates a divine authority that becomes the foundation for many other traditional materials. Whereas the Judeo-Christian creation myth features an absolute God as creator, the corresponding Chinese myth recounts how the goddess Nüwa repaired the toppling sky and created people. The goddess Nüwa seems to validate the existence of a primitive matriarchal culture before the advent of phallocentrism. An episode in *The Classic of Mountains and Seas* describes a country inhabited only by women. The brief description gives no detailed explanation of this strange place, but identifies its two basic elements, women and water. Based on this fantastic description, later vernacular fictions such as *Journey to the West* (*Xiyou Ji*, ca. 1592) and *Flowers in the Mirror* (*Jing Hua Yuan*, ca. 1827) reimagine such a kingdom of women by depicting it either as an all-female community or as a kingdom whose power structure is matriarchal. Many contemporary novelists find an emancipatory potential in the goddess Nüwa and a matriarchal utopia. Employing the strategy of defamiliarization to reverse the power relationships between the sexes, the imagination of a matriarchal society requires readers to recognize the sexist ideologies of the real world. However, literary construction of female-dominated societies is still based in binary opposition, often without enough interrogation. Chapter 3 critiques a select group of contemporary Chinese matriarchal fiction.

Chapter 4 examines the metamorphoses of a folkloric script of interspecies romance, as exemplified by "The Legend of the White Snake." Folktales function as a form of sociocultural heritage and offer models for interpreting experience in everyday practices, but the beliefs and values conveyed by many folktales are those ingrained in patriarchy. Thus, the models they offer are challenged by the modern emphasis given to women's perspectives. The well-known story of the White Snake has been transformed to cater to modern progressive attitudes on gender and sex. By focusing on the modern adaptations of the White Snake legend by female authors—Hong Kong author Li Bihua's novel, *Green Snake* (*Qingshe*, 1986), Chinese American author Yan

Geling's novella, "White Snake" ("Baishe," 1999), and two online novels—this chapter examines how contemporary female authors incorporate and adapt old folktales in their separate narratives. These novels challenge inherited literary and cultural tradition, interrogate and question its gendered discourse as defined by the heteronormative patriarchal family structure, and suggest ways in which non-normative sexuality and gender roles can be imagined and practiced by female members of the society.

Chapter 5 turns to strange tales epitomized by the Qing dynasty author Pu Songling's works. The chapter mainly deals with the adaptation of two iconic tales, "Painted Skin" ("Hua pi") and "Nie Xiaoqian," both of which feature otherworldly female characters. Unlike the primary sources from chapter 4, which are fictions produced by elite and popular authors, this chapter's focal texts are visual media products, including blockbuster films and animations. The discussion of the melodramatic film *Painted Skin* (2008) and the carnivalesque animation *Xiaoqian* (1997) shows that these works are capable of reflecting social issues as well as questioning ideological attitudes. In a society primarily dominated by male authority, age-old conventional burdens preserved in various traditional stories still restrain and inhibit the realization of agency and fuller development of the marginalized members of the society, and subversive and innovative adaptations that diverge from familiar scripts can encourage a more critical and reflective view of traditional stories and their implicit values.

Chapter 6 introduces another type of power imbalance, intergenerational conflict between children and adults. The primary texts under analysis here are two children's fantasy novels, *My Mother Is a Fairy* by Chen Danyan (*Wo de Mama shi Jingling*, 1998) and *Jiujiu from the Ghost Mansion* by Tang Tang (*Laizi gui zhuangyuan de Jiujiu*, 2010). Both novels feature a marginalized otherworldly female/child character. An intersectional approach allows us to see the interconnections between patriarchal ideology, parental authority, and anthropocentrism: to see how these characters are subject to a triple rejection, being simultaneously female, nonhuman and nonadult. These two novels are found to construct a binary opposition between the fantastic-female-child and the rational-male-adult, with the latter dominating both the female and the child by repressing their propensity for imagination and fantasy. However, although these fantasy novels might seem to conform to the ideological status quo in terms of the patriarchal family structure, they also have a subversive edge in the way that the binary opposition between male and female is transgressed. Such novels point to the formation of a new kind of intersubjective relationship that is based on understanding and acceptance rather than refusal and dominance.

This book examines the processes by which contemporary Chinese authors and film directors reshape traditional fantastic tales to develop new narratives. In order to interrogate the hierarchy of male over female within traditional Chinese stories, contemporary adapters employ innovative narrative techniques to create transgressive space. This investigation of the process of textual transformation also takes into consideration shifting social-historical contexts and seeks to discover ideologies behind old stories and their ideological implications for modern society. The relationship of fantasy to reality in the adaptation process allows for some retellings of older materials to interrogate and resist conservative gender ideologies. This book does not intend to determine whether particular adaptations are faithful to their original texts but rather seeks to explore what new meanings are generated in the new texts, and why they are being generated.

1

Feminist Adaptation in the Contemporary Chinese Context

This book examines adaptations of traditional stories in the contemporary Chinese context. The influential theory of intertextuality informs us that the meaning of a work of literature is not produced by its self-contained linguistic system but built from systems, modes, and traditions established by previous works of literature and art forms, as well as more general social and cultural discourse. In other words, the intertextual web of narrative proliferation does not exist in a conceptual, economic, and political vacuum. Therefore, the investigation of the process of textual transformation should also take into consideration shifting social-historical contexts and seek to discover the changing and unchanging messages behind stories as well as the ideological implications inherent in stories for contemporary society. Different adaptation strategies, exemplified by changes to the familiar plots and characters, and various choices of narrative voice, perspective, and language styles, ineluctably contribute to the reinforcement and distortion of ideological frames preserved in the traditional stories and genres.

This chapter sets up the coordinates that frame the study. I begin with a discussion of different academic terms in recent adaptation studies and articulate their input for my research. Since this study scrutinizes adapted texts for their critical deconstruction of power structures inherent in the source materials, a mapping of the three predominant ideologies behind Chinese traditional stories, and a delineation of the cultural context of contemporary China upon which old and new ideologies are contested in myriad adaptations and retellings are needed. Among several power relations, gender inequality is the main focus of this book. However, I employ a broadly intersectional approach to examine the gender politics behind adaptations. An intersectional approach will allow us to see the interconnections between patriarchal ideology, parental authority, heteronormativity, nationalism, and anthropocentrism in their construction of hierarchical structures. Following the delineation of several basic concerns in my study of adaptation and retellings, I will situate this study in relation to previous scholarship within adaptation studies, taking into account the East Asian context in order to counterbalance the polarized East-West divide. The major theoretical framework upon which my book is grounded is cognitive and affective narratology. I will show the benefit of introducing these theories into adaptation studies by two brief cases.

Key Concepts in Adaptation Studies

The impulse to tell a story over and over is perhaps an inherent human propensity: the folklore within the oral traditions of many cultures is formulaic in its patterns. Children, especially at a very young age, tend to listen to their favorite story again and again. The popularity of genre fiction lies in its predictability. In a way, repetition is at the heart of adaptation. However, the same element is never precisely the same. Therefore, adaptation is the same with a difference, or as Hutcheon notes, adaptation is a form of "repetition without replication" (*A Theory of Adaptation* 176).

What is an adaptation? In the broadest sense, adaptation describes "the capacities for human, cultural, and biological adjustments as a way of surviving, advancing, or simply changing" (Corrigan 25). It primarily refers to a text that reworks an older story or several stories to suit a new purpose or environment. I refer to earlier versions of adapted texts as "pre-texts."[1] To recognize or suspect a pre-text (or more than one pre-text) establishes a horizon of expectations with which to interrogate the focused adaptation. In this book, adaptation is viewed as both a process and a product (Hutcheon, *A Theory of Adaptation* 15–16) as well as an aspect of reception (Corrigan 23) and critique

---

1. According to Stephens and McCallum, "to be a retelling a text must exist in relationship to some kind of source, which we will refer to as the 'pre-text,' though it is perhaps only a minority of cases in which this source is fixable as a single work by an identifiable author. Even when this is so, few retellings are simple replications, even when they appear to reproduce the story and point of view of the source" (*Retelling Stories* 4).

(Venuti 38). I use the terms *adaptation* and *retelling* interchangeably, in their broad senses, to refer to the "repetition with variation" of texts across time, culture, and all media types.

The prevailing impression concerning adaptation is premised on a change of media, notably from print to film. Recent developments in adaptation studies have moved beyond the unidirectional movement of literature to film and toward a broader scope of transmedia creation (Cartmell and Whelehan, *Screen Adaptation* 13; Murray 41; McCallum 2). In this new era of globalization and online communication, the boundary between professional and amateur, reader and writer, is radically blurring, and retellings and adaptations are becoming more and more transmedial and intertextual. A core and original text has become less and less visible; instead, multiple texts form a network of intertextuality.

Multiple linguistic terms are associated with adaptation and retelling. The most noticeable include *intertextuality, sequel, spinoff, fan fiction, remade*, and *transmedia storytelling*. In the following sections, I offer a preliminary clarification of the literal denotations and cultural connotations of several key words in adaptation studies and enunciate their relationship to my study.

Intertextuality

Intertextuality has become an essential component of contemporary adaptation theories, as the adapted text is compared with not only the pre-text but other adaptations and similar texts in an ongoing dialogical process. In the postmodern cultural milieu, the concept of originality has also lost currency, and it has been suggested that originality, "the notion of beginning as singular, definable, and stable is severely problematic" (Bennett and Royle 6). Hierarchies and precedents lose their privilege as texts "create a prismatic environment of intersections, overlappings, and misdirections" (Corrigan 30). Phyllis Frus and Christy Williams also argue that "lack of originality is no longer considered a weakness" but audiences rather find pleasure in "detecting a plurality of voices" and assume that "the more echoes we hear, the richer the text, and . . . that richness is a sign of value" (13). Therefore, an understanding of the concept of intertextuality is essential to the discussion of adaptation theories.

Intertextuality as a literary concept was introduced by Julia Kristeva and Mikhail Bakhtin. Its central hypothesis is that texts are produced and readers make sense of them only in relation to the already embedded codes that dwell in texts and readers (Wilkie 131). French post-structuralists such as Julia Kristeva and Roland Barthes posit intertextuality as an intrinsic, universal attribute of texts, and thus, for them, all texts are inherently intertextual (Moraru 257). However, it should also be noted that in its poststructuralist form, intertextuality constitutes a threat to the establishment of a viable discipline of adaptation studies, since in an all-pervasive intertextuality "everything becomes definable as an adaptation" (Allen 206). In a sense, this universalist view of intertextuality is unhelpful in adaptation studies, and therefore intertextuality should be restricted to the interplay of identifiable or traceable texts.

Christine Wilkie identifies three main categories of intertextuality: quotation, imitation, and genre texts (132). Among the three categories, the last is the closest to universalist intertextuality, and whether it qualifies as strict adaptation or transformative texts remains questionable. In this book, most of the chapters are confined to intertextuality in its limited sense, dealing with texts that rewrite with clear and direct textual references to other texts. However, in chapter 3 I do include discussion of genre, dealing with texts grouped together in recognizable patterns and sharing clusters of codes and literary conventions.

Sequel, Spinoff, and Fan Fictions

One reason why adaptation is prevalent in almost all cultures is people's predilection for the continuation of a story. If a story enjoys enormous popularity, readers yearn to know "what happens next," and sequels emerge in response to this demand. Prequels and sequels include both written texts and media products. As Martin W. Huang's edited volume on Chinese sequels (*xushu*) in the Ming and Qing dynasties states, "*xushu* should not be singled out for their presumed 'derivativeness,' because direct 'textual borrowing' is a quality shared by almost all major works of the traditional Chinese vernacular *xiaoshuo* [novel]. After all, many of them were the products of repeated rewriting by multiple authors based on preexisting sources" ("Introduction" 3). In a more general sense, works featuring "continuations" (*xu*), "supplements" (*bu*), "rewritings" (*gai*), and "imitations" (*fang*) should be subsumed in the category of adaptation.

Spinoff, also known as sidequel, refers to new products and stories based on popular television programs, films, novels, and so on. In *Literary Spinoffs* Birgit Spengler examines the rewriting of nineteenth-century classic English literature in the contemporary context, initiated by Jean Rhys's rewriting of *Jane Eyre* (1847) in *Wild Sargasso Sea* (1966), and emphasizes the subversive and marginal stance these literary spinoffs take toward the original works. Spengler observes that literary spinoffs share essential features and preoccupations with fan fiction, another notable phenomenon in the contemporary media landscape (102). Indeed, to extend the scope of adaptation studies to include fan-produced texts, images, and videos will be beneficial to a more comprehensive and inclusive understanding of textual transformation.

Fan fiction is a new branch of this broad retelling/adaptation process, in which fans of a specific creative work produce their own transformative stories derived from the text. For fan fiction critics, the concept of fan fiction could be as broad and innovative as myth storytelling millennia ago, or could be as narrow as the 1920s Austen and Holmes societies and 1960s *Star Trek* fanzines (Derecho 62). The phenomenon of fan fiction, as adaptation, could be seen as part of the long history of retellings, but their foregrounding in modern cultural studies could not achieve independence without the development of new technology: film and the internet. Adaptation studies in media discourse started after the emergence of film, and fan fiction became visible in the eyes of public and academia only after the revolution of communications media in the new century.

Fan fiction refers to the source material on which its transformative work draws as canon. Fan fiction usually diverges radically from the canon, most notably exemplified by changing the fantasy and sci-fi genres into romance, a prominent example of this being slash fiction. The criterion of fidelity holds little currency in fan fiction compared to its influence on general adaptation.

Remade and Transmedia Storytelling

To differentiate between remake and adaptation is sometimes invalid, since many literary texts, especially classic ones, have been adapted to films more than once, which makes the latest film version naturally a remake of an earlier one. In adaptation studies, research into remake is a significant though narrow category, since remake usually concerns only one medium, while adaptation is concerned with movements between different media forms. However, there is growing consensus to "understand the practice of remaking as one of several industrial and cultural activities of repetition (and variation) which range from quotation and allusion, adaptation and parody, to the process-like nature of genre and serial filmmaking" (Loock and Verevis 2). Among various cinematic remakes, cross-cultural remakes receive relatively more academic attention, as books on the transnational remakes of Chinese cinemas illustrate (Kenneth Chan; Yiman Wang). Sarah Woodland's book investigates both intercultural and intracultural remakes in Chinese-language films. She views the film *A Chinese Ghost Story* (2011) as a remake of the 1987 version with the same title, and my analysis (chapter 5) views both of them as cinematic adaptations of Pu Songling's short story "Nie Xiaoqian" from his *Strange Tales from Liaozhai*.

Another term that is closely related to adaptation is transmedia storytelling. Henry Jenkins articulates the prototypical model of transmedia storytelling in *Convergence Culture* as a story "unfold across multiple media platforms, with each new text making a distinctive and valuable contribution to the whole" (293). Jenkins's theory of transmedia storytelling has had a profound impact on academia and the media industry. However, his model is by and large a commercialized and corporate-oriented one exemplified by American media products. Studies of American transmedia franchises underline the dominant role that the film industry has played in these intellectual properties, as with Jenkins's representative example of *The Matrix* trilogy.

In the Chinese media landscape, however, the film and TV industries rely heavily on the adaptations of novels published both in print and online. Therefore writers, instead of directors and producers, become the hub around which transmedia storyworlds are built and subsequently expand (Wang and Hu 110). Recent academic explorations advance the notion of a "cultural specificity model," in relation to understanding transmediality, which takes into account "the politics, peoples, ideologies, social values, cultural trends, histories, leisure and heritage of individual countries and their smaller communities" (Freeman and Proctor 4). It sees transmediality as being beyond storytelling as a commercially oriented industry, and, rather, as a socially, politically, and ideologically profound cultural practice.

The model of transmedia storytelling constructed by Jenkins is idealistic and preoccupied with its distinctiveness, which cuts off the connections with the more traditional adaptation. Adaptation is regarded as mere repetition of the story, and is thus excluded from transmedia storytelling. This opinion shared by some transmedia theorists is based on a narrow understanding of adaptation, which treats adaptation as a copy of the original and only involves the participations of two media (literature and film). However, as discussed above, through the perspective of intertextuality, the scope of adaptation studies in recent years has greatly expanded to encompass multiple media forms. The request for fidelity has also lost its central status in examinations of adaptation products. Therefore, studies of transmedia storytelling and adaptation "are asking a related set of question," though with different terminological and methodological assumptions (Jenkins, "Adaptation, Extension, Transmedia" n.p.). More work remains to be done to promote the collaboration between two fields.

Adaptation and Ideology

The retelling and adaptation of traditional stories "serves important literary and social functions, inducting its audience into the social, ethical, and aesthetic values of the producing culture" (Stephens, "Retelling Stories" 91). Tradition, which automatically implies continuity with the past, seeks to inculcate certain values and norms of behavior by repetition. Behind the linguistic and semiotic cues of any story is the latent attitude toward issues such as gender, ethnicity, and class. In the process of storytelling, circulating, and retelling, ideologies have continuously shaped the form of stories over time.

Scholars in adaptation studies have proposed various categories to classify the different types of adaptation (Wagner 222–27; Genette 30; McCallum 20). The categorization is not especially productive since the boundaries between types are usually fluid. Therefore I tend not to distinguish between taxonomic categories such as expansion and transposition. What I am interested in is the distance between the narrative discourse of adaptations and their pre-texts, and how this kind of distance reflects the shifting social and cultural contexts.

Based on the different attitudes in adaptation practice toward the ideology of pre-texts, it is possible to discern, albeit roughly, a reinforcing type and a subversive type. The adaptation that is more faithful to an identifiable pre-text is not necessarily more conservative in maintaining the traditional ideologies than other radical adaptations, although this is often the case. The changes in the mode of discourse are much more potent in interrogating the ideological perspective in the pre-text than changes in the plot and content.

Three essential components of narrative discourse are the temporal and spatial chronotope, the focalization, and the language style. Any retelling of a pre-text needs to make its own choice regarding these three parts. Stephens identifies two significant changes in narrative strategy that could facilitate retellings to interrogate their pre-texts: telling the story from the point of view of one (or more) of the characters and telling the story through a first-person narrator ("Retelling Stories" 95). Hong Kong author Li Bihua's *Green Snake* (1986) uses the first-person narrator to rewrite "The Legend of the White Snake" through the perspective of Green Snake, the young sister of the White Snake. This change of narration successfully challenges the morals and manners of traditional Chinese culture presented in the legend. As I argue in chapter 4, Li Bihua's retelling exemplifies changes in the mode of discourse that have a powerful impact in destabilizing and subverting the ideology of traditional stories.

The fidelity debate has lost currency in adaptation studies primarily because by slavishly imitating the source materials adaptations inevitably bring back the latent ideologies behind the traditional stories, which may not be suitable for modern and contemporary social and cultural environments. As Simone Murray observes, "fidelity criticism was deemed not only a woefully blunt instrument with which to examine adaptations, but wilful infidelity was in fact the very point: adaptations interrogated the political and ideological under-pinnings of their source texts, translating works across cultural, gender, racial and sexual boundaries to secure cultural space for marginalised discourses" (10). The appearance of revisionist or subversive retellings becomes more fre-quent and visible, as Western feminist fairy-tale scholarship shows (Zipes, *Don't Bet on the Prince*; Haase, *Fairy Tales and Feminism*; Schanoes; Sellers).

Although the transgressive potential is included in the action of some subversive rewritings, this function should not be too exaggerated. Liedeke Plate alerts us to the possibility that "rewriting may challenge very little, being actually an integral part of the literary and cultural life of texts—and hence, of canonicity and marketing" (11). Diane Purkiss also argues women's rewriting of myth in contemporary poetry may have the paradoxical function of endors-ing the original myth. In other words, rejuvenation of past materials some-times causes the unreflective appraisal and restoration of traditional values.

Feminist literary criticism is closely related to the research on retelling and adaptation, with influential articles such as Adrienne Rich's "When We

Dead Awaken: Writing as Re-Vision" and Alicia Ostriker's "The Thieves of Language: Women Poets and Revisionist Mythmaking" as the starting point. Among feminist literary criticism, rereading, reinterpretation, revision, and rewriting are all essential terms in subverting a male-centered literary tradition and reclaiming a literature of its own.

Adaptation and translation share some similar concerns about derivativeness and secondariness, and for some feminist translation theorists, "'women' and 'translator' have been relegated to the same position of discursive inferiority. The hierarchical authority of the original over the reproduction is linked with imagery of masculine and feminine; the original is considered the strong generative male, the translation the weaker and derivative female" (Simon 1). Adaptation shares this inferior status with translation, as well as the request for fidelity, which also has strong resonances in the history of marital mores and gender politics (Simon 11; Johnson 142). Feminist adaptations attempt to interrogate the gendered hierarchy and destabilize the structure of originality and authority, and they rebel against mainstream ideologies through their infidelity and unfaithfulness.

Intersectional Feminism in the Chinese Context

The perspective of gender is particularly salient for the examinations of the transformation of Chinese traditional stories, since their source materials are produced in the context of Confucian culture, which is notorious for its debasement and disenfranchisement of women. It is generally agreed that two types of canon existed in premodern China. Confucian classics, including the Four Books and Five Classics, the primer texts for children (*Three-character Classic* [*Sanzi jing*] and *Thousand Character Classic* [*Qianzi wen*]), and the educational textbooks for women (*Lessons for Women* [*Nü jie*] and *Biographies of Exemplary Women* [*Lie nü zhuan*]), constitute the primary canon. At the core of Confucian values is *sangang* (the three cardinal guides), namely, "the ruler guides his subject, the father guides his son, and the husband guides his wife." The three cardinal guides were first articulated by Dong Zhongshu (179–104 BC), a West Han philosopher, and thereafter became the ideological base of feudal China (Baoyun Yang 78). The three cardinal guides codify a natural order of superior-inferior between rulers and subjects, parents and children, and husbands and wives. Another type of canon is formed by literary writings, "whose language was often more vernacular and whose content was often less concerned with Confucian values" (Hartman 95). However, these literary works are still produced and circulated within the Confucian cultural context and implicitly legitimatize hierarchical order and obedience to authority.

It should be noted that among the premodern literary canon, this book uses the genre of fantastic and supernatural (discussed in detail in the next chapter) to examine its contemporary transformation. The Chinese supernatural, according to Meir Shahar, is "an upside-down image of the Confucian ethos," which "placed men above women, old above young, learning above physical heroism, and etiquette above spontaneity" (198). Their deviation from accepted social and cultural norms can function as a safety valve that provides the society a temporary liberation from the Confucian ethos, yet without necessarily challenging the ethos itself (Shahar 205). The existing order of men over women, old over young, and rulers over subjects remains solid throughout ancient China and configures all genres of writing and social classes. Furthermore, both elite classic literature and vernacular popular texts are produced by male authors, and, as Dorothy Ko argues, "the fact that the Chinese literary tradition consisted almost entirely of writings by men meant that the woman writer had to be initiated into a world in which she had no rightful place and no distinct voice" (18). Contemporary adaptation provides opportunities to expose and reflect on these ideological implications, and gives the silenced female group a voice to express their feelings and desires.

This tripartite paradigm of male and female, child and adult, subject and ruler is inherently interlocked. Li-Hsiang Lisa Rosenlee (88) elucidates this interconnectedness in Confucian culture as follows:

> The connection between kinship hierarchy and gender disparity has begun to emerge as a critical area in Chinese gender studies; the problem of gender is no longer perceived as a uniform subordination of woman to man in all aspects of life. Instead, gender disparity is situated in the complex web of kinship relations where the disparity between genders forms only part of the social inequality between the senior and the junior kin. Gender by itself cannot determine one's position in life. Gender must also be combined with age, generation, marriage, and class, etc. to amount to anything significant.

With such insights, this book employs a broadly intersectional approach to gender politics (Lorde; Crenshaw). If feminism can be generally categorized as "the struggle to increase women's access to equality in a male-dominated culture" (Gamble viii), it should also be noted that feminist thought is not a monolithic ideology and "resists categorizations into tidy schools" (Tong and Botts 11). "Intersectional" has thus became an adjective that best captures feminist thinking. An intersectional approach will allow us to see the interconnections between patriarchal ideology, parental authority, heteronormativity, nationalism, and anthropocentrism in their construction of hierarchical structures. Kimberlé Crenshaw explores how race and gender intersect to shape the violence against women of color (1244). Following her lead, intersectional theory has developed out of "a critique of gender-based and race-based research," which fails to "account for lived experience at neglected points of intersection" and tends to "reflect multiple subordinate locations as opposed to dominant or mixed locations" (McCall 1780). Among the multiple burdens, the intersection of race and gender receives much more academic interest than others (Nash 2). To counter this unevenness, in implementing intersectionality in studies of literature and adaptations, this project will take into considerations of cultural specificity.

In ancient China, family defined by polygynous marriage and patrilineal inheritance as a social organization and ideological construction is the predominant space where gender, age, and ethnicity intersect. Patricia Hill Collins (65) notes that age and seniority, apart from gender, are fundamental principles of family as social organization, and her observations of the close correlation between traditional family ideal and American national identity are also applicable to the Chinese context. In the traditional Chinese family, domestic hierarchical orders between husbands and wives and parents and children are suggestive of public order. The centrality of the family in Chinese traditional culture is so obvious that it has been manifested in many Chinese words. For example, the ruler is called "the son of heaven" and "parent-official" by his subjects.

After the end of feudal society, around the turn of the twentieth century, feminist thought awakened in China. But the early feminist movement was part of a larger project of enlightenment, national strengthening, and modernization, which was not necessarily opposed to the nationalist discourse. The Republican era also saw the first generation of women writers who contributed to literary feminism by "composing numerous narratives portraying Chinese women's daily lives, dilemmas, struggles, and revolutionary aspirations and practices" (Zhu and Xiao 8). After the Chinese Communist Party (CCP) took power in 1949, the state-sponsored socialist feminist movement aimed at achieving gender equality through a series of campaigns promoting women's educational, legal, and economic rights. But socialist gender norms are built on "official denial of a female identity independent from class," which emphasizes gender sameness and suppresses sexual desire (Wu and Dong 476). With conventional femininities downplayed and masculinized women celebrated, the socialist legacy on the women's movement is a double-edged sword for later generations.

After the reform policy launched in 1978, China embraced the market economy and consumer culture. The drastic economic transformation toward marketization and globalization brought new opportunities as well as problems for the new generation of women. Contemporary Chinese women are trapped in a gender dilemma "in the wake of the paradigmatic transformation of the state's agenda from equity-centered socialist revolution (including egalitarian women's liberation) toward an efficiency-driven marketization and privatization" (Zhu and Xiao 21). On the one hand, after the promotion of a market economy that praises "competition and efficiency," a "self-reliant individualism" is generally accepted and internalized (Jackson, Liu, and Woo 16). This competitive economic environment demands women to be financially and psychologically independent. On the other hand, traditional patriarchal ideology has not faded with the advent of the reform, and women are still expected to fulfill the role of a wife and mother, who is responsible for doing the housework, taking care of children, and maintaining family harmony. Domestic duties and responsibilities inherited from Confucian culture are combined with the chances and free choice brought about by the neoliberal economy and individualized postfeminism.[2] Moreover, the new economic and political contexts in a postsocialist China have led to the entwinement of gender and class, which renders the category of gender a stand-in for class. Through this displacement, "conflicts (such as class) perceived by ruling elites as more threatening have been absorbed by those seen as more manageable

2. Postfeiminism recognizes young women as empowered consumers, but disavows a feminist subject position. The application of postfeminist theories to the Chinese context is justified, as Sue Thornham and Feng Pengpeng (195) and Tingting Hu (27) illustrate.

(such as gender discontent)" (Wu and Dong 486). Meanwhile, media and academic attention are often preoccupied with concerns "mainly pertaining to young urban professional women and appear to be less resonant with other women's everyday struggles and problems" (Zhu and Xiao 22). The intersection of gender and class in the contemporary Chinese context provides the backdrop upon which literary and cinematic imaginations emerged.

Children and adolescents find themselves in a situation similar to that of women, especially the generation who grew up under the one-child policy (1979–2016). They "have enjoyed better living standards and educational resources but also shouldered heavier pressure of parental expectations for their academic success and upward mobility" (Xiao 39–40). Yet their career success and upward mobility are conditioned by class, ethnicity, and gender-specific statuses, and failure in this neoliberal competitive society leads to despair and depression. As Hui Faye Xiao observes, "themes of alienation, loss, and disillusionment have prevailed in an (ironically) thriving youth culture in the new millennium" (18). The explosion of youth literature (*qingchun wenxue*) written by and for post-80s writers, and their popularity, are symptoms of this particular social context.[3] Through either realism or fantasy, post-80s writers address themes such as loneliness, alienation, and self-identification and also write about their rebellion against adult authority and the doomed painful failure of youth rebellion.

The intersection of gender and age in the Chinese patrilineal system puts adolescent girls in a particularly vulnerable position (chapter 6), and this precariousness is probably the reason why a certain kind of melancholy is pervasive in many coming-of-age stories of girls written by modern and contemporary Chinese female authors (Xu 322). Young lesbians and queer girls who defy gender norms and heterosexual relationships are often the victims of structural oppression generated by gender and sexuality, but their literary expressions of alternative imaginations and practices of gender and sex indicate the possibility of the formation of an assertive subject (chapter 4).[4]

---

3. By "post-80s" I refer to the generation born between 1980 and 1989 in mainland China, especially in urban cities, after the introduction of the one-child policy.
4. Studies of Chinese schoolgirl romance by Fran Martin (12) and Japanese girl's culture by Deborah Shamoon (*Passionate Friendship*, 33) observe that a temporal logic tends to govern literary expressions of same-sex intimacy among female adolescents, whose same-sex desires function only as a detour, followed by the ultimate adoption of a heterosexual identity in

Traditional stories sometimes bear the mission of creating and reinforcing a national or cultural mythology, which makes them a possible accomplice of a cultural nationalist agenda. As Yingjie Guo contends with reference to several groups of cultural nationalists in contemporary China, their goal is "the rediscovery of cultural authenticity and the activation of the historical community" (133). Such a trend is manifested in many ways, including the dramatic increase in the last decade or so in "the publication of Chinese classics, historical TV drama and film, historical novels, and general interest in qigong, fengshui, and traditional costume" (136). For example, the rhetoric of neo-Confucianism was introduced to a mainland Chinese audience in the 1980s, with its favorable contents being utilized by the official discourse. The Confucian love of order, "obedience to one's superior, the devotion to the state and the protection of the family" helps to "promote the desperately needed social order and stability" (Meissner 19). However, as Xianlin Song cautions, "with only a few exceptions, the destructive role that Confucianism had played historically in oppressing women is hardly mentioned" during this Confucian renaissance (98). The often repressed tension between women and nation makes the relationship between feminism and nationalism dangerous and sometimes paradoxical. Chen Shunxin observes feminists can either be critical toward nationalist discourse or actively participate in this discourse (4), and in Chinese history, women often have chosen the latter position. Therefore, the feminist critique and challenge of nationalism and the patriarchal structure remains crucial (chapter 3).

If the power of tradition lies in its repetition and its acclaimed continuity with the past, then radical revision and transformation of a traditional text have huge liberating potential on an ideological level. Nevertheless, the demand for cultural authenticity may preclude the subversive and parodic adaptations of some canonical works, which would restrict their interpretative richness. Indeed, the state strives to reclaim control over the usage of these traditional canons as national icons. For example, in the 52rd Order issued by the State Administration of Radio, Film and Television (SARFT, 2006), the following policies are emphasized: films and other media products that include plots and contents that "deliberately debase and parody revolutionary heroes,

---

adulthood. However, this linear mode of homoeroticism as "just a phase" has been rejected by some new queer-themed literature and film (Monaghan 3; Cathy Yue Wang, "'You Two'" 135).

important historical figures, and important literary figures from Chinese and foreign masterpieces" should be censored and revised (article 14).[5] Such regulations actually prohibit any subversive adaptations of literary canonical works, deprive readers and audiences of the possibilities of multiple and open interpretations of certain works, and also deny any criticism and interrogation of implicit ideological assumptions in these canonical works.

Under such a social and political context, fantasy narratives that adapt traditional stories ineluctably show signs of the power struggle between male and female, child and parent, local and global, and also between state and market, and tradition and modernity. The adaptations analyzed in this book aim to destabilize the traditional stories, which are male-, adult-, and human-centered, and thus provide alternative scenarios and possibilities that interrogate the socially and culturally defined attitudes toward gender, sexuality, and other identity issues.

Transformation of a Specific Story Cycle

There is a body of case studies on the textual transformation of a particular tale in different historical periods of China. Lan Dong's monograph *Mulan's Legend and Legacy in China and the United States* is an extensive case study of Mulan's story, which features a cross-dressed female heroine. Dong uses Genette's trope of the palimpsest to conceptualize the transformation of Mulan stories, and the concept of the palimpsest "conveys the multiplicity of different versions portraying Mulan in a variety of guises" (7). A strength of Dong's research lies in its cross-cultural scope and its close attention to the "richness and variety of Mulan's story in China before the heroine's journey across the Pacific Ocean" (6). Thus, it highlights the complexity and problematics underlying the issues of cultural authenticity. Compared to Dong's cross-cultural study, Louise Edwards's work on Hua Mulan is specifically grounded in the

---

5. www.gov.cn/ziliao/flfg/2006-06/06/content_301444.htm. The State Administration of Radio, Film and Television (SARFT) existed between 1998 and 2013 and then transformed into the State Administration of Press, Publication, Radio, Film and Television (SAPPRFT). In 2018, the SAPPRFT was abolished and its functions subordinated to the Communist Party of China Central Committee's Publicity Department instead of the State Council of the People's Republic of China.

Chinese context. She astutely observes that in the Mulan story cycle, the opposition to central government authority evident in pre-twentieth-century versions is erased in later adaptations through "the subsuming of filial piety into a statist discourse" ("Transformations of the Woman Warrior" 178). The materials she discusses are drawn from different historical periods and a diverse range of genres, and hence the transformation of the core themes could be observed. Sookja Cho's *Transforming Gender and Emotion: The Butterfly Lovers Story in China and Korea* addresses the love story of Liang Shanbo and Zhu Yingtai and investigates the story's capacity to "evolve and multiply over the centuries and across continents" (5). A shared issue of Mulan's story and the Liang-Zhu story is that they both touch upon the empowerment and complexity cross-dressing brings to female agency, and therefore the discussion of their retellings and adaptations ineluctably touches on the changing gender politics of different historical periods and cultural environments. Liang Luo's *The Global White Snake* traces the modern and contemporary adaptations of one of China's foundational folklores, "The Legend of the White Snake," in the multicultural context. The anthology *Retelling Fantastic Tales in the East Asian and Global Contexts*, which she edited, manifests the rising academic interest in adaptation of fantastic stories in East Asia and the global context with special attention to the political potential and affective power of these multimedia texts.

These studies by Dong, Edwards, Cho, and Luo provide extended and detailed case studies of one specific story cycle. Although such diachronic readings offer meticulous examinations, they nevertheless are sometimes inclined to ignore the synchronic relationship between contemporary adaptations of various traditional works. As opposed to these studies that devote a whole book to one particular tale and its evolution and transformation across time and place, *Snake Sisters and Ghost Daughters* is inevitably less detailed and particular in the presentation of a story's mutating trace. Although I acknowledge that the source texts on which contemporary novel and film adaptations are based are by no means singular and fixed, I have no intention to give a comprehensive delineation of the history and diverse versions of these narratives. Instead, I place more emphasis on the present and contemporary adaptations, and on the social and cultural contexts. The focus of this monograph is not on the premodern stories, and I do not view adaptation as evidence of the canonical status of certain literary works, in which the multiple existences of adapted versions are proof of a work's everlasting appeal. This study does not intend to answer the question of whether an adaptation is faithful to its pre-text, but rather seeks to explore what new meanings are generated in the adapted text and for what purpose. Moreover, by juxtaposing several case studies, this book provides a more nuanced observation of the hidden themes and contentions behind the prevailing cultural practices of old story retellings in contemporary China.[6]

Adaptation as a Transcultural Practice

The cultural nationalist agenda inherent in some Chinese adaptations is a natural reaction to the unidirectional flow of Western culture to China brought by economic reform and global exchange. Reclaiming a local cultural legacy may function as a positive resistance to the monologue of Western culture represented by Disney animation and Hollywood superhero block-busters. As Murray contends, adaptation studies have overwhelmingly focused on English-language texts (21). This book attempts to counter this westernization of adaptation studies and brings Asian texts into the picture.

Some studies of transcultural adaptation put Asian texts and Western traditions into dialogue. Murai Mayako's *From Dog Bridegroom to Wolf Girl: Contemporary Japanese Fairy-Tale Adaptations in Conversation with the West* is informed by Western feminist fairy-tale scholarship and tries to "emphasize the gain, rather than the loss, in adopting a cross-cultural approach" and to

---

6. Many studies of Chinese adaptation have been devoted to the specific relationship between two mediums (most notably film and literature), and they tend to emphasize medium specificity even though not prioritizing one over the other. Liyan Qin's dissertation, "Trans-media Strategies of Appropriation, Narrativization, and Visualization: Adaptations of Literature in a Century of Chinese Cinema," and Hsui-Chuang Deppman's monograph, *Adapted for the Screen: The Cultural Politics of Modern Chinese Fiction and Film*, are such examples. Qin's study is not so much on adaptation per se, but on film history from the perspective of adaptation. Deppman's book investigates Chinese film-literature interaction and the cultural politics it reflected, among which gender politics is the most prominent one. The limitations of these two works are reflected in the fact that the adaptation phenomenon has exceeded the scope of two-way traffic of novels and films and extends to all other media forms and genres, including, but not limited to, video games, picture books, graphic novels, and even theme parks. The two works also lack the comparative perspective between premodern literature and contemporary films, since the novels and movies under examination are entirely modern and contemporary ones.

"test the validity of the critical approaches in the West by applying them to the examination of non-Western material and identify both the limitations and the advantages of such methodologies" (4). Her study is a feminist scrutiny of how fairy tales are received and transformed in contemporary Japan, and it is insightful to the critical explorations of gender depictions and patriarchal ideologies in Japan as well as a wider East Asian context. Similar attention to gender issues is also discernible in Lucy Fraser's *The Pleasures of Metamorphosis: Japanese and English Fairy-Tale Transformations of "The Little Mermaid."* Fraser carefully scrutinizes the way gender is imagined in retellings of Andersen's famous tale, particularly across different cultures. Anna Katrina Gutierrez's *Mixed Magic: Global-Local Dialogues in Fairy Tales for Young Readers* employs theoretical methods from cognitive narratology to address the cross-cultural adaptation of Western fairy tales in Asian works. Her methodology proves to be notably productive, especially in its challenging of the unidirectional flow of Western culture to the rest of the world and recommending a more nuanced form of globalization framed as an exchange rather than a monologue (xv). One advantage of Gutierrez's project is its introduction of concepts from cognitive literary criticism into adaptation studies. Since cognitive narratology is an area of criticism that examines readers' mental processing of narrative fiction in terms of "a narrative pattern that our minds understand intuitively and recognize as recurring across literary traditions" (*Mixed Magic* xviii), it is particularly beneficial to adaptation studies in its emphasis on readers' mental processing of familiar narrative patterns.

The studies from Murai, Fraser, and Gutierrez are significant in their bridging of the gap between East and West, global and local; however, by highlighting and using the Western genre "fairy tale" as a starting point, they run the risk of overlooking the long and flourishing local literary histories and genres that are neither identical nor totally distinct from westernized fairy tales.

Traditional stories such as myths and folklore are employed and retold by Chinese diasporic and immigrant authors who have written in English. Maxine Hong Kingston's *The Woman Warrior: Memoirs of a Girlhood among Ghosts* (1976) retells the Mulan story as well as other traditional Chinese tales, especially the ghostlore. Amy Tan's several novels, such as *The Hundred Secret Senses* (1995) and *The Bonesetter's Daughter* (2001), weave Chinese ghost stories and the trope of reincarnation into her narratives. For these authors, Chinese traditional stories help them to formulate a cultural identity and express their cultural difference as a minority group. They also contribute to articulating the in-betweenness of the diaspora, who struggle between two cultures and languages (Ken-fang Lee 106). Deborah Madsen articulates the difference between "an essentialist diasporic paradigm, which draws on an understanding of singular national allegiance and ethnic blood identity," and "a hybrid transnational paradigm of identity that refuses singular allegiances and essentialist myths of blood kinship" ("Mo No Boy" 100). According to Madsen, Wayson Choy's and Amy Tan's works are representative of the first paradigm, whose rhetoric is characterized as double negative, belonging neither here (host land America and Canada) nor there (homeland China). Traditional tales and Chinese cultural practices inevitably contributes to this essentialist myth of an authentic China.

A new generation of diasporic authors like Larissa Lai, as Madsen argues, promote "a local-global dynamism through a 'both/and' paradigm for diasporic identity" ("The Rhetoric of Double Allegiance" 29). Lai's generation was born during the civil rights movement and grew up in the 1980s and 1990s, when multiculturalism was accepted by most people, and therefore their cultural orientations and values tend to be diverse. An obsession with Chineseness does not take a strong stand in their works. Instead, they highlight the heterogeneity and multiplicity of the Asian subject in the diaspora. Lai employs Chinese myths and folklores in an innovative way. Unlike Amy Tan's *The Hundred Secret Senses*, which brings the past represented by the ghost back to the present in a linear way through the trope of reincarnation, Lai's *When Fox Is a Thousand* (1995) and *Salt Fish Girl* (2002) put the past, the present, and the future in juxtaposition and "construct a narrative world in which ghosts and the living participate equally, a world where the supernatural is present in all places and times" (Madsen, "The Rhetoric of Double Allegiance" 40). In this fictive world, the past and the present, China and Canada, the Orient and the Occident "share the same ontological status" rather than standing in opposition, and the diasporic subjectivity is "constructed transnationally across time and space" (Madsen, "The Rhetoric of Double Allegiance" 40). Lai's critique of a single nation-state identity is intersected with her interrogation of the patriarchal ideology, as chapter 3 will illustrate. This intersectional critical perspective is also shared by Chinese American author Yan Geling, who writes mainly in Chinese.

Some distinctions need to be made between adaptations written in English by the Chinese diaspora and those written in Chinese by mainland Chinese and Sinophone authors. A crucial problem is whether the target reader is familiar with the materials being adapted. We can generally assume that Chinese-speaking readers are familiar with traditional stories when they read contemporary adaptations written in Chinese, although it is not always the case. After all, myth, fairy tale, and folklore by their very nature "depend on a communality of understanding" (Sanders 45). But when English-speaking readers read ethnic literary texts that adapt traditional tales, they experience something new and fresh. In other words, they are the unknowing audiences, in Hutcheon's term, who "experience the work without the palimpsestic doubleness that comes with knowing" (*A Theory of Adaptation* 127). Ignorance of the original text can be viewed as a loss from one perspective: a loss of the similarity and difference between the original source and the rewriting. From another perspective, this experience forces the monolingual reader to "confront multicultural discourses" (Ken-fang Lee 107). Two types of heteroglossia can be experienced by different readers. For Chinese-speaking readers, adaptations written in Chinese bring the freshness of telling a familiar story in a new way. For English-speaking readers, reading ethnic adaptations is enjoying a new story written in a familiar language. Bilingual readers experience both. It should be noted that this book is not primarily concerned with transcultural adaptation and dialogue, although Western cultural influence, globalization, and cross-cultural communication are indispensable parts of it.

Employing Cognitive and Affective Narratology to Adaptation Studies

The research on the process of adaptation from traditional genres and literary works to new narratives in multiple media forms is a burgeoning field and has already witnessed a flurry of academic works across the world. Critical attention to text-screen exchange is often concerned with Renaissance, eighteenth-century, nineteenth-century, and modernist Anglophone literary canons (Cartmell and Whelehan, *Adaptations*; Stam and Raengo). Pre-modern texts, such as myths, fairy tales, and folklore, on the other hand, are spongy texts, leaving enough room for reinterpretation and elaboration. Among the various traditional genres, fairy tales perhaps receive more focus than other genres (Bacchilega, *Fairy Tales Transformed?*; Zipes, *The Enchanted Screen*). Apart from folk and fairy tales, other genres, including mythology, epics, legends, and early canonical fictions and dramas, have also gained scholarly attention (Rogers and Stevens; Attebery, *Stories about Stories*). With a more specific focus on fantasy, Brian Attebery's *Stories about Stories: Fantasy and the Remaking of Myth* focuses on the ways writers use fantasy to reframe myth, an umbrella term representing various oral narrative forms (2).

Since twice-told stories are prevalent in children's literature, research on the relationship between old stories and contemporary children's books is abundant (Lefebvre; McCallum). My book also includes several primary texts whose target readers are children and young adults. John Stephens and Robyn McCallum's 1998 seminal book *Retelling Stories, Framing Culture: Traditional Story and Metanarratives in Children's Literature* is a forerunner in introducing adaptation studies to children's literature scholarship. A large component of their analysis deals with retellings of myths, legends, and folk and fairy tales. Their work draws attention to the complex interaction between pre-text, retellings, and the context within which these retellings are produced and consumed. Their special focus on the ideology behind the process of retellings is provoking for any study of adaptation.

The common methodology employed by many adaptation studies, according to Murray, is textual analysis (4). She also observes that "the importation of concepts from post-structuralism, post-colonialism, feminism and cultural studies broke down one part of the self-isolating critical wall built up around the text, and opened up adaptation studies to concepts of audience agency" (9). When the function of readers and audience is taken into consideration, cognitive and affective narratology become apt tools for examining the process of adaptation. The collective cultural knowledge shared by readers and writers helps readers to comprehend stories on the basis of very few textual or discourse cues (Herman, "Cognitive narratology" 49). For example, the following excerpt from Li Duan's novella "Fox Medicine" ("Hu yao," 2007) could be fully comprehended only with help from the readers' world knowledge and literary scripts:

Cheng was intoxicated by her amazingly beautiful smile and got the courage to ask: "At night the Cowherd is lonely, and he wonders where the Weaver Girl goes."

Upon hearing this, the smile disappeared from the girl's face, and she solemnly replied: "How could you as a gentleman try to flirt with me?" (3)[7]

Scripts in literature study refer to knowledge about prior texts readers have consumed or encountered, since "literary genres, fictional episodes, imagined characters in narrated situations can all be understood as part of schematised knowledge negotiation" (Stockwell 79). Scripts in general are stereotypical knowledge drawn from experiences in everyday situations, such as dining at a restaurant or going to the cinema. In other words, the ideas of scripts and schemas are used to describe knowledge representations stored in past experiences, either in static (schema-like) or dynamic (script-like) form (Herman, *Story Logic* 89). To understand why the girl is angry at Cheng's words, readers must draw on their stored knowledge of the script "The Cowherd and the Weaver Girl" ("Niulang zhinü," also the two stars known as Altair and Vega), which is a famous Chinese local legend about star-crossed lovers. The comparison between Cheng and the girl and the protagonists from a famous love story works to imbricate another script from everyday experience, the script of courtship. Although courtship activity is universal, its codes and norms are historically and culturally specific, and the impropriety of the young intellectual's action would be grasped with the background knowledge of the Confucian social code, in which courtship between young people is usually strictly regulated by authoritative community members such as parents. A subtler layer of the girl's angry reaction lies in the implicit attribute behind the "night" schema, whose relationship with sexual intercourse is grounded on complex assumptions and may be activated only by experienced adult readers. Lack of knowledge of these literary and everyday scripts will not prevent readers from making sense of this scene, but the thorough appreciation of this conversation, its implications for characterization, and its embedded ideological burden can be achieved only with the help of knowledge of multiple scripts.

Since the theory of scripts and schemas sees these knowledge structures as dynamic and experientially developing, literary narratives, "by presenting

---

7. All English translations from the Chinese original are mine unless otherwise noted.

atypical, norm-challenging, or physically impossible fictional scenarios, inter-mix processes of script recruitment, disruption, and refreshment" (Herman, "Cognitive Narratology" 50). As Herman proposes, script theory may help to investigate "how literary narratives, through their forms as well as their themes, work to privilege some world models over others" (*Story Logic* 113). These world models are essentially ideologies behind the stored stereotypical knowledge of scripts.

The repetition of a certain script works to manipulate a reader's belief system. For example, the recurrent narrative outcome in many European fairy-tale scripts is "the prince and the princess lived happily ever after," which teaches the reader a belief system based on patriarchal and heterosexual assumptions. Similarly, tales that are instantiations of an interspecies romance script in many Chinese *zhiguai* tales (records of the strange, see the next chapter for more details of this genre) whose normative form is the romance encounter and marriage between a male human scholar and a beautiful fox spirit or ghost also end with the couple living happily ever after, but with the addition that the son of the couple succeeds in the imperial examination and becomes a high government official. The recurrence of this narrative outcome is expressed only through the successful male offspring, and thereby the status of the otherworldly mother could be legitimated. The outcome reinforces two primary principles inherent in Confucian ideology: the patriarchal assumption that women are merely tools to produce a male descendant for the family of their husbands, and the pragmatic opinion that the only meaning in life for men is the pursuit of an official career. The aforementioned excerpt from "Fox Medicine" works as an example of schema modification. When information about the girl's true identity as a fox spirit is given, the culturally imbued schema of "fox-woman" as seductive and flirtatious is overturned, as the young intellectual Cheng now initiates improper sexual jokes and is rebuked by the fox girl. In a more general sense, the plot of "Fox Medicine" is an adaptation of this interspecies romance script.[8] Li Duan begins the instantiation of this

---

8. The precise pre-text, I suppose, is the tale "Qingmei" from Pu Songling's *Liaozhai* collections. The story features Qingmei, as a hybrid child of a mortal father and a fox mother, who is sold to be a maid in a rich family. Unlike Li Duan's protagonist, Qingmei does not possess any supernatural power in Pu's text. According to Rania Huntington, Pu did not demand consistency in his fox tales. In some stories the interspecies children "will be purebred humans, but sometimes the half-breed children are means of taming their fox mothers" (*Alien Kind* 248).

script with a normative opening, that is, with a young scholar who failed in the imperial examination, a beautiful and elegant girl whose true identity is a fox spirit, and a deserted old temple, but the further development of this script turns to an irregular path, with an abnormal ending that is dissonant with its literary conventions in many aspects:

1. The fox spirit marries Cheng and gives birth to a daughter instead of a boy. The girl possesses certain supernatural abilities inherited from her mother and is troubled and experiences discrimination because of her hybrid identity.
2. The fox spirit does not act as a devoted and caring wife and mother according to Confucian social standards. She is always absent-minded and misses her natural world.
3. When Cheng takes another wife in quest of male offspring, the fox spirit disappears.
4. Cheng dies from a disease two years later, in poverty and without male offspring.

All these divergences are not without ideological implications. When a text refuses to follow a script or makes a radical change to a script, it conflicts with the script readers have stored in their mind, and hence pushes readers to embark on a process of cognitively resolving the conflict. In this process, the old ideology underlying a script may be rendered visible and may then be interrogated. Divergence 1 confronts the absurd obsession with a male heir in traditional feudal society, and divergence 2 scorns the model wife of the patriarchal Confucian paradigm and also the anthropocentric ideology in many *zhiguai* tales, which position the human world as more socially desirable than the natural and animal world. In this divergence, influence from European otherworldly maiden tales may be discerned: for example, the reluctant Selkie wives in Celtic Selkie girl tales. In traditional tales, the male scholar usually takes both human and otherworldly wives and the women are normally in a harmonious relationship. Divergence 3 targets the institutionalization and normalization of polygamous behaviors and values, with special

For a translation of Pu's "Qingmei," see *Strange Tales from Liaozhai* [translated by Sondergard], vol. 2, 610–23.

attention on women's compliance with this system. Divergence 4 abandons the concern with a male heir and shatters the promise of a happy ending. Therefore, Li Duan's atypical, norm-challenging ending renders her novella a modern revisionist adaptation of an interspecies romance script, as illustrated further in chapters 4 and 5; the manipulation of the familiar script will challenge the script's representation of female subjectivity as either monstrous or passive. Therefore, ideology, through the repetition of stereotypical knowledge as scripts and schemas, influences readers' beliefs about gender, race, nationality, religion, and so on (Gutierrez, *Mixed Magic* 14). Even if readers are not entirely convinced by the new script and affirm their culturally stored ideology thoroughly, at least they start to think reflectively and critically about something that previously they may not even have realized was an issue. Adaptation, as "repetition with variation" (Hutcheon, *A Theory of Adaptation* 176), in a broad sense, is about the ways old scripts are updated to relate to changing social, economic, and cultural contexts.

This case aptly illustrates the appeal of employing script theory from cognitive narratology to adaptation studies, for it shows precisely how texts interact with readerly experience (Stockwell 76) and views the production and circulation of literature as a dynamic communication between readers and writers, based on shared knowledge as scripts and schemas. Besides, in the adaptation process, a reader of the pre-text could become an author of a new text, and the unfixed priority between author and reader renders the chronological order less important than the scripts shared between the texts they produce. Therefore, a script-based approach to adaptation studies may suggest a shift away from the diachronic investigation of the pre-text and the new texts to a synchronic investigation of how different adapters use one script to develop new stories regardless of chronology.

A primary method to achieve script refreshment is through blending. Conceptual blending, according to Mark Turner, is "the mental operation of combining two mental packets of meaning—two schematic frames of knowledge or two scenarios, for example—selectively and under constraints to create a third mental packet of meaning that has new, emergent meaning" (10). "Slaying Dragons" ("Tu long"), Shen Yingying's 2008 short story, combines Chinese mythology about mermaids and modern medical surgery and tells a chilling tale about the mutilation and commodification of mermaids. The archetypal mermaid-type creature first appears in *In Search of the*

Supernatural (*Sou shen ji*), a compilation of Chinese strange tales written by Gan Bao during the Eastern Jin dynasty (317–420 AD). It refers to a type of fishlike creature living in the South China Sea as *jiaoren*. These creatures are technically gender neutral, weaving miraculous, intricate cloth, and, when sad, they cry tears that turn into pearls (Hayward and Wang 130). Other sources state that they could be used to produce oil that will burn and never go out (Fraser 21). Chinese *jiaoren* seem quite different from Western mermaids, which are prized for their practical uses. In Shen's tale, dragons refer to *jiaoren*, and dragon slayers are a group of people who live by performing a highly skilled surgery that splits the tail of *jiaoren*. Surgically modified *jiaoren* with two legs become sexual toys for noblemen and wealthy people and sell for a good price. The author, Shen Yingying, who is reputedly a medical doctor, describes the surgery in all of its dreadful and precise details. But the story is narrated through a young girl named Su Mian, who aspires to become a doctor. As a member of another species that is feuding with *jiaoren*, she shows inborn hatred toward these aquamarine creatures and views them as nonhuman monsters. Therefore, she has witnessed the complete surgical procedure full of brutality, blood, and pain but remains indifferent until the end. This tale weaves premodern mythical sources with modern medical science. Readers are presented with a cognitively blended scenario. The schema of mermaid also blends attributes of fish with women. Shen's narrative depicts a young mermaid as if she is a fish, for both the dragon slayer and the onlooker Su Mian. Her description of fin cutting and belly opening is similar to how a fresh-caught fish is prepared for cooking. But most readers will interpret and view this poor creature as a girl, an intelligent kind who can speak, think, and feel. Thus, the story has an emotional effect on readers through shock and dread. Moreover, readers' dread and shock contrast sharply with the unfeeling indifference of the narrator. This contrast prompts the initial interrogation of racial discrimination embodied in Su Mian. The mutilation and commodification of *jiaoren* by humans stems from their racial differences, their consumable and precious bodies, and their unusual beauty, giving their persecution and servitude a gendered lens. This case illustrates that adaptations can elicit certain emotions in their audiences through verbal and visual details. These emotional reactions are part of the complex narrative comprehension process of readers and spectators, through which interrogation and reflection can take place.

The affective turn in literary and media studies helps to shift the focus of adaptation practices away from what stories say to what stories do—in other words, to what stories arouse from reader and audience. John Hodgkins proposes a way to understand adaptation as "a flow of affective forces between texts, a generative drift of intensities between mediums" (12). This change of focus could displace the traditional concentration on fidelity in adaptation discourse, and shed light on how literature and cinema give rise to feelings and thoughts that speak to the lives and times of readers and spectators (19). With an eye toward cognition and affect, we can shift the critical energy away from what an artwork means, to how it works and what it does.

2

Chinese Fantastic Narrative Tradition and Its Contemporary Revival

Fantasy as a literary genre is protean and elusive, and thus hard to define. However, the common understanding of fantasy is predominantly an Anglo-American one. This chapter examines the conceptualization of fantasy as a Western genre in contemporary China in the early twenty-first century. The Chinese understanding of fantasy as a literary genre, and the production of texts, is influenced by an unbalanced cultural exchange brought about by globalization, but the influence of traditional texts is noticeable. Particularly, East Asian contexts are brought in to aid in the effort to counterbalance this unidirectional cultural exchange between East and West. This chapter delineates a Chinese literary tradition of the fantastic and supernatural before the notion of fantasy as a modern Western genre came into China. This tradition starts with ancient myths, then goes into strange tales (*zhiguai*) in the Six Dynasties, Tang tales (*chuanqi*), vernacular novels in the Ming and Qing dynasties represented by *Journey to the West* and *Flowers in the Mirror*, and martial arts fiction, which flourished in the Republican era.

After a brief review of the genre studies of fantasy in Western academia, I then connect studies of retelling and adaptation discussed in the first chapter with fantasy literature. By virtue of its generic characteristics, fantasy literature shows more affiliations with traditional stories than realist fiction does. The gender issue in fantasy is also examined, by questioning the genre's ideological stances. Overall, this book takes an inclusive and synthetic attitude toward fantasy, encompassing works for both adults and children as well as literary and commercial genres. It also wishes to promote a more comprehensive understanding of fantasy, taking culture-specific characteristics into consideration, in an attempt to counterbalance the westernization of this genre on the global scale.

The Conceptualization of "Fantasy" as a Genre in Contemporary China

Although China enjoys a rich literary tradition dealing with the subject of the supernatural, consisting of short stories, novels, and dramas, fantasy as a modern genre is generally grounded on influential Western works such as J. R. R. Tolkien's *The Lord of the Rings* trilogy. English fantasy dominates the contemporary world, at least in sheer numbers, and especially in conceptual framing. As Farah Mendlesohn and Edward James comment, a great deal of translation from English fantasy into other languages as well as original English-language material is read by fantasy fans around the world. In contrast, fewer translated fantasies enter the Anglo-American market (6), and those that do enter the Anglophone world are usually works from Europe, such as works by E. T. A. Hoffmann, Astrid Lindgren, or Michael Ende.

The Lord of the Rings trilogy by J. R. R. Tolkien and the *Harry Potter* series by J. K. Rowling were translated into Chinese at the start of the twenty-first century in mainland China. Chinese fans quickly embraced this new genre and produced localized works. However, finding or creating an accurate Chinese word to translate the term *fantasy* has been a challenging problem for scholars. Unlike the clear-cut term for science fiction, which is translated unambiguously into *kehuan*, two characters respectively standing for science and imagination, the situation with the translation of *fantasy* is much more difficult since no Chinese word directly corresponds to the English term. Grounded on the particular social and cultural context of contemporary China, ultimately, there are four corresponding Chinese words for the one English word *fantasy*, and different terms are used by different communities with different cultural connotations.

Qihuan (the strange and the imagined) is a type of fantasy for the adult market, and is usually found on the same shelves as science fiction, horror, and thrillers. Along with *qihuan*, there are two other, similar terms for fantasy in the adult market, *xuanhuan* and *mohuan*. According to Zheng Xiqing, the differences between the three words ending with *huan* (imagination) are as follows: *qihuan* is overall Western-mode fantasy, exemplified by second-world fantasy from Tolkien and George R. R. Martin, while *xuanhuan* is fantasy with an explicit Eastern style, usually including Daoist mysterious power and mixed with martial arts. Since this type of writing is particularly popular online, the work is indicative of low cultural esteem and low literary value. *Mohuan* is mainly used as a term that corresponds with the *magical* in *magical realism*, which is not relevant to fantasy as a commercial genre but as a type of literary fiction (86). The term *huanxiang xiaoshuo* (fiction of imagination) or *huangxiang wenxue* (literature of imagination) is discussed and used mainly in the field of children's literature. For Zheng, a crucial fault in the discourse of Chinese fantasy, including *qihuan, xuanhuan, and mohuan*, is their neglect of children's fantasy (81). But the reason for this oversight is the lack of communication between the study of fantasy literature and the study of children's literature in China. Children's fantasy and adult fantasy are produced, criticized, and circulated in separate fields, by separate people, and their mutual ignorance is the biggest hindrance for the development of a more tolerant and inclusive understanding of fantasy as a literary genre in the future.

The paths between child-oriented and adult-oriented fantasy have been separated since the early stage of the introduction and conceptualization of the English word *fantasy*. Children's literature scholars and critics, including Chen Danyan, Zhu Ziqiang, and Peng Yi, enthusiastically promote fantasy literature, *huanxiang xiaoshuo*, and writers of this type of literature receive support from academia and publishing institutions. In contrast, the development of fantasy for adults, *qihuan/xuanhuan*, has occurred at a more grassroots level and is primarily fan-based, and the criticism it has received from mainstream academia is also controversial.

Huanxiang Xiaoshuo, Children's Fantasy, and Didacticism

After translations of classic Western children's fantasy novels became available in China and then received critical attention from a number of Chinese scholars, including Chen Danyan, Zhu Ziqiang, and Peng Yi, these same scholars were responsible for initiating a discussion about the new genre and urging local writers to try producing their own versions of it. The term "fantasy" was initially translated as "modern fairy tale" (Chen Danyan, "Rang shenghuo" 199) or "novelized fairy tale" (Zhu, "Xiaoshuo tonghua" 63). Using E. B. White's *Charlotte's Web* (1952), Oliver Butterworth's *The*

Enormous Egg (1956), and George B. Selden's *The Cricket in Times Square* (1960) as examples, Chen Danyan describes these narratives as containing a "multi-sided depiction of a complex personality, . . . the harmonious combination of the novelized realistic story and fairy tales," and concludes that "they are half novel and half fairy tale, a hybrid of the novel and the fairy tale" ("Rang shenghuo" 200–202). Chen also translated E. B. White's *Stuart Little* (1945) into Chinese herself in 1984. Her interest in this new genre persisted until 1998, when she wrote her own fantasy novel for children: *My Mother Is a Fairy* (see chapter 6). In his 1992 article Zhu Ziqiang claimed, "from fairy tales to literary fairy tales to fantasy are three developing phases of unrealistic children's literature" (64). The phrases "novelized fairy tale" and "fairy tale novel" indicate that fantasy is seen as an evolved form of traditional fairy tales; it shares the same content as fairy tales but is written in the form of the novel. Later, the scholarly understanding of fantasy broadened and deepened. It was no longer seen as an extension of fairy tales but as an independent new genre. Scholars later began to use the term *huanxiang xiaoshuo* (fiction of imagination) to refer to narratives that could be categorized as modern fantasy. Although the conceptualization of fantasy has advanced from "fairy tale in novel form," we should note that all of these discussions still have children's fantasy as their sole focus.

This kind of children's fantasy was positively received by scholars of Chinese children's literature, because children's literature in China has suffered from the bonds of realism ever since its first appearance (Lifang Li 81), and thus fantasy is viewed as liberating authors to promote a more child-oriented, less didactic discourse. In 1997 and 1998, two series of "Great Fantasy Literature" ["Da huanxiang wenxue"] which included fifteen novels, were published by the 21st Century Publishing Group, a publishing house specializing in children's literature. Out of the fourteen writers of these novels, only two of them, Peng Yi and Ban Ma, had a persistent interest in fantasy literature. Most of the authors published in the series earned their reputation as children's writers through writing realist fiction, short or long. For them, fantasy literature from the West was an alien concept.

The fifteen novels in the "Great Fantasy Literature" series share many similarities. The narratives are all everyday stories that incorporate fantastic elements instead of secondary-world fantasy; the narrative modes are more realistic than fantastic; and the supernatural creatures that are depicted are ghosts, fairies, and monsters. They were not particularly popular with young readers and, like a flash in the pan, they soon disappeared into obscurity. Among the fifteen novels, Zhang Zhilu's *For Whom the Cicada Sings* (*Chan wei shui ming*, 1999) remains the most popular and is also exemplary in many aspects.

The protagonist is a girl who is troubled by her bad scores on a school exam. She accidentally picks up a fountain pen that can magically help her write the right answers on her exams. Later she realizes that a boy who is physically dying, and who is also indebted to her father, has put his spirit and soul into this pen in order to help her. Although the separation of body and soul in this narrative is fantastic, most of the novel's content is devoted to realistic depictions of the girl's daily life at school and with her family, with the focus on the exam and the importance of gaining good scores. Similarly, in Peng Xuejun's *Endless Piano Sound* (*Zhong buduan de qinsheng*, 1998), the elder son of a middle-class family dies in a car accident and then turns into a ghost to reunite with his younger sister. The accident happens because his mind is occupied with a thrilling adventure book he has half read, and he is too eager to know what happens next to notice the approaching car. He has little time to read because his mother forces him to practice piano, which is a torture for a boisterous boy. These two novels both touch on a social issue, the conflict between the heavy burdens of study put on children's shoulders by their teachers and parents and the playful and carefree nature of childhood. This conflict resonates with Lifang Li's observation about Yang Hongying's realistic fiction, the *Ma Xiaotiao* series, in which she argues that a crucial problem that still prevails in the Chinese education system is the nature of the authority and control that adults wield over children (88). Thematically these fantasy works are very similar to their realistic counterparts. Each author spends more narrative space on the description of the daily life of children than on the intrusive supernatural elements. The realistic narrative mode continues to haunt fantasy writing for Chinese children. The lack of success of this series is largely caused by the external impetus the authors received from editors, scholars, and the market. The development of children's fantasy in China is less spontaneous than that of its Western counterparts and is also overshadowed by the realistic works produced by the same authors. The genre of children's fantasy has "not yet developed very far," as Lifang Li accurately notes (90).

Qihuan, Pulp Magazines, and Collective World Building

The development of fantasy outside children's literature is much more spontaneous and dynamic. It is considered to be more of a grassroots phenomenon in China, since works produced for older readers were initiated by fans, translators, and pulp magazine editors. In 1992, a Taiwanese avid computer game fan, Zhu Xueheng (Lucifer Chu), established a column called "Fantasy Library" in a Taiwanese computer game magazine. In this column, he began to translate fantasy novels such as Margaret Weis and Tracy Hickman's *Dragonlance* series, based on the game of Dungeons & Dragons, which he subsequently published in 1998. This was the first-ever translation that advertised itself as a translation of fantasy fiction in Taiwan, and hence it marked a breakthrough for fantasy works detached from the field of computer games and emerging as an independent literary form (Rehling 78; Chung 10). In 2001, Zhu Xueheng published a translation of *The Lord of the Rings* trilogy. This Taiwanese version, along with the mainland Chinese translated version (2001), appeared at almost the same time as the first episode of Peter Jackson's *The Lord of the Rings* movie trilogy (2001). One year earlier, J. K. Rowling's *Harry Potter* series (1997–2007) was also translated into Chinese in mainland China, and the cinematic adaptation of the first volume, *Harry Potter and the Sorcerer's Stone*, was released at the same time as Jackson's *The Lord of the Rings: The Fellowship of the Ring*. The *Harry Potter* series achieved huge success among Chinese readers, as in the other parts of the world (Henningsen 275; Erni 139). The availability of these Western fantasy novels in Chinese and their extremely popular movie adaptations signaled that fantasy literature and film had become a new cultural hotspot in a globalized China.

Under the influence of Western fantasy series, Chinese authors began to write *qihuan/xuanhuan* in their own style. Unlike with the initiation of children's fantasy, in which academic institutions and publishing houses played important roles, Chinese fantasy novels for adults were published online and supported by pulp magazines. *Qihuan* is generally the term used to refer to Western-style fantasy written in the Chinese language, whereas *xuanhuan* is the term used to refer to fantasy with Chinese characteristics. Here I add another distinction into the demarcation of these two genres, with *qihuan* being works published in traditional print forms (books and magazines) and *xuanhuan* being online novels. There are some differences between these two groups of writing in form and style. Works published in magazines and books, which include many short stories and novellas, are generally shorter than online works. As a continuation of the traditional print industry, *qihuan* also shows affinity with earlier popular literary genres such as martial arts. In contrast, online fantasy novels are often much longer.

The formation of the Western fantasy genre has been significantly influenced by magazines like *Weird Tales* and *Unknown*, and this is certainly also true in the Chinese situation. In 2003, *Science Fiction World* (*Kehuan Shijie*, aka SFW), a magazine based in Chengdu, Sichuan Province, launched a branch magazine—*Fantasy World* (*Fei·Qihuan Shijie*)—that soon became a robust platform for China's local fantasy writing. This magazine survived for ten years. These ten years also mark the golden age of Chinese indigenous fantasy writing. Works published in print media such as magazines and books generally are of higher literary quality than works published online, and hence these ten years saw the production of a group of canonical texts of local Chinese fantasy. These canonical works, exemplified by the *Novoland* series (*Jiuzhou*, 2001–) and the *Cloudswild* series (*Yunhuang*, 2005–), showcase many characteristics of their era.

Both *Novoland* and *Cloudswild* are secondary-world fantasy, with the history, geography, and religions of their storyworlds created collaboratively by several similar-minded writers. The *Novoland* project was initiated by a group of young writers in 2001. Their aim was to create an Eastern Middle Earth world, which had its own unique setting of astronomy, history, geography, and religions (Mingwei Song 395). In the early stage of this project, writers used a short story solitaire game to explore and enrich their world system. Races, cities, and supernatural creatures were added one by one. Up to now, forty-six books have been published that are set in the *Novoland* world, in conjunction with more than one hundred magazine issues.[1] Since 2016, several cinematic and television adaptations of *Novoland* novels have appeared.

The *Novoland* series opens the database of their settings to the public, and hence anyone new who is interested in this world can join and produce their own creative works. From the beginning, *Novoland* abandoned the distinction between original and fan work, pre-text and adaptation. Its pre-text is not an identifiable text but a secondary world setting system, and as long as a new author is using this setting, he or she can create their own characters and plots.

---

1. See the fan-generated wiki website for Novoland: jiuzhou.huijiwiki.com/wiki/

This radical intertextuality based on world building instead of characters and plots shows a natural affinity with the transmedia storytelling proposed by Jenkins, a new mode of storytelling that extends across multiple media. Colin Harvey and Dan Hassler-Forest demonstrate that nonrealist genres such as science fiction and fantasy are particularly favored by transmedia storytelling and world building, and *Novoland* could be viewed as a Chinese example of this trend.

Unlike the male-author-dominant *Novoland* series, the *Cloudswild* project was initiated by three female writers, Cang Yue, Shen Yingying, and Li Duan. Up to now they have produced more than twenty books. As women writers, their protagonists are usually girls who travel around the land, have adventures, and fall in love. Unlike some books in *Novoland* that focus mainly on masculine activity such as battles and wars, books in the *Cloudswild* series lay more emphasis on the mental maturation and interpersonal relationships of female characters. A similarity between these two series, however, is that they both use myths and legends from Chinese culture to structure their secondary world.

Although *Novoland* authors attempt to create an Eastern Middle Earth, one crucial problem lies in the localization of secondary-world fantasy in Chinese contexts. There is a deeper reason for the prevalence of realistic fantasy and the rarity of secondary-world fantasy in children's literature, as presented by the "Great Fantasy Literature" series published by 21st Century Publishing Group. Traditional Chinese fantastic literature is marked by its mingling of the mundane and the supernatural. Yu-Ling Chung observes that "cases of 'the secondary world' in Western fantasy works with an independent operating system including history, geography, races and languages, such as Middle-earth in *The Lord of the Rings*, are very rare in Chinese fantasy works" (43). For Tolkien, a fantasy writer must be a "sub-creator," who makes a "Secondary World" differentiated from "Primary World" (37). Such a distinction between the outer, objective primary world and the inner, imaginative secondary world, is indeterminable, or even nonexistent in the Chinese tradition. The Chinese do not have a myth of an ultimate creator, and authors are usually not designated as an ultimate initiator. Therefore, Chinese readers and authors have a natural affinity for novels that mix the fantastic with the realistic. Brian Attebery views this mixed type as a subgenre that emerged within fantasy in the 1960s and "promises to reshape the genre most significantly" (*Strategies of Fantasy* 126). This subgenre is characterized by the avoidance of the enclosed fantasy world and describes "settings that seem to be real, familiar, present-day places, except that they contain the magical characters and impossible events of fantasy" (126). This subgenre is far from recent in the Chinese case, and is the norm rather than the exception. Secondary-world fantasy, in contrast, presents a challenge to the mindset of Chinese readers familiar with traditional fantastic literature. Even the dazzling and overwhelmingly fantastic storyworld of *Journey to the West* is still firmly grounded in a historical background (the Tang dynasty) and features a real life figure (Tripitaka).

Contemporary secondary-world fantasy novels, such as the *Novoland* and *Cloudswild* series, emerge out of the Western influence, but they are closer to historical novel than high fantasy. The third volume of Jiang Nan's *Novoland: Eagle Flag* (*Jiuzhou: Piaomiao lu*) series is titled *World Famous Generals* (*Tianxia mingjiang*, 2007), and its core plot is a crucial battle that decides who will sit on the throne. It reads like another version of *Romance of the Three Kingdoms* (*Sanguo yanyi*), with all of its detailed descriptions of tactical strategy and Machiavellian politics. The secondary world it constructs is inextricably bound up with Chinese dynastic history even though not a particular period in actual history. The richness and longevity of Chinese historiography act as both a blessing and a burden for fantasy writers.

It is hard to decide whether the *Novoland* series and *Cloudswild* series belong to adult fantasy or young adult fantasy, since both the authors and the readers of these texts are young adults in their twenties. Apart from a small number of explicit sexual or violent descriptions, many novels in these series could be seen as a bildungsroman in a fantastic world. For example, Jin Hezai's *Novoland* work *The Legend of Feathers* (*Jiuzhou: Yu chuanshuo*, 2005) pivots on the maturation of its young protagonist, Xiang Yichi, a name that literally means "different wings," who is marginalized in his community because of his unusual black wings. His lonely life is transformed by his meeting with a girl, Feng Lingxue (Snow), who has the purest white wings and best combat skills in the community. Their friendship gives him the courage to find out his real identity and evoke his hidden potential. Eventually, he becomes the hero who is destined to save his race and the world. The novel blends bildungsroman and romance, with attractive fantasy settings, and achieved huge popularity among adolescent readers.

However, it is not easy to identify these writings as young adult fantasy since these authors do not intend to write with an edifying message, as is expected of Chinese children's and young adult literature. Although children's fantasy writers in the "Great Fantasy Literature" series view fantasy as a less didactic mode for expression, they still assume they are writing for a group of readers who are cognitively and intellectually inferior and in need of guidance and education through books. Writers of the *Novoland* and *Cloudswild* series are instead writing without explicit didactic intentions. Since they are young adults in their twenties or early thirties, their works are apt to attract attention from readers of similar age groups (or a little younger). This lack of didactic intention provokes critical controversy. In 2006, Tao Dongfeng, a literature professor, attacked the authors of three popular online fantasy works in an article. In addition to highlighting their low aesthetic value, he also criticized what he perceived as a lack of moral value in the narratives and thus labeled the works as *zhuang shen nong gui*, a derogatory Chinese phrase that means "pretending gods and ghosts playing tricks." What is lacking in these works, according to Tao, is the didactic and educational function of literature. He accuses the novels of being "morally ambiguous, indifferent to political issues, and demonstrating a lack of public concern" (9). The three novels mentioned by Tao are works originally posted online, and they are attacked as representatives of the newly emerged yet highly popular *xuanhuan* genre. He believes that the readers and writers of *xuanhuan* novels belong to the post-80s generation, who also indulge in playing computer games. The interconnection between *xuanhuan* novels and computer games in Tao's accusation is noteworthy.

Xuanhuan and Internet Literature

Around the start of the twenty-first century, the germination of Chinese fantasy writing coincides with the flourishing of Chinese internet literature. Chinese internet literature does not refer to works of electronic art with innovative uses of hyperlinks, video, and audios but rather is simply fiction written by amateur and professional authors that is posted online (Lugg 121). Most of this is genre fiction for entertainment. The launching of several literary websites and forums since 1997 plays an important role in the vigorous online writing. Major online literature websites include *Qidian* (www.qidian.com) and *Jinjiang* (www.jjwxc.net), with a demographic division of consumers. *Qidian* primarily caters to the tastes of male authors and readers, with fantasy, science fiction, detective fiction, and horror the most popular genres. *Qidian*-style fantasy and adventure novels have become representative works of Chinese online literature, and eclipse the more female-oriented genre of romance, including BG (heterosexual), *danmei* (or BL, boys' love), GL (girls' love). *Jinjiang* is more female-oriented and is famous for its romance novels.

Online fan communities have played an essential role in the early development of Chinese internet literature (Tian and Adorjan 883). But commercialization and genre hybridity are new trends in Chinese internet literature. *Qidian* was the forerunner in charging a fee for online novels, and it has been followed by other websites. The ever-escalating commercialization of online literary websites requires broader readership and longer works, since the income of authors depends on the readership size. The length of online novels has expanded exponentially, since the amount a reader has to pay and the length of the novel are correlated. Longer novels can incur greater profits for both the authors and the websites that publish their works (Schleep 66). Genre hybridity is also a logical consequence from the perspective of genre evolution. The fully matured generic conventions and clichés inevitably lead to repetition and boredom. Genre hybridity marks the increasing formal and thematic sophistication of certain genres.

Nonrealist genres are proving to be the most popular among online writing and reading, with *xuanhuan* being the most representative. Other genres related to fantasy include *xiuzhen* (immortality cultivation), *daomu* (grave robbing), and *chuanyue* (time-travel). *Xuanhuan* novels blend the Daoist cosmic system with martial arts fiction and are often referred as Eastern fantasy. According to Zhange Ni, "at the heart of the *xuanhuan* type is a new fantasy subgenre named *xiuzhen* (immortality cultivation), which draws from the repository of Daoist alchemy in particular and Chinese religion and culture in general to build an imaginary world in which cultivators pursue immortality through rigorous self-training, fierce competition with rivals, and strenuous fighting against monsters" ("Xiuzhen [Immortality Cultivation] Fantasy" 2). The story arc is generally repetitive and predictable and depicts an underdog boy who "successfully accomplished tasks and adventures and has been rewarded with high socio-political status, wealth and women" (Chao 132). Some male-oriented *xiuzhen* novels emphasize "the self-possessed, self-governed, and self-enterprising" cultivator who "seeks constant ascension" in the hierarchical cultivating system (Ni, "Xiuzhen [Immortality Cultivation] Fantasy" 20). These male protagonists show little moral concern and treat women as trophies. *Qidian*-style *xuanhuan* and *xiuzhen* novels are adept at world building but are generally not very good at depicting the psychological and emotional dimensions of characters. Like Western sword and sorcerer novels, gender stereotypes and sexism are prevalent. Recently, female authors have started to reclaim these male-oriented genres by challenging and rewriting their literary conventions (Wang and Alberto).

Grave-robbing (*daomu*) fiction, initiated by Tianxia Bachang's *The Ghost Blows out the Light* (*Gui chui deng*) series, blends horror, adventure, and fantasy with history. Although inspired by American adventure films like the *Indiana Jones* series, the author of *The Ghost Blows out the Light* grounds his writing in Chinese premodern literature on ghosts and the supernatural (Macdonald, "Notes on the Fantastic" 18). Time-travel (*chuanyue*) fiction depicts contemporary characters who travel back to China's dynastic past, and often features plots that "emphasize the protagonist's romantic liaisons and pursuit of power and social recognition" (Rojas 1). It is argued that online perceptions of fragmented spatiality and simultaneity have contributed to the popularity of the time-travel and fantasy genres (Duan 677). More generally, Chinese internet fantasy novels are flourishing in both the domestic area and at an international level, as the leading Chinese-to-English novel translation website, Wuxiaworld (www.wuxiaworld.com), illustrates (Yuxi Wang 1). Contemporary Chinese fantasy novels are hybrid works with multiple cultural inputs, blending traditional Chinese narratives such as mythology, folklore, historiography, and martial arts fiction with Japanese ACG (anime, comic, and game) cultural elements and Western fantasy tropes. Conversely, they are positively received in the English-speaking world. The two-way cultural exchange and dialogue contribute to dismantling the unidirectional flow of Western culture to other parts of the world.

Traditional Chinese literature, Japanese media products, and Western fantasy are three resources from which contemporary Chinese fantasy novels draw and develop their hybrid form and content. Each of the three types of input and their historical and cultural contexts are the topic to which we now turn.

Traditional Chinese Literary Works with Fantastic Elements

The traditional Chinese literary works with fantastic elements enjoy a strange position in twenty-first-century Chinese literature. They do not belong to a modern fantasy genre based on Western criteria, and they do not have a clear and strong lineage in the current literary context, since modern and contemporary Chinese literature after the May Fourth Movement has generally employed the Europeanized realist novel as a paradigmatic model. Therefore, as Ming Cherng Duh notes, under the hegemony of Western culture, "the category of high fantasy suggests Tolkien's *Lord of the Rings* trilogy, Lewis's *Chronicles of Narnia* series, and Le Guin's *Earthsea* books, but not . . . Wu Chen An [Wu Cheng'en]'s *Journey to the West*, or Hsu Jong Ling [Xu Zhonglin]'s *Creation of Gods*. Perrault, the Grimms, Andersen, and Wilde have long been considered great figures in fairy tales, while Pu Sung Ling [Pu Songling], the creator of *Strange Tales from Liaozhai*, which contains voluminous stories of fox fairies and mysteries, is ignored" (10). In other words, genres, or categorizations in Duh's terminology, are culturally contingent. Genres such as legends and folklore can be found in the Chinese oral narrative, and genres such as epics and chivalric romances may exist only in the Western context,[2] while certain written genres are indigenous and corresponding Western categories are not easily identified. In this section, I primarily focus on the premodern Chinese narrative tradition whose contents include supernatural elements, and I use "the fantastic" or "the supernatural" to refer to these narratives and leave "fantasy" as a term to describe a modern genre developed much later with interaction with Western traditions.

As discussed in the previous section, the lengths and styles of contemporary Chinese fantasy novels published in print and on the internet are different. Of higher literary quality and shorter length, print works correspond with the premodern genre of *zhiguai* tales, while online fantasy novels show more similarity to the premodern long vernacular chapter fiction represented by *shenmo xiaoshuo* (fiction about gods and demons). Written in classic Chinese language, *zhiguai* as a genre is more elite than vernacular fiction, and this distinction can also be applied to contemporary print and online works.

Rania Huntington provides an overall portrait of Chinese fantastic narrative in premodern times in the article "The Supernatural." According to her,

Elements of the supernatural are found throughout the history of Chinese literature, cutting across genres. It has differing importance in different genres: it

---

2. It is generally agreed that Han Chinese lack an epic tradition. See Jaroslev Prusek, "History and Epics in China and in the West."

is the preeminent topic of the classical tale, one important topic of vernacular fiction and drama, and a specific mode in poetry. Each genre explores different territory of the supernatural. (111)

Chinese traditional fantastic narratives distinguish themselves from other traditions mostly by the permeable boundaries between ordinary and strange, real and unreal realms, and hence many scholars have noticed the inappropriateness of employing Western theories of the fantastic to analyze Chinese traditional narratives. Karl S. Y. Kao observes that the Chinese supernatural and fantastic are "never caught in the experience of alienation from nature . . . [n]or are they tormented by any indeterminacy in the character's or the reader's attitude towards the supernatural manifestation in the human world that characterizes the Western fantastic" (3–4). Huntington points out that although she uses the word "supernatural," its meaning in Chinese contexts is different from in the West, for "in pre-modern China such events and creatures are not beyond or apart from nature; instead the odd and exceptional is an inherent part of the natural system" ("The Supernatural" 111). Judith Zeitlin based her observations on Pu's *Liaozhai* tales, and remarks that these tales are "deliberately left ambiguous" and "erase the border between reality and illusion, history and fiction," and the expectation from Todorov that "the reader must inexorably choose between a supernatural cause or a rational solution is entirely absent" (*Historian of the Strange* 10). This feature makes Chinese premodern fantastic narratives a forerunner of Western modernism and postmodernism: as Ming Dong Gu argues, "the epistemology of Chinese fiction anticipated the rise of surrealistic, and magically realistic novels of modern times" (327). These arguments on the essential difference between the Chinese and Western fantastic traditions run the risk of oversimplifying two rich histories without consideration that inside these two separate traditions there are also multiple and changing particularities caused by different historical and social contexts, but which nevertheless capture a primary essence that needs further theoretical and empirical exploration.

The Chinese word for prose fiction, *xiaoshuo*, became fixed as a descriptor for the novel and modern short story as understood throughout the world only in the late 1910s and 1920s following the May Fourth Movement (Zeitlin, "Xiaoshuo" 258). Before that time, the premodern Chinese narrative tradition is long and autonomous, with many special cultural traits. As Zeitlin notes, there are two separate yet intermingling systems in Chinese narrative: narratives composed in classical Chinese, "the standard written language in China until the modern vernacular reform movement of the 1910s and '20s," and narratives written in vernacular (or in a mixture of vernacular and classical) (253). Both classical language literature and vernacular enjoy a bundle of works dealing with supernatural elements. Works of fiction in the classical language are usually short story collections, also known as *biji xiaoshuo* (jotting fiction), and include the subgenres of *zhiguai* and *chuanqi*. Vernacular fiction, though developed much later, flourished in the Ming and Qing dynasties, when several full-length masterpieces appeared that could be seen as representative of Chinese novels.

Zhiguai and Chuanqi

Chinese narratives with supernatural themes first appear in the form of short stories and anecdotes written in the classical language, commonly acknowledged as the genre of *zhiguai* (records of the strange). The earliest and one of the founding works in this genre is *The Classic of Mountains and Seas* (*Shanhai jing*, from the fourth century BC to the second century), which is "the most representative and influential in the preservation of ancient mythic and folkloristic material" (Xiaohuan Zhao 23). The Six Dynasties period played a significant role in the maturation and popularization of the *zhiguai* genre. Its exemplary work, *In Search of the Supernatural* (*Sou shen ji*), was produced around the fourth century, and includes 464 short pieces. Its narrative style resembles factual accounts rather than fiction. In the preface, the editor, Gan Bao, claims that he has collected pieces from earlier written and oral sources to "show clearly that the spirit world is no lie" (*yi faming shendao zhi buwu*). Fictionality in Chinese narrative had not yet gained a legitimate and autonomous status in this period, and to justify its existence it had to emulate the forms of historiographic writing, which enjoyed the highest status in the rigid generic hierarchy of discourses (Henry Y. H. Zhao 70–72; Anderson 23). Nevertheless, early collections such as *In Search of the Supernatural* served as repositories of popular characters and plots, provided a legacy of schemas and scripts—character stereotypes, plot devices (e.g., demon impersonators, celestial intervention), and favorite props (e.g., magical mirrors, stones, gems, and swords)—and contained the earliest versions of a number of Chinese folk legends (DeWoskin, "Gan Bao" 652). A famous story from *In Search of the Supernatural* is "Li Ji Beheads the Serpent" ("Li Ji zhanshe" in Gan Bao 424–25), which is unique in its progressive depiction of a brave and active female character. The tale is featured in *The Serpent Slayer: And Other Stories of Strong Women*, retold by Katrin Hyman Tchana and illustrated by Trina Schart Hyman, a collection of tales from around the world about strong girls and women.

Tang tales (*chuanqi*, tales of the marvelous) have a broader subject matter than *zhiguai*. Many tales deal with "the trials of the literati in the capital, their love affairs or political vicissitudes" (Nienhauser xiv). But impressive tales usually include unrealistic elements, such as "The Biography of Liu Yi" ("Liuyi zhuan," in Zhang Youhe 31–38) and "The Biography of Miss Ren" ("Ren-shi zhuan," in Zhang Youhe 1–6). The former is a tale about a human male's rescue of the daughter of the dragon king, and the latter an archetypical tale about the romance between a human male and a female fox spirit. Compared with "records of the strange," Tang tales tend to be longer and more artfully crafted and elaborated, though they still "take the historical biography as their formal model and still credit hearsay and eyewitness accounts as sources" (Zeitlin, "Xiaoshuo" 251). Again these tales prove to be rewritten and retold continuously, in the form of either drama, opera, or vernacular stories.[3] Later, *chuanqi* also designated a form of Chinese opera popular in the Ming and Qing dynasties, and plays with supernatural and ghost themes were still prevalent.

Classic language short fiction in the Ming and Qing dynasties began to blend features from "records of the strange" and "tales of the marvelous" and innovate conventions, with Pu Songling's *Liaozhai* tales as the epitome of this genre. This work provides numerous stories about ghosts, foxes, immortals, and demons. It spawned many imitations at the time, and attracted multiple adaptations in later generations. Chapter 5 deals with adaptations of Pu's works, with a special focus on ghost stories.

All of these collections of short stories about the supernatural are highly intertextual, both inside their particular literary tradition and outside with other discourses. As Kenneth DeWoskin illustrates, Chinese premodern fiction came into being by "picking from the public record, collecting and

---

3. On the rewriting of Tang tales, see Huang Dahong, *Tangdai xiaoshuo chongxie yanjiu* [*Studies on Rewriting of Tang Tales*].

borrowing from earlier versions, revising and adding commentaries" ("The Six Dynasties Chih-Kuai," 51). Among the more than four hundred tales of *In Search of the Supernatural*, half come from formerly written records, either reproduced without change or rewritten as adaptations (Lin 134). The resources are miscellaneous, including books about history, philosophy, rituals, religion, geography, and art. Subsequent collections of *zhiguai* draw freely and broadly from previous collections, and one story type can be found in more than one written source. *Zhiguai* tales engage in a dynamic dialogue with vernacular literary works, oral storytelling, and performing arts, with continuous mutual borrowing and retellings. Karl S. Y. Kao observes that in the process of genre shift from Six Dynasties *zhiguai* to Tang *chuanqi*, topoi, or motifs, "which may be defined as units or sequences of events identifiable as adapted from existing literary or cultural sources, or sequences recognizable as recurrent in contemporary works of Tang literature," reappear by two basic operations, accretion and transformation (40–41). This formulation of textual adaptations displays an earlier awareness of the important role rewriting has played in Chinese fantastic narratives.[4]

Fiction of the supernatural written in the classical language not only engages with its vernacular sisters but also engage with other higher discourses in the cultural hierarchy, such as philosophy and historiography. For example, Pu Songling's authorial comments at the end of his tales are a parody of the convention created by Sima Qian in *Records of the Grand Historian* [*Shiji*] (ca. 91 BC). He changes Sima's phrase, "The Grand Historian (*taishigong*) says," to "Historian of the Strange (*yishishi*) says," which is also an active assurance of an alternative tradition that departs from dogmatic historiographies. Similarly, the title of Yuan Mei's *What the Master Would Not Discuss* [*Zi bu yu*] (1788) is an allusion to Confucius's famous dictum, "the subjects on which the Master did not talk, were extra-ordinary things, feats of strength, disorder, and spiritual beings" (*zi bu yu guai li luan shen*, Legge 201). Through this explicit titular allusion, Yuan's tales of the strange and the spiritual consciously resist the orthodoxy promoted by Confucianism and its moral conservatism (Louie and Edwards, xxiii). Therefore, this group of literary works is a many-tongued

---

4. Kao's structural analysis of a single story-type and its representation in both *zhiguai* and *chuanqi* narrations also shows an earlier engagement of cognitive criticism in his introduction to the concept of frame from Goffman (45 n.54), which is the equivalent of scripts and schemas in later critical discourse.

genre, with innate heteroglossia, in Bakhtin's term. Each work incorporates a dialogue with previous models of this genre and with other discourses in the cultural milieu.

Apart from classical short stories from *zhiguai* and *chuanqi*, vernacular literature also warmly embraces supernatural content, in either short stories (*huaben*), full-length novels, or drama. In terms of stories dealing with the fantastic, they share a common system of scripts and schemas with their classical language counterparts. For example, the basic character type (an alien woman, a mortal man) and story line (the romance between them) of "The Legend of the White Snake" shares many similarities with tales in the *zhiguai* genre that feature interspecies romance encounters, such as the romance between male humans and female fox spirits described in Pu's collections. But "The Legend of the White Snake" is mainly developed in various semivernacular forms, from *huaben* in the Song and Yuan dynasties to Ming and Qing dramas. Although they share a story prototype, the shift in form is not without thematic influence. As Huntington stresses, the interspecies romance in the *zhiguai* genre is "viewed only from the male and human side," and remains "primarily a pleasure for male readers." Thus, the alien women in these tales do not inspire sympathy among female readers because they are not "emotional creatures in their own right with whom one could identify." "The Legend of White Snake" is an exceptional case, since the story was developed mainly in vernacular genres, and she "was a figure of sympathy" (*Alien Kind* 288–89). To further address this difference in readers' emotional reaction to the same story written in the different discourses, we need to take into consideration the social background of readers in both genres, generally elite male intellectuals versus middle- and lower-class audiences, as well as the different narrative strategies used in the two forms. The higher class *zhiguai* tales are usually narrated from the limited third-person perspective of the male characters (Yang Yi 214) and thus the emotions of the alien female characters remain opaque to readers. In contrast, vernacular stories generally use an omniscient and intrusive storyteller as narrator, whose narrative voice is sometimes explicitly manipulative in arousing certain moral and emotional judgments in readers, and the arias sung by female characters in dramas can give a direct display of their emotional status, all of which contribute to a more sympathetic attitude among readers in response to the characters. The analysis of modern and contemporary adaptations of the White Snake story in chapter 4 further illustrates the potential to subvert ideology that is inherent in changes of narrative perspective and voice.

Shenmo and Wuxia

Chinese full-length vernacular novels flourished in the Ming and Qing dynasties. Among the towering works from this period, *Journey to the West*, *Investiture of the Gods* and *Flowers in the Mirror* are in a fantastic mode, and each is a cultural palimpsest with layers of prior texts. They have been labeled as *shenmo xiaoshuo* (fictions about gods and demons) by Lu Xun (187). Even in generally accepted realistic novels, such as *Romance of the Three Kingdoms*, *Water Margin* (*Shuihu zhuan*), *Dream of the Red Chamber* (*Honglou meng*), and *The Plum in the Golden Vase* (*Jin ping mei*), there are numerous instances of miraculous and fantastic happenings (Gu 325). In other words, vernacular novels that contain no hint of supernatural elements are a rarity, as Huntington remarks ("The Supernatural" 126).

After myths, folklore, short story collections of the strange, and full-length novels about gods and demons, martial arts fiction (*wuxia xiaoshuo*) is the next step in the development of a Chinese fantastic literature tradition. Martial arts fiction is a popular genre rooted in historical narrative, but fully matured and stereotyped in the Republican era. Most martial arts novels contain supernatural elements, including supernatural powers such as "walking and flying in the air, otherworldly beasts, drugs and healing techniques beyond any modern scientific explanations" (Zheng 83). These elements endow martial arts fiction with some of the criteria for Western fantasy, but in most cases they are not considered to be equivalent to Western fantasy because most have explicit historical references, "so concrete that the supernatural and the historical come to a perfect mixture" (Zheng 83). But one feature the genre shares with Western fantasy is dense intertextuality, in that every single storyworld of the novels in this genre constitutes a shared world of *jianghu*, which literally means "the rivers and lakes," and a liminal space between real and imagined, and between civilized and barbarian. Clan names and martial arts movements created in earlier works are recycled by later writers, along with narrative conventions and plot clichés. Therefore, I tend to see martial arts fiction as an indigenous popular genre corresponding to Western fantasy, and it is the only genre of traditional popular fiction that has survived beyond the imperial era in China and is still being written today (Wan 1), and hence it provides us with a good case study of the adaptation of traditional motifs and tropes in the contemporary era.

It seems that multiple authorship of a similar plotline is a common feature of traditional Chinese literature, fantastic or not. Barthes points out that the original meaning of the word "text" is "a tissue, a woven fabric" (159). Similarly, the Chinese character *wen*, which denotes "text," is also etymologically perceived as "a motley of tissues thrown together" (Jing Wang 2). For Jing Wang, in a culture where tradition and history hold as privileged a position as they do among the Chinese, the idea that "no text escapes the confinement of its age-old literary tradition is a truism so familiar to traditional critics that a notion such as 'intertextual relationship' has long been taken for granted and needs little justification" (3). This intertextual penchant, exemplified by the popularity of rewriting in narrative, by the emphasis on allusion in poetry, and by the focus on the past in literary criticism, aptly illustrates the ultimate paradoxical nature of originality in the Chinese tradition. The apparent lack of enthusiasm for innovation in Chinese culture is perhaps, by virtue of the unwillingness to make a distinction between creator and creature, manifested by the lack of a creation myth (Martin Weizong Huang, "Dehistoricization and Intertexualization" 46). This paradoxical implication for originality explains the reason why many successful literary innovations in traditional China were made in the name of "restoring antiquity" and "transforming antiquity," through a process of synthesis. As Martin Huang ("Dehistoricization and Intertexualization") remarks, for the Chinese,

> The "innovative" value cherished is gauged in terms of its relation to tradition. Innovation is never an isolated or purely individual phenomenon, because while the Chinese do not have a myth of ultimate creation, they do believe that humanity is a major participant in cosmic change. What is stressed is continuity—an open process of change; no one can be designated as the ultimate initiator. (47)

Where the Judeo-Christian creation myth features an absolute God as creator, the corresponding Chinese cosmological myth is the story of how Nüwa repairs the toppling sky with colorful stones. The insight this myth gives Chinese ancient authors is "supplement" rather than "creation":

Thus, "supplement" is meant in the sense of "filling in the holes"—of placing new material where it belongs within a pre-existing structure, of mixing small doses of fiction with history. In this metaphor [Nüwa repairs the sky], literary invention bolsters and reinforces order rather than distorting and subverting it. This is not the Western image of the writer who freely imitates the Creation but rather a view of the writer as an assistant to the natural process of creation who selectively fills in gaps as needed. (Zeitlin, *Historian of the Strange* 25).

This emphasis on "synthesizing" and "supplement" reflects an early awareness of intertextuality in Chinese culture. Although the past is respected, the emphasis on the strategy of "transforming antiquity" is fundamentally to "make the tradition accommodate contemporary inspirations," and "creative possibility lies in the subtle manipulation of various données of a given tradition," which then transcends the older literature (Martin Weizong Huang, "Dehistoricization and Intertexualization" 48). Therefore, traditional Chinese literature provides ample examples from which to study the process of retelling and adaptation.

The propensity to use old materials in traditional Chinese literature is not exceptional. Walter Ong comments that the manuscript culture of medieval Europe had taken intertextuality for granted: "It was still tied to the commonplace tradition of the old oral world, it deliberately created texts out of other texts, borrowing, adapting, sharing the common, originally oral, formulas and themes, even though it worked them up into fresh literary forms impossible without writing" (133). This culture of the palimpsest lost its currency in the modern West when ideas such as originality and intellectual property came into existence. Similarly, this propensity to reproduce familiar tropes and motifs has been less prevalent in modern and contemporary China: after Western literary concepts such as mimesis and realism were introduced and widely accepted, a new sense of originality replaced the old accumulative tradition.

The Oppression and Rejuvenation of the Fantastic

Many traditional genres that have been closely bound to the fashion for retelling, such as popular historical romances, scholar-beauty romance, and the fantastic, have lost or are losing their grounding social and cultural contexts in the twentieth century—feudal society, dynasty cycling, arranged marriage, religious superstition, and so on. The disappearance of traditional literary genres with fantastic elements and the loss of the retelling traditions are a common product of the modernization of Chinese literature that occurred during the early twentieth century. The authentic modern literature of the May Fourth Movement "was expected to highlight themes such as enlightenment and revolution," and "in a discourse largely modelled after nineteenth-century European canons of realism, ghosts, together with other supernatural beings, find no place" (David Wang 264). Modern Chinese literature canons are dominated by Europeanized realist fiction, and alternative writing other than realism, such as satiric fantasy, myth-retelling, fairy tales, and fables, is neglected even though it is written by the same big names in literature history. Thus, Lu Xun's "A Madman's Diary" ("Kuangren riji," 1918) is counted as a classic, yet his *Old Tales Retold* (*Gushi xinbian*, 1936) receives lesser attention. The same could be said of Ye Shengtao's fairy tales (for example, *Scarecrow* [*Daocao ren*], 1923) compared to his autobiographic realistic novel, *Ni Huanzhi* (1929). Shen Congwen's *Border Town* (*Biancheng*, 1934) is viewed as one of the best modern Chinese fictions, yet his adaptation of Lewis Carroll's classic fantasy novel, *Alice's Adventures in China* (*Alisi zhongguo youji*, 1928), is viewed only as an early and failed experiment of a literary genius. Although this novel, compared to the elegantly styled and poetic *Border Town*, is weak from an aesthetic standpoint, it remains an interesting case if we view it as a cross-cultural adaptation and position it in relationship with the Swiftian satiric fantasy tradition. In a similar vein is Lao She's *Cat Country* (*Mao cheng ji*, 1933), a dystopian satire overshadowed by his more realistic novels represented by *Rickshaw Boy* (*Luotuo xiangzi*, 1939). A similar neglect happens in the West, as Attebery notes: "people conveniently forgot that Woolf also wrote fantasy (*Orlando*), James ghost stories, and Forster science fiction. *Bleak House* and *Huckleberry Finn* overshadowed their own creators' *A Christmas Carol* and *A Connecticut Yankee in King Arthur's Court*" (*Stories about Stories* 98–99). More research should be conducted addressing these neglected alternative writings in modern Chinese literature.

This oppression of the fantastic reached a higher level after the establishment of Communist rule, with Marxist materialism promoted as the orthodox ideology, although the real situation is much more paradoxical and complicated. Some canonical literature masterpieces, such as *Journey to the West*, were sanctioned after reinterpretation as an allegory of class struggle and an appraisal of the power of the proletariat, and some folktales that fit within a revolutionary framework were also accepted (Farquhar 255–256). Yet certain new renditions of ghost literature are highly risky. As Maggie Greene observes, ghost stories linger over the Chinese literary landscape, even in the Maoist era (3). Proponents argue for the inclusion of ghost literature on their didactic merits, but the opposing viewpoint connects them with superstitious practices that would not be tolerated by the CCP (Greene 4). Meng Chao's new Kun opera, *Li Huiniang* (1961, an adaptation of a Ming drama), which features human-ghost romance and ghost vengeance, was banned by the state authority, and the banning was a prelude to the Great Cultural Revolution (David Wang 265). The debate surrounding ghost opera and the subsequent total ban on it on 1963 illustrate the tension between modernity and superstition; they also demonstrate that socialist culture was less monolithic than commonly assumed (Wilcox 5; Smith 424).

The vigorous return of traditional fantastic literature to China became visible only in the 1980s. This literary renaissance is coincident with a revival in the so-called feudal superstition, including "a rush to rebuild temples and ancestral halls, the resurgence of spirit mediumship and exorcism, renewed interest in divination and geomancy, [and] the reemergence of heterodox religious cults" (Smith 405). David Wang is correct in pointing out two crucial factors at work in this revival: "the importation of Western fantastic discourse from the Gothic romance to magical realism," and a comeback of "pre-modern Chinese ghost narrative tradition in the postmodern literary scene" (266). A considerable amount of research has been undertaken on authors such as Mo Yan, Gao Xinjian, Yu Hua, Su Tong, and Wang Anyi, whose works incorporate supernatural materials within a realistic social context.[5]

Instead of focusing on works of so-called pure literature in Chinese discourse, I turn my attention to works belonging to a more popular spectrum, such as children's and young adult books, online literature, commercial fantasy, and live-action films and animations. I suggest that these works deserve serious attention since they are no less rich and subtle in their incorporation of traditional materials and contemporary issues and blending

5. See David Wang's "Second Haunting," Haiyan Lee's *The Stranger and the Chinese Moral Imagination* (particularly chapters 1 and 2), and Jefferey C. Kinkley's *Visions of Dystopia in China's New Historical Novels.*

of realistic concerns and fantastic tropes than their more serious companions. With the dissolving of the once clear-cut boundary between high and popular culture in the postmodern era, the dialogue and interaction between these two discourses should be encouraged and promoted.

Intra-Asian Cultural Flow

Apart from East-West dialogue, contemporary Chinese fantasy implicates intra-Asian cultural flow with special focus on Japanese popular culture. Many scholars have pointed out that fantasy literature in China evolved under the impact of Japanese manga, animation, and games, although the Western roots of some Japanese media cannot be ignored (Chung 66; Tse and Gong 104). The fact that international consumers of translated Chinese fantasy are mostly former fans of Japanese manga, animation, and light novels also confirms the affinity between contemporary Chinese fantasy and Japanese media products (Yuxi Wang 1). In fact, intra-Asia cultural exchange is more entangled and multidirectional than a one-way influence.

For example, Japanese author Tanaka Yoshiki's fiction series *Legend of the Galactic Heroes* (*Ginga Eiyū Densetsu*, 1981–87) is known to be highly influential to the development of contemporary Chinese fantasy works. But Tanaka's work itself blends *Romance of the Three Kingdoms* (a Chinese classic historical novel) with space opera (a Western science fiction subgenre). Works from Japanese author Yumemakura Baku are another example. His fiction *Śramaṇa Kūkai* (2004) features a Japanese Buddhist monk, Kūkai (774–835), who has traveled to China during the Tang dynasty to study Chinese esoteric Buddhism. This work has been adapted into a fantasy mystery film, *Legend of the Demon Cat* (*Yaomao zhuan*, 2017), by Chinese director Chen Kaige. The life experience of Kūkai aptly illustrates the process of cultural exchange among Asian regions based on religion. A Japanese fantasy novel with him as the protagonist and its Chinese cinematic adaptation further exemplify this intra-Asian dialogue. Another fantasy series by Yumemakura, *Onmyōji* (1988–), has had a significant impact on contemporary Chinese fantasy authors. In mainland China, it has been adapted by the NetEase Company into a mobile phone game, and subsequently into two films. Composed of episodic short stories, this series depicts the legendary *onmyōji* (a practitioner of *onmyōdō*, Way of yin-yang) Abe no Seimei from the Heian period (794–1192) solving mysteries and crimes of supernatural origin. Way of yin-yang is a system of divination, magic, and sorcery developed in Japan and based on the Chinese philosophies of *yin* and *yang* and *wuxing* (five elements), which have interacted with Japanese indigenous religion. Many of the demons and monsters Seimei confronts in the *Onmyōji* series belong to the general category of *yōkai*. *Yōkai* (monster) culture in Japanese manga and anime also illustrates close intra-Asia cultural exchange (Foster 169; Shamoon, "Yōkai in the Database" 276). *Yōkai* culture in premodern Japan, with Toriyama Sekien's *Gazu Hyakki Yagyō* series (1776, 1779, 1781, and 1784) as its epitome, according to Michael Dylan Foster, is influenced by the encyclopedic mode imported from China and initiated by *The Classic of Mountains and Seas* (*Shanhai jing*) (Foster 229). Contemporary manga artists such as Mizuki Shigeru and Takahashi Rumiko have drawn on Toriyama Sekien's work to develop their manga series about monsters, and like the "database animal" otaku[6], they have combined some elements to produce new *yōkai*. In the adaptation process, the entries on mythical plants, animals, and weird countries in *The Classic of Mountains and Seas*, like the catalog of *yōkai* in Toriyama Sekien's work, become modular units of information that can be categorized, rearranged, or used to create new narratives.

---

6. Japanese cultural critic Hiroki Azuma proposes a "database mode" that he observes in the appropriation of animation, manga, and games by Japanese readers, and that is effective in breaking old ideologies and engaging actively with postmodernity. Hiroki Azuma's theory of the database is grounded in the context of Japanese *otaku* culture. Azuma claims that *otaku*, the obsessive fans of anime and manga, are no longer interested in the grand narrative of their favorite fictions but focus instead on organizing details of the characters and fictional worlds into a database (53). Azuma uses the "tree model" as the metaphor of the desire for a grand narrative, and he coined the term *database model* to describe the postmodern form of knowledge arrangement and narrative generation. This database is composed of different character types popular in *otaku* culture, and these character types can be further dissected into different *moe* (affective) elements, and new characters are designed "as a result of sampling and combining popular elements" (Azuma 42). These elements are the defining features in physical appearance, personality, and idiosyncrasy. In his example, the *moe*-elements of popular anime character Ayanami Rei include quiet personality, blue hair, white skin, and mysterious power. New Rei-type characters are born out of the rearrangement and combination of these and other *moe*-elements. From the tree model to the database, the previous hierarchy between up and down and center and periphery is erased in the multilinked nest.

Although the Gothic novel was initially a Western concept that may be traced to Horace Walpole's 1765 supernatural romance, *The Castle of Otranto*, it could also serve as a translation term for a similar tradition observable in Eastern culture (Hughes 87). In his detailed survey of Japanese Gothic tradition, Henry Hughes acknowledges that Eastern Gothic has a long tradition stretching back centuries to origins in ancient China, embodied in the narrative genre *zhiguai* (records of the strange collected during the fifth and sixth centuries) and *chuanqi* (tales of the marvelous composed in the Tang dynasty). Traditions represented by the Six Dynasties *zhiguai* and Tang *chuanqi* found new expression in the work of Pu Songling (Hughes 63), whose collection of short stories, *Strange Tales from Liaozhai*, was published posthumously around the same time as Walpole's incipient Gothic novel. Hughes argues that the post-1949 demands of Marxist discourse effectively restrained the growth of Gothic literature in mainland China, and this Eastern Gothic tradition initiated by ancient Chinese narratives continued and flourished across the sea in Japan, represented by the writing of Izumi Kyoka, Akutagawa Ryunosuke, and Mishima Yukio (64). However, as discussed above, this Eastern fantastic tradition was interrupted but not eradicated by the years dominated by the Mao regime, and the reactivation of already-existing indigenous genres became interwoven with trends in Western and world literature.

Novels by Tanaka Yoshiki and Yumemakura Baku, *Yōkai* (monster) culture, and Eastern Asian gothic tradition are all examples of this reciprocal cross-border learning process among Asian countries (Iwabuchi 24). Due to the close cultural exchange of earlier periods, the fantastic culture in East Asia shows many overlapping and close intertextualities. As Koichi Iwabuchi argues, based on shared experiences of forced modernization, inter-Asian comparison is "less hierarchical relationships than the prevailing West-Asian comparison" (26). Given the fact that "translation of theories derived from Western experiences in a non-Western context still tends to be confined to a West-Rest paradigm," he proposes inter-Asian referencing as a method to go beyond "the Euro-American dominance of—or the parochial regionalism/nativism in—the production of knowledge" (31). The closely connected East Asian fantastic texts from the ancient to the contemporary period serve as a vehicle for the nuanced negotiation between the specificity and universality of East Asian cultures.

Theorizing Western Fantasy

Neither Chinese nor Japanese fantasy narratives in the modern era could exist without the influence of translated Western fantasy novels, be they oriented toward adults or children. Thus it is necessary to briefly examine the understanding of this genre in the Western context. It is generally acknowledged that, as a self-conscious literary mode, fantasy emerged in the middle and last decades of the eighteenth century as a response to the Enlightenment and to the contemporaneous rise of literary mimesis (Clute 921; Mendlesohn and James 3). Academic discussion of Western fantasy oscillates between two poles, the literary and the commercial.

In the literary mode, theorists of fantasy literature employ structural and psychoanalytic tools to explore relevant narratives. Tzvetan Todorov employs reader hesitation as the core criterion of the literary fantastic, which revolves around two neighboring choices, the uncanny and the marvelous (25). According to Todorov's distinction, fairy tales, and much modern fantasy, especially secondary-world fantasy, belong to the marvelous. Rosemary Jackson emphasizes the ideological impact of fantasy, as from her psychoanalytic perspective the literary fantastic has subversive power toward mainstream dominant ideologies (9). On the other hand, academic works, as represented by Jamie Williamson's study, investigate fantasy as a market label and commercial genre, and they demonstrate that fantasy as a discrete genre (as a sibling of science fiction and horror) emerged in the 1960s and 1970s through the publishing project of the Ballantine Adult Fantasy Series (BAFS) edited by Lin Carter.

J. R. R. Tolkien's *The Lord of the Rings* trilogy (1954–55) is beyond doubt the primary genre-shaping text, and his famous critical essay "On Fairy-Stories," though titled as "fairy stories," is actually a key essay on the definition and discussion of modern fantasy literature. His many opinions, including the emphasis on the subcreation of a secondary world and the promotion of eucatastrophe as the highest function of fantasy, have substantial influence on later scholars' attitudes toward the generic characteristics of fantasy. Attebery articulates the concept of "fuzzy set" to define fantasy not by boundaries but by central examples (*The Strategies of Fantasy* 12). Although fantasy is an all-age genre, the category of fantasy for children and young adults as "a semi-autonomous existence" came into critical prominence at the end of the twentieth century (James and Mendlesohn 4).[7] Fantasy literature also enjoys an unusually higher status in children's literature than in mainstream literature.

If we accept an inclusive understanding of fantasy, as Kathryn Hume suggests, which encompasses both the commercial genre and the literary mode and enacts a "departure from consensus reality" (21), then it is vitally important to bear in mind that what constitutes reality is contingent upon the beliefs and worldview held by a person or a community in changing historical and cultural contexts. Therefore, it is only after the Enlightenment, which established scientific rationality and delineated the boundaries of the possible, that fantasy could become a self-conscious art. Engaging with religious studies, Zhange Ni notes that "scholars of fantasy have yet to study the genre with reference to the modernist triad of science, religion, and magic/superstition" ("Fantasy / Magical Experiences" 4), and she argues that fantasy is not only opposite to science but also incompatible with the modern Protestant model of religion, which is interiorized, privatized, and depoliticized. Therefore, fantasy is a postsecular genre. Ni's study combines literary and religious studies, which can benefit fantasy criticism by reinvigorating the forgotten magic and superstition.

Fantasy literature is radically intertextual. Fantasy as a modern literary genre closely links to genres from premodern times, such as myths, epics, legends, folklore, fairy tales, chivalric romance, and Gothic fiction. Contemporary fantasy plays with the conventions of traditional stories. The traditional narrative modes underlying fantasy, including myth, epic, saga, and romance, whose availability to modern readers was the result of scientific research originated in eighteenth-century antiquarianism, were, as Williamson reminds us, largely unknown before 1750 (37). Therefore, modern fantasy writing is on the same line with academic research, translation, and adaptations of archaic literature. Zooming in on myth, Attebery observes that the history of fantasy writing and the modern scholarly engagement with myth are the two sides of the same coin. Therefore, he defines fantasy as modern myth-making (*Stories about Stories*). Both Williamson and Attebery have demonstrated the close relationship between premodern texts and modern fantasy, as well as the creative writing of fantasy and scholarly research.

---

7. For studies on children's fantasy, see Levy and Mendlesohn; Hunt and Lenz; and Gates, Steffel, and Molson.

Fantasy as a literary genre relies more on previous cultural artifacts than does realist fiction, and therefore the presence of preexisting literary scripts is crucial to its content and form. From a cognitive perspective, these literary schemas and scripts could be either a specific character type (fox spirits, ghosts) or a story type from folklore (interspecies romance tale), and readers' stereotypical knowledge about these scripts has an impact on their interpretation of a new narrative. The major tropes in fantasy writing, such as vampires (blending of a certain kind of bat and human) and mermaids (blending of fish and women), are new perceptual frames born out of the integration of impossible and possible entities. They no longer strike us as odd or strange since they have been repeated and calcified into familiar schemas firmly stored in our minds. To arouse a sense of novelty in readers, writers need to confront and orient these stereotyped frames innovatively and critically, and the best fantasy writers are those who draw broadly and reflectively on the genre's rich literary traditions. The adaptation process, in essence, is an exciting game that oscillates between familiarity and novelty, and the (im)balance between familiarity and novelty has implications for readers' view of issues that may or may not exist in realistic society. Cognitive narratology, as a combination and update of reader-response theory and structuralism, is apt at identifying what, precisely, makes genre fiction endlessly pleasurable despite its alleged repetition and predictability.

Fantasy, Ideology, and Gender

After the examination of fantasy in different cultural contexts and their cross-cultural interaction, it is necessary to address some common assumptions about this genre. First and foremost, ideology comes under scrutiny. If we see the whole genre of fantasy as the modern descendant of traditional literary forms, then when modern fantasy makes use of traditional materials and structures, it stands a fair chance of also bringing back the traditional assumptions about issues such as gender and class, which usually are not very progressive from the modern viewpoint. As Lisa Tuttle reminds us, "fantasy as a genre is generally perceived as more hospitable to women than science fiction and horror, and more flexible in the choices it offers than historical fiction or romance, yet the standard patriarchal bias imposes limitations which are seldom subverted or even questioned" (393). Likewise, female characters of Chinese *xuanhuan* novels published on the website *Qidian* are often portrayed as submissive and marginalized, generally appearing together as a "harem" that is dependent on men (Yuxi Wang 8). For Tuttle, the reason behind fantasy's gender bias lies in its looking to the past and its reuse of old patterns and archetypes. Therefore, to advocate a feminist reshape of fantasy necessarily requires reading and dealing with traditional and folkloric materials critically. Focusing on fantasy as a popular genre, Anne Cranny-Francis identifies three types of it in order to write about the experience of women in contemporary Western society: second-world fantasy, fairy tale reworked, and horror. Each of the three types has to "rely on the constant comparison with traditional narrative to construct a feminist reading position" (94). Therefore, the study of fantasy through a gender perspective is inevitably linked with the studies of rewriting and adaptation.

The recurrent tendency of women writers to use the fantastic as a tool to interrogate social and political meaning is not limited to only Western culture.[8] As David Roas observes, "a feminist use of the fantastic, then, is becoming increasingly widespread among authors across different countries, languages, and art forms" (9). Women writers from Latin America, Japan, and Italy combine gender and fantasy to form a feminist standpoint by highlighting the potential of the supernatural to subvert gendered expectations and norms.[9] Chinese female authors are no exception. This book tries to move beyond mere critique of fantasy texts that reinforce existing gender norms and provides detailed analysis of fantasy that operates both in opposition to and in collaboration with patriarchy. As my analysis of Chen Danyan's *My Mother Is a Fairy* (1998) in chapter 6 illustrates, as a fantasy located within everyday life it envisages some alternative ways of understanding the world and modern life for young Chinese readers but does not fundamentally disturb the prevailing social gender norms. The mother from another world has been

---

8. On this subject, see, among others, Lucy Armitt's *Contemporary Women's Fiction and the Fantastic*, and *Gender and Sexuality in Contemporary Popular Fantasy* edited by Jude Roberts and Esther MacCallum-Stewart.

9. See, Danielle Hipkins's *Contemporary Italian Women Writers and Traces of the Fantastic*; *Fantastic Short Stories by Women Authors from Spain and Latin America* edited by Patricia García and Teresa López-Pellisa; and Mayako Murai's *From Dog Bridegroom to Wolf Girl: Contemporary Japanese Fairy-Tale Adaptations in Conversation with the West*.

depicted as weak, delicate, and marginalized, with neither power nor agency, and has been deserted by her husband and daughter in the end. However, her existence and the memory created by her for her daughter gives the young girl ways to look beyond the pragmatic and conforming society. Moreover, the first-person narration and the questioning young narrator continue the story when its folklore archetype stops and also give voice to characters that cannot be heard in traditional tales. It is a work compromised between conflicting powers surrounding modernity and tradition, male and female, and indigenous and global.

Fantasy is not innately particularly conservative nor innately particularly subversive; it has the potential to be transformative since it always imagines an alternative world. As Dan Hassler-Forest argues, "the radical potential of fantastic genres is constantly being contradicted and curtailed" by their ideological opposite (10). Whether this potential is actualized depends on many variable factors, including, but not limited to, the author's attitude, the narrative mode the text employs, readers' expectations, and the social and cultural context from which the text was born. And the realization of this potential is achieved not only through content innovation but also through the development of a polyphonic narrative mode. For Bakhtin, the high and straightforward genres, such as "epic, tragic, lyric, [and] philosophical," are monotonic (*The Dialogic Imagination* 55). The conservative nature of these traditional stories is grounded more on their "third-person narration told from the singular point of view of an all-seeing narrator" and does tend to "leave a text's assumed core values unaddressed and hence unchallenged" (Stephens, "Retelling Stories" 94). Or, in Rosemary Jackson's words, the narrators of fairy tales are omniscient and have absolute authority, "making the reader unquestioningly passive" (154). Therefore, the effective strategy for breaking fairy tales' authorial control must be done through the change of narrative mode, through the transformation from monotonic to polyphonic. The object of this book is to scrutinize the changes in both content and the narrative discourse during the process of retellings and adaptations of traditional fantastic texts, and then explore the influences of these changes on the gender politics of their pre-texts.

Researchers of Chinese internet literature highlight the wish-fulfillment function of many online novels, encapsulated in the term YY, an abbreviation of the word *yiyin*, which means mental porn. According to Heather Inwood,

"YY is essentially wish-fulfillment fiction that allows the subjective fantasies of authors and readers to be realized through plot devices such as time travel, gender swapping, futuristic technologies, magic and the supernatural, and sheer good luck" (438). The erotic indication of *yiyin* reminds us of Judith Butler's defense of pornography as a type of fantasy: "within psychoanalytic theory, fantasy is usually understood in terms of wish-fulfillment, where the wish and its fulfillment belong to the closed circuit of a polymorphous auto-eroticism" (110). Either as a literary genre or as a mental activity, the wishes fulfilled by some fantasy narratives may be firmly in line with dominant power relations and social norms, as expressed by the endings of many Chinese popular fantasy novels, which grant high sociopolitical status, wealth, and women to their male protagonists. It is easy to denounce them as toxic male fantasy, but what is reflected by the popularity of these novels is a cruel reality that economic resources, social status, and romantic relationships are beyond the scope of most individuals in a highly competitive and unequal society. These novels thus become "forms of refuge and escape in that they . . . [make] up for what people . . . [cannot] realize in society" (Zipes, *Breaking the Magic Spell* 196). However, there are other types of wishes that are not restricted by the hegemonic social-cultural discourse, which imagines less repressive power relations and alternative ways of living. In these imaginations, competitive rivals are transformed into lovers; being different does not lead to discrimination and isolation; no boundary is impassable; and gendered bodies are free and empowered. The true magic power of fantasy lies in them.

3

Goddess, Matriarchal Utopia, and the Remaking of Chinese Mythology

The mythology of a certain culture, usually its earliest oral or written records, initiates a divine authority that becomes the foundation of many other traditional materials. This is not to say that folk and fairy tales are simply the diminished remnants of once flourishing mythology, but rather that myths deal with grand subjects that fulfill culturally important functions for a specific community or nation (Teverson 16), and myth is thus anticipated to provide a specific kind of cultural capital. Furthermore, in the case of Bible stories, as Stephens and McCallum comment, they are "the bearer of an interpretive tradition which informs all acts of interpretation involving traditional stories" (*Retelling Stories* 26). This interpretive authority might not be as powerful in the Chinese context, for the preserved repertoire of Chinese mythology is amorphous and scattered, lacking an overarching system. However, modern and contemporary adaptation of and scholarship on Chinese mythology still fulfill culturally significant functions in the various historical periods. Therefore, this book on feminist adaptations of traditional stories starts with a discussion of the transformation of mythical texts in contemporary fantasy works, ranging from online novels to commercial films.

Where the Judeo-Christian creation myth features an absolute God as creator, the corresponding Chinese cosmological myth is the story of how the goddess Nüwa repairs the toppling sky and creates people.[1] The goddess Nüwa seems to validate the existence of a primitive matriarchal culture before the

---

1. Apart from Nüwa, there are other accounts of creation (Pan Gu and Hundun) in Chinese mythology.

invasion of the phallocentric order. In *The Classic of Mountains and Seas*, one episode describes a country inhabited by only women. The brief description gives no further explanation about this strange place, but only identifies two basic elements, women and water. Based on the fantastic description, later vernacular fiction such as *Journey to the West* and *Flowers in the Mirror* reimagine such a kingdom of women by depicting it either as an all-female community or as a kingdom whose power structure between the two sexes is reversed. It should be noted that stories of kingdoms of women and the story of Nüwa are not directly textually connected. Many contemporary novelists find an emancipatory potential in the goddess Nüwa and a matriarchal utopia. This chapter examines a group of contemporary fiction and film that features women's dominance in a matriarchal society. In its employing of the strategy of estrangement to reverse the power relationships between the sexes, the literary imagination of a matriarchal society forces readers to recognize the sexist ideology in the real world. However, as I argue, such a construction of a female-dominated society is still based on binary oppositions without interrogating them.

The Nature of Chinese Mythical Narrative

That the Chinese mythmaking imagination has been shackled is seemingly a well-accepted argument, for which Confucian rationalism is frequently blamed (Yuan Ke xi). The negative attitude of Confucian scholars toward fantastic elements has the consequence that fewer myths were preserved in written records, but instead were either deleted or rationalized. Although a mythical world might be kept alive through oral traditions, myths "did not undergo the enhancing process of being transformed into literature or being systematized by creative authors," as Homer, Hesiod, and Ovid did for Greek and Roman mythology. Instead, mythological material "was absorbed, and thereby preserved in literary amber, in a disorganized way in a number of miscellaneous books" (Yuan Ke xii). Though Confucius disapproved of stories of the supernatural, philosophers from contending schools, especially the Taoists Laozi and Zhuangzi, tended to use fantastic stories as fables to illustrate their doctrines. Buddhism from India, since the Han dynasty, has spawned many animal fables and fantastic stories that enrich the pantheon of Chinese mythology.

By virtue of the nature of Chinese mythical narrative, which is "an amorphous, untidy, lapidary, fragmentary, and scattered congeries of archaic expression" (Birrell, "Myth" 62), it is hard to summarize a consensus ideology in Chinese mythology. A patrifocal ideology is also not innate in the earliest Chinese myths. Some scholars, by studying the pictograms of Chinese characters, argue that the initial denotations of words such as *god* (*shen*) and *emperor* (*di*) referred to females rather than males (Ye and Sun 1–16; Ye 288–302). Nevertheless, the patriarchal social paradigm ultimately pushes goddesses out of their high status and into the marginalized corner of the pantheon of Chinese mythology through the euhemerizing strategy employed by Confucian historians and scholars. However, the amorphous and obscure nature of Chinese mythology renders its characters and plots as a whiteboard, which is open to various and even conflicting interpretation and reorientation. Therefore, the retellings of myths in a contemporary context become the sites of contestation on which ideologies of altruism, heroism, cultural superiority, and misogyny are simultaneously reproduced and interrogated.

The Loss and Revival of a Goddess: Nüwa

In the earlier mythological texts, Nüwa is not only the creator of human beings but also the savior of humankind by mending the damaged sky and stopping the flood. She appears as early as in *The Classic of Mountains and Seas*, a treasured repository of ancient Chinese myths whose time of completion ranged from the fourth century BC to the second century AD. Chapter 16 describes, "There are ten gods who named Nüwa's gut. Nüwa's gut turned into spirits. They took different routes and settled into the wilderness Liguang" (Yang and An 7). This brief description heralds the creation of humans credited to her. It also points out the transformative ability of Nüwa. The annotations of this passage by Guo Pu (276–324) explain that "Nüwa, is an ancient goddess and empress, who has [a] human's face and [a] serpent's body. She can transform seventy times daily; whose guts metamorphose into these spirits." Many of Nüwa's myths center around two themes—metamorphosis and fertility. The creation of humans is detailed in another ancient writing, *Fengsu Tongyi* (*Popular Customs and Traditions*, second century AD). This text relates how Nüwa created human beings by molding them from yellow earth with her hands. Exhausted by the work, "she took a cord and pulled it through the mud, then she lifted the cord and shook it. All the sludge that fell down from the cord became men and women" (Yang and An 172).

Nüwa is also a savior of humankind from extinction caused by disasters. *Huainanzi* (139 BC) states that:

> In remote antiquity, the four poles supporting the sky collapsed, and the land of the nine divisions of ancient China broke up. The sky could not completely cover the earth, and the earth could not totally carry the world. Fires raged fiercely and did not go out. Floodwater ran everywhere and did not subside. The fierce beasts devoured kind people, and violent birds seized the old and the weak. Nüwa then melted stones of five different colors to patch the sky, cut the legs off of a huge tortoise and set them up to support the four extremities of the sky, slaughtered the Black Dragon to save the people, and collected ashes of reeds to stop the flood. (Yang and An 11)

These two feats of Nüwa, creating humanity and repairing the Pillar of Heaven, show her high status as a primeval deity. She is the Great Mother of humans, a culture heroine, and one of the most essential and influential primeval goddesses in Chinese mythology. However, in the following centuries, the figure of Nüwa was overshadowed by the hegemony of patriarchal gender politics, and she began to be paired with a male god named Fuxi. Their brother-sister marriage made them the progenitors of humankind, as recorded in *Duyi zhi* (*A Treatise on Strange Beings and Things*, 846–74). In this much later narrative, the goddess "has been demoted from primal creatrix to a mortal subservient to God in Heaven, and also a lowly female subservient to the male in their marital relations" (Birrell, *Chinese Mythology* 34).

The image of Nüwa also endures transformation. In early Chinese literature and grave paintings, Nüwa was depicted as having a lady's head and a serpent's body. She gradually became an elegant and graceful goddess in full human shape in later developments (Yang and An 174). The change from zoomorphic deity to human form coincides with Nüwa's subordination to male gods, due to both "the contempt of some eminent and educated men for animalian gods and the increasing domination of masculinity in elite social doctrine" (Schafer 29). After the Han dynasty, Nüwa gradually vanished from the institutionalized religions such as Daoism and Buddhism, and survived only in folk religious practice. She is worshipped as the inventor of marriage and as a divine matchmaker. According to Yang Lihui's fieldwork research, the folk practice of Nüwa worship provides an alternative space for women who are excluded from the Confucian domain, and the folk dance during the worship ritual is usually performed by women and passed on matrilineally (161).

A theory about the existence of a prehistorical matriarchal society booms in the West, since the publication of Johann Jakob Bachofen's *Mother Right* (*Das Mutterrecht*, 1861) and further elaborated through the writings of Marija Gimbutas and Riane Eisler. However, as Cynthia Eller cautions, the existence of such a matriarchal utopia in history not only lacks concrete archaeological evidence and is subject to interpretive bias, but also runs the risk of essentializing the difference between men and women and reinforcing stereotypes that link women with the body, nature, and childbirth (*The Myth of Matriarchal Prehistory* 6). In the Chinese context, the existence of a primitive matriarchal culture before the invasion of phallocentric ideology seems to be validated by the figure of Goddess Nüwa. Earlier mythical texts assert Nüwa's independent status, and later texts couple her with the male god Fuxi.

But employing this linear trace of matriarchal utopia and patriarchal takeover into Chinese history should be circumspect, as Eller reminds, and there is no shortage of loopholes and contradictions. For example, in a funeral stone carving from the Han dynasty, the Wuliang Shrine, Fuxi and Nüwa were portrayed with human heads and upper bodies and serpents' lower bodies, with tails intertwined. The paring of Fuxi and Nüwa in the mural painting ostensibly supports the replacement of female independence by male dominance, but at a closer look it is evident that both Fuxi and Nüwa are represented with snakes' bodies, and their hands are holding a compass and a ruler. If the animal body represents their close connection with nature, and the compass and ruler represent "human forms of knowledge, notably scientific and technological skills" (Peter Huang 368), then there is no distinct correspondence between female/nature and male/culture. Instead, all of these symbols are displayed in a harmonious rather than a hierarchal way.

The late imperial era might have seen the construction of a more rigid gender hierarchy and more severe repression of women, but earlier porous and obscure mythical texts left room for both repressive and liberal interpretation of female agency, as exemplified by the image of Nüwa. Among the two feats of Nüwa, creating humankind was perhaps related to her female body as nurturing mother, but repairing the sky had nothing to do with her maternity. Eller asserts that "though there is nothing inherently feminist in matriarchal myth, this is no reason to disqualify it for feminist purposes" (*The Myth of Matriarchal Prehistory* 7). Instead of employing the separatist view of primitive and civilized, and matriarchal and patriarchal, one could view the group of mythical texts about Nüwa not as a clear and linear trace of the falling of a goddess from almighty to marginal but as a deposit of obscure and porous texts whose language and meaning are complex, paradoxical, and inclusive. As Alicia Ostriker contends, "all myth central to a culture survives through a process of continual reinterpretation, satisfying the contradictory needs of individuals and society for images and narratives of both continuity and transformation" (*Feminist Revision* 27). It is such dynamics and flexibility of myth that make the diverse interpretations and adaptations of Chinese myths possible, although not every interpretation is imbued with progressive gender ideology.

As both Edward Schafer and Andrew Plaks observe, after her debut in mythical texts, Nüwa enjoys a relatively inconspicuous status in medieval Chinese literature. But she reappears in several vernacular novels of the Ming and Qing dynasties. *Investiture of the Gods* (*Fengshen yanyi*) is a sixteenth-century Ming novel that combines fantasy and historical romance. The novel details the fall of the Shang dynasty (1600–1046 BC) and the rise of the Zhou dynasty (1046–771 BC), but opens with a mythical framework, as many Ming and Qing vernacular novels do. King Zhou of Shang visits a Nüwa temple, and he is sexually aroused at the sight of a statue of Nüwa. The infuriated goddess then swears to destroy King Zhou and his dynasty. She sends a female fox spirit down to earth who is disguised as a beautiful girl, Daji, to seduce King Zhou of Shang. Daji as a femme fatale summoned by Nüwa seems to emphasize that Nüwa, as a goddess, is capable of employing feminine beauty and sexual attraction to corrupt men and destroy their kingdom. Daji is blamed for the fall of the Shang dynasty through corrupting King Zhou and distracting him from state affairs and causing him to rule with tyranny and cruelty. The existence of Daji provides an excellent excuse for the demise of the dynasty from the patriarchal perspective. This framework seems to reinforce the sexual connotations of the goddess Nüwa.

The opening chapter of Cao Xueqing's *Dream of the Red Chamber* also uses a mythical framework focusing on Nüwa, but the treatment is very different from that of *Investiture of the Gods*. In this novel, the male protagonist Jia Baoyu is originally a colorful stone left by Nüwa when she repaired the sky. As Li-Chuan Ou argues, in classical Chinese literature, the feat of patching the sky functions as a metaphor for the ideal of the Confucian intellectual to govern the state and serve the people, and the stone's inability to repair and disqualification from repairing the sky becomes a metaphor of self-pity and mourning from frustrated literati who fail in an official career (119). Imperial examinations and official careers were available only to men in ancient China, and therefore, repairing the sky serves as a metaphor for social achievement belonging mainly to the male domain. If the creation of humankind underscores Nüwa's female fertility, while the repair of the sky is a more masculine feat, thus Nüwa's combination of these two feats indicates an androgynous nature. Interestingly, In *Dream of the Red Chamber*, Jia Baoyu as the main male character shows little interest in attending imperial exam- inations and pursuing a masculine career path, but embodies many qualities associated with the women of his society (Edwards, *Men and Women* 38). The connection initiated by the mythical framework between Nüwa, the colorful stone, and Jia Baoyu tends to emphasize this kind of androgyny. *Dream of the Red Chamber* also portrays a female character, Wang Xifeng, who expresses the preference to be a man. However, as Edwards aptly observes, "Baoyu's fem- inine activities, such as his predilection for cosmetics and female company and his disdain for the civil service career path, are ultimately less reprehensible than Xifeng's foray into the masculine world" (*Men and Women* 86). Xifeng is physically and spiritually destroyed for her ambition for power, and the novel "depicts female transgression of acceptable boundaries as more constricting than male transgression" (*Men and Women* 86). Although *Dream of the Red Chamber* depicts Nüwa's repair the sky of in its opening mythical chapters, in its mimetic main section, it provides a rather bleak picture for women who transgress gender boundaries.

In the late Qing dynasty and the Republic of China, the goddess Nüwa was summoned by the intellectuals who promoted the women's liberation movement and the authors of new fiction as the epitome of female hero- ism, and thus she embodies a distinctive feminist creed. For example, the vernacular novel *The Stone of Goddess Nüwa* (*Nüwa shi*, 1904), which details female assassins resisting the bankrupt Qing regime, opens with a mythical framework about the goddess Nüwa. However, the feminist movement in

early-twentieth-century China arose "in the context of national modernization projects that swept the country in the wake of European and Japanese
imperialism" (Dooling 17–18). In other words, it was only through the align-
ment with nationalist pursuits that women's liberation could be legitimated.

As Qingyun Wu observes, the myth of Nüwa as sky-mender and flood-
conqueror "gives Chinese women a continuous sense of responsibility in family
or national crisis, cushioning the moments of patriarchal collapse" (6). In a
similar vein, there is the tradition of women warriors represented by Hua
Mulan. Yet Chinese women warriors breaking into the masculine world of
war are generally doing so in the name of father and nation, and are therefore incorporated by the patriarchal principle (Edwards, "Transformations of
the Woman Warrior"). Many contemporary novelists find an emancipatory
potential in the goddess Nüwa as well as women warriors, and they need to
construct their literary imagination very carefully to fully evoke the potential
as well as to avoid the pitfalls. In the next section, I examine Canadian Chinese author Larissa Lai's novel *Salt Fish Girl* (2002) to explore the literary
imagining of a goddess and its thematic implications for gender politics in
contemporary society.

A Radical Return to the Serpentine Goddess

Salt Fish Girl employs the myth of Nüwa and other folkloric scripts. By innovatively blending and transforming mythical, folkloric, and literary materials,
this novel effectively frees female subjectivity from the repression of the patriarchal order crystallized in its multiple pre-texts. Set alternatively in China
from the pre-Shang dynasty to the early 1900s and a futuristic North America constituted by the corporate-controlled towns of Serendipity and Painted
Horse and an Unregulated Zone, Lai's novel is structured by separate chapters
narrated by a mythical and reincarnated Nüwa and by future Miranda. Nüwa's
part unfolds around her elopement with Salt Fish Girl and their impoverished
life in the earlier-twentieth-century Canton, while Miranda's narration pivots
on her strange stinking disease, her family life, her internship at a clinic, and
her encounter with her lover, Evie, and final awakening. It is arguable that
the part of Nüwa is primarily based on mythology, while the part of Miranda
is patterned after the conventions of science fiction, with high-technology

scenarios and new invented gadgets. Thus, the novel manages to "fuse the trope of reincarnation in folklore and myth to that of cloning in science fiction" (Joo 57). However, as Michelle N. Huang observes, these two threads of stories are eventually one narrative "in a knotted, intertwined form," and "Lai's splicing of pre- and postmodern genres—mythology and science fiction—formally enacts the novel's meditation on genetic modification" (119). As Paul Lai also notes, "*Salt Fish Girl*'s juxtaposition of a prehistorical past, historical moments, and a speculative future creates a hybrid narrative that is at once myth, history, fairy tale, and science fiction" (169). Lai alternates the voices of the goddess Nüwa (as well as her incarnation) and Miranda to intertwine a story of female sexuality and subjectivity. Nüwa's mythic voice and Miranda's science fictional voice collaboratively inscribe a full and cyclical story.

Such a generic hybrid narrative is constructed by multiple generically and culturally diverse intertexts, among which two groups of source materials are identified in Lai's novel: the first group includes Chinese and Christian creation myths and their literary descendants, including Mary Shelley's *Frankenstein* and Shakespeare's *The Tempest*. The other is the interspecies romance tale type, including the Japanese folktale "The Crane Wife" and Hans Christian Andersen's literary fairy tale "The Little Mermaid."

Lai's polymorphous narrator begins as Nüwa, the serpentine creator goddess, with the sentence, "in the beginning there was just me" (1). The phrase "in the beginning" alludes to the Bible, the Western counterpart of Nüwa's creation myth. In the Bible, the evil snake tempts Eve and then causes the loss of Eden, which establishes the association between female, serpent, and evil. In the Chinese creation myth, however, the half-female, half-snake goddess, Nüwa, is not the embodiment of evil but rather the power of creation. As a female creator of humankind, Nüwa also contrasts sharply with the God in the Christian myth, for she has more sympathy and affection toward her creations. According to Genesis, God floods the Earth, for he is furious at the sinful state of humankind. In Chinese mythology, some recorded fragments describe Nüwa as the savior of humankind by mending the damaged sky and stopping a flood. Lai finds profundity and potential in the tales about Nüwa by showing that even though narrator-Nüwa considers her creations to be "monstrous" and "disgusting" (3–4), she still endeavors to help them to survive and prosper. She does not consider herself superior to mortals, but rather feels a longing to become one of them. In contrast, Dr. Flowers, the male creator of human clones in Lai's novel, ruthlessly exploits his creations, for he does not view these clones as human (Lai, *Salt Fish Girl* 255). This attitude is reminiscent of Frankenstein's contempt for his monster. As Robyn Morris remarks, Lai's usage of Nüwa mythology directly links reproduction to the maternal rather than the technological, and "allows for a contestation of historically embedded textualizations of human origins as a natural, Western, and paternal creation" (91). In Lai's reorientation of the creation myth and her depicted contrast between female tolerance and male indifference, her novel successfully empowers female subjectivity through the image of Nüwa.

The degradation and disempowerment of Nüwa from a powerful goddess to an abject victim starts with the bifurcation of her tail into two legs, an event that overtly reminds readers of Andersen's "The Little Mermaid." Lai's description of the splitting of Nüwa's tail consciously draws attention to Andersen's pre-text:

> "I saw a young man's face," I told her, "I want to go up into the world as a human being."
>
> She said, "I can give you legs, but the bifurcation of your tail will be very painful."
>
> "I don't care," I said, "I am not afraid of pain." (Lai, *Salt Fish Girl* 8)

Another reference to Andersen's tale occurs when Nüwa later comes back from the Island of Mist and Forgetfulness, a floating city in the sky that symbolizes the Western world in contrast to Nüwa's impoverished homeland, Canton. Upon her return, her parents and lover cannot understand her anymore, for she has lost her native language. Both the loss of the language and the loss of the tail could be seen as the impairment of the agency of Nüwa. A third similarity with "The Little Mermaid" is that she "will never again be without pain" (Lai, *Salt Fish Girl* 8). In a scene at the beginning of the novel, when a young man on a boat looks down at the lake and sees Nüwa, his face triggers Nüwa's desire to become human and consequently leads to her bifurcation. Although the young man on the boat is reminiscent of the Prince in Andersen's story, Lai gives the episode a disturbing twist. After Nüwa gains legs, she sees that "on a nearby rock sat another woman, also stroking her legs and marveling at their newness" (Lai, *Salt Fish Girl* 9). Another woman indicates there is a companion mermaid for Nüwa. But the following sentence, "her face was remarkably like the face I had seen gazing down at me from the boat," disrupts the familiar script (Lai, *Salt Fish Girl* 9). The resemblance of the woman's face to the young man's blurs the difference between female companionship and heterosexual romance. Readers need to create new mental models to comprehend the distorted script. Subsequently, in her first reincarnation, Nüwa meets and falls in love with Salt Fish Girl. In her next reincarnation as Miranda, Nüwa meets and falls in love with Evie, a human clone that is a mixture of woman and 0.3 percent freshwater carp, a supposedly reincarnated Salt Fish Girl. The initial blurring signified by the facial resemblance is ultimately asserted and transformed into replacement, for there is no longer a place for the Prince in Lai's novel. Lesbian desire based on sameness and equality triumphs over heterosexual union based on difference and hierarchy.

The ultimate empowerment of female subjectivity is achieved by the ending of the novel, which depicts Nüwa/Miranda and Salt Fish Girl / Evie in the water with tails coiled together, returning from human to mermaids. The gesture alludes to the famous funeral stone carving in Wuliang Shrine dated back to the Han dynasty, which portrays the god Fuxi and goddess Nüwa half-human half-snake with tails intertwined. In the modern story, the male god Fuxi has been replaced by another female—Salt Fish Girl / Evie. The provocative ending of the novel, which depicts Miranda going into labor and giving birth to a baby girl underwater while she and Evie have their tails interlocked, is a final assertion of queer kinship and female power. Miranda was impregnated not by insemination but by eating fruit from a mutated durian tree, showing that men are no longer necessary for reproduction. Not only is the creation of humankind rendered as maternal and non-Western in Lai's retellings of the Nüwa myth but reproduction is also achieved through an alternative means, which has the effect of "enforcing their bond with nature and stating their independence from the male principle" (Villegas-López 36). Therefore, the subordination of female to male is replaced by liberating female same-sex desire.

Even though Nüwa/Miranda is the unchanging first-person narrator, Lai titles her feminist dystopian novel *Salt Fish Girl*. Salt Fish Girl / Evie is more radical and rebellious than her partner, while Nüwa/Miranda is torn between a still-effective patriarchal system with a loving nuclear family and a thriving corporate economy and a radical female community that fights against the abusive biotechnology developed by male capital holders and scientists.

Miranda used to work as an intern for Dr. Flowers, who is the creator of illegal human clones—including Evie— used for sweatshop labor. Miranda also sells her mother's songs to the Pallas Company for profit and creates an advertisement for the Pallas Company in which "shoes replaced the handsome prince as objects of [the little mermaid's] desire" (Lai, *Salt Fish Girl* 236). Miranda acquiesces to the institutional exploitation of female labor that builds on the intrinsic link between patriarchy and capitalism until she gradually realizes the hidden truth. Her awakening is accomplished through active reinterpretation and rewriting of familiar stories. A crucial moment is an allusion to the Japanese Swan Maiden tale, "The Crane Wife," when Miranda's only friend from Serendipity, Ian Chestnut, invites her to attend a party, where she sees several weird shows. In one of these, a female stripper sings a version of the crane wife story:

> The woman opened her mouth and began to sing a song about a crane woman who bathes in a rocky pool while an unscrupulous young student peeps through some bushes. She waits for him to leave so she can get out of the water, but he steals her feathered dress. She yells into the forest, begging him to bring it back, but the only response she gets is the wind sighing through the trees. (Lai, *Salt Fish Girl* 195)

This paragraph alludes to a folktale well known across East Asia, but it should be noted that this is a version retold by Miranda, and her voice shows a startling awareness of the implicit repression of female characters inside the tale. In the canonical version of "The Crane Wife," a poor man saves an injured crane and releases it. Several days later, a beautiful woman visits this man and asks him to marry her. She weaves a silk brocade for the man to sell. The woman is the crane who has been saved, and she marries the man to return the favor. When her true identity is exposed, she disappears forever (Murai 46). Miranda's retelling apparently deviates from this common version, and infuses it with another Japanese Swan Maiden tale, "The Feather Garment" ("Hagoromo"), which features the cloth-stealing plot. By adding this cloth-stealing plot, Miranda changes a voluntary marriage into a forced one. Words such as "unscrupulous" indicate her condemnation of the young student, and the use of the words "yells," "begging," and "sighing" shows she feels sympathy for the helpless crane woman. Miranda then realizes that the stripper's face resembles Evie's, which implies she is also one of the enslaved human clones. Later in the party, when Miranda is forced to come to the stage to perform her mother's song for the elite audience, a parallel between her, the clone stripper, and the crane woman in the tale has been constructed—for all of these female characters are exploited by the patriarchal society in tandem with corporate capitalism. Therefore, Swan Maiden stories such as Andersen's "The Little Mermaid" and the Japanese "The Crane Wife" are submitted to severe scrutiny in Lai's rewriting, with their latent repression of female subjectivity foregrounded and then criticized. The domesticated little mermaid and victimized crane wife are replaced by the rebellious Evie and the powerful Miranda, and the subversion of phallocentrism is completed by Lai's returning and restoring the once-powerful-but-lost Chinese serpentine goddess Nüwa.

A Matriarchal Utopia in Mythology

Another trope thematically connected with the goddess is that of a prehistoric matriarchal society. The Amazons in Greek mythology might be the earliest imagined realization of such a matriarchal society. Jessica Amanda Salmonson observes that such fantasies are cross-cultural and universal: "Chinese myth tells of 'the Women's Kingdom,' their rich and unapproachable capital existing near a distant sea, possibly referring to the same Themiscrya in Amazonia, located on the Euxine" (*Encyclopedia of Amazons* n.p.). The first mention of a country inhabited only by women appeared in *The Classic of Mountains and Seas*: "The Country of Women lies north of the country of Shaman Xian. Two women live there with water surrounding them. One author says that the two women live together within the same house gates" (Birrell, *The Classic of Mountains and Seas* 116). The brief description gives no further explanation of this strange place, identifying only two basic elements, women and water. The third-century commenter on *The Classic of Mountains and Seas*, Guo Pu, enlarges on these two basic elements by linking them logically: "There is a yellow lake, where women bathe and then emerge pregnant. Any sons they give birth to suddenly die after three years" (Strassberg 173). Based on these fantastic descriptions, later fiction such as *Journey to the West* (*ca.* 1592) and Li Ruzhen's *Flowers in the Mirror* (*ca.* 1827) reimagine such a kingdom of women.

The depiction of the Kingdom of Women of West Liang in *Journey to the West*[2] (chapters 53–54 in Wu Cheng'en 643–66) generally follows mythical texts and Guo's annotation. On their pilgrimage, a small group passes through a country where not a single male lives. Female citizens in this country become pregnant through drinking water from the river called Child-and-Mother River. Tripitaka and Pigsy accidentally become pregnant by drinking from this life-giving river, and Tripitaka is also forced to marry the empress of the Kingdom of Women. Though exhibiting the humor and wit of the author Wu Cheng'en to its full extent, this episode nevertheless contributes to the larger theme of the narrative, in that it emphasizes and praises Tripitaka's dedication to Buddhism as evidenced through his resisting sexual temptation. In this way, the group's experience in this kingdom is just another ordeal in their quest. The temptation of the beautiful empress of this kingdom and its strange customs are obstacles to be overcome.

Flowers in the Mirror, especially the first half of the novel, is a witty and humorous Chinese version of Swift's *Gulliver's Travels* (1726). This first part depicts a sea voyage to foreign nations, undertaken by three male characters: an intellectual, Tang; his brother-in-law Lin, a merchant; and an old helmsman, Duo. The group encounters many strange plants, monsters, and bizarre countries, whose names and habitus are apparently borrowed from *The Classic*

2. Like many other Chinese novels from the Ming and Qing dynasties, *Journey to the West* is a work with multiple antecedents prior to the sixteenth century. The novel is an extended account of the pilgrimage committed by the Tang monk Xuanzang (Tripitaka) and his four disciples (Sun Wukong, aka Monkey; Zhu Bajie, aka Pigsy, Sha Wujing, aka Sandy; and a dragon prince). The basic pilgrimage plot comes from the life stories of Xuanzang, a monk living during the Tang dynasty, who traveled alone from China to India to collect and bring back Buddhist scriptures. One of his disciples, Bianji, compiled the book *Datang xiyu ji* (*Great Tang Records on the Western Regions*) in 646 according to his master's dictation and based on his nineteen-year journey. This book is acknowledged as the earliest and prototypical version of *Journey to the West*. Another significant rendering in the evolving history of this story is *Datang sanzang qujing shihua* (*The Story with Poems of How Tripitaka of the Great Tang Obtained the Buddhist Sutras*) from the Northern Song dynasty, the first in which a monkey figure joined the group of pilgrims. The next step is a dramatic version, *Xiyou Ji Zaju* (*Variety Drama of Journey to the West*) written during the Yuan dynasty (fourteenth century). The sixteenth-century novel version, absorbing many elements from preexisting oral and written versions, with the help of the author's literary genius, has become the canonical text of this pilgrim narrative. Along with the generational accumulation of oral and textual records, the story evolves from a primitive shape to a more extended and sophisticated form. For a detailed analysis of the previous versions of *Journey to the West*, see Dudbridge.

of Mountains and Seas, while the voyage mode is patterned after *Journey to the West*. However, *Flowers in the Mirror* reverses conventions from the two earlier texts, *The Classic of Mountains and Seas* and *Journey to the West*. The most extended and climactic episode of the first voyage, the Kingdom of Women episode (chapters 32–37 in Li Ruzhen 218–55), is an excellent example of Li's development and subversion of the two previous texts.

Li innovatively rearranges the logical relationship between the three elements: women, men, and water. His schema switches the exclusion of men to inclusion and then reverses the power structure between the sexes. His Kingdom of Women changes from a single-sex domain to a gender-reversed society. In this kingdom, women assume the dominant role, as do men in a patriarchal feudal society. They work as empresses, officials, soldiers, and breadwinners, while men play the domestic role as wives, concubines, and mothers. The inclusion of males in the society renders the fertilizing function of water unnecessary. Instead, Li turns the water into a flood, thus inverting it from a symbol of female fertility to a vehicle for male accomplishment, since in Chinese mythology the myth of controlling the flood is credited to the male hero, Yu. Although the mythology of Nüwa mentions her collecting the ashes of reeds to stop the flood, this tale is overshadowed by the more prevailing (male) version of "Yu the Great controls the flood." In Li's carnivalesque episode set in a female-dominated society, it is Tang's controlling of the flood that saves Lin from the fate of becoming a concubine of the empress. The handsome merchant Lin catches the eye of the empress of this kingdom. Imprisoned in the palace, he is subjected to a process of torture aimed at making him a proper concubine of the empress, including ear piecing and foot binding. The unbearable pain caused by foot binding drives Lin almost to suicide.

In this episode, the sarcasm is obviously directed against the traditional subjugation of women in China, represented by its most hideous practice—foot binding. Therefore, in its unrelenting depiction of the brutality associated with the objectification of women, this episode in *Flowers in the Mirror* effectively dismisses the Buddhist quest theme evident in *Journey to the West*; it also successfully reveals the barbaric side of gender politics in the seemingly civilized nation of China. In the later part of Li's fantasy novel, talented girls are allowed to attend a special imperial examination supported by Empress Wu Zetian. Unlike the imagined king of a country of women, Empress Wu Zetian acted as the ruling empress of China from 684 to 705, during the Tang dynasty. The criticism of the Confucian conservative gender paradigm and the positive appraisal of women's intellectual achievements ostensibly constitute feminist features in Li's novel, and the chapter concerning the Kingdom of Women is therefore included in Estelle B. Freedman's *The Essential Feminist Reader* (37–46). However, closer scrutiny reveals Li's contradictory perspectives in addressing the agency of women. As Maram Epstein argues, the novel "is less about the lives of, or possibilities for, actual women and girls than a highly patterned fantasy in which the gender complementarity builds on the contradictory meanings associated with the symbolic feminine" (271). The novel ends with the overturn of Empress Wu's rule by male Tang loyalists, and the novel's ambivalent attitude toward Empress Wu's usurpation of the throne casts a doubtful light on the novel as a feminist manifesto.

Journey to the West and *Flowers in the Mirror* represent two types of matriarchal utopias, "either on the grounds that no men were present in the population or that women served as heads of state" (Jay 220). The former is in a separatist mode and the latter is in a power reversal mode. Contemporary Chinese speculative fiction and film generally follows these two narrative modes, but innovatively plays with their tropes and motifs. As Eller notes, "the myth of matriarchal history is, at heart, an enormous thought experiment, a play with reversals, an endeavor to visualize a past radically different from the present" (*Gentlemen and Amazons* 8). In the following section, I examine a group of texts that actively engage with these two modes of matriarchal utopia rooted in ancient Chinese myths, and investigate their legacy and their deviation from old tales.

The Separatist Paradigm

Separatist matriarchal utopias usually depict a society with female citizens only. However, these narratives always involve encounters with men from the outside. The Chinese mythical tale of a kingdom of women, as detailed in *Journey to the West*, depicts the encounter between the empress and her subjects and the four male members of the team of pilgrims. The empress tempts Tripitaka with a marriage proposal, which Tripitaka steadfastly rejects. This encounter and marriage proposal function as a trial, testing Tripitaka's abstinence and religious piety. The romantic element is not included in the Ming dynasty novel; however, the empress's sexual desire toward Tripitaka is indicated. Minimal information about the politics, economy, history, and culture of this kingdom is revealed. Nevertheless, the novel portrays it as a prosperous and civilized country.

Inspired by Greek Amazon mythology, Charlotte Perkins Gilman's feminist utopian novel *Herland* (1915) imagines a country undiscovered by the outside world, Amazonian in nature and resembling the kingdom of women as detailed in *Journey to the West*. Both the Kingdom of Women in *Journey to the West* and Gilman's Herland are populated entirely by women, who give birth parthenogenetically. In both narratives, the arrival of a group of men disrupts the women's relative peace. However, neither the Ming novel nor later adaptations depict one of the women leaving her homeland to visit the outside world, as Ellador does in Gilman's novel. Another key difference between the Chinese and Western imaginaries about an exclusively female society is that the Chinese text lacks the utopian view evident in Gilman's book, partly because China has never had a strong utopian literary tradition in general (Qingyun Wu 9). Later adaptations have more interest in portraying the love affair between the empress and the monk than in particularizing the history and geography of the women's country and its economic and cultural system.

Modern and contemporary rewritings and adaptations of this episode in the women's kingdom from *Journey to the West* generally choose one of two paths, carnivalization or romanticization. A vulgar farce about a nymphomaniac lurks beneath the Buddhist allegory, warning against carnal desire, as manifested in an episode in the fourteenth-century variety drama *Xiyou Ji Zaju* (Chen Jun 96–103). A drama in twenty-four acts, *Xiyou Ji Zaju* is more an entertaining farce for the mass audience than a creation for the literati. Its handling of the Kingdom of Women is carnivalesque, portraying the empress as a horny woman, who tries to marry and rape Tripitaka by force. The ribald lyrics of the drama are amusing and humorous, which effectively dispels the solemnity and sacredness of the original religious allegory.

One of the earliest cinematic adaptations of this episode from *Journey to the West*, Ho Menghua's *The Land of Many Perfumes* (*Nüer guo*, 1968), follows this line. This film belongs to *The Monkey Goes West* series (consisting of four films) produced and released by the Shaw Brothers Studio in Hong Kong in the 1960s. *The Land of Many Perfumes* develops the nymphomaniac theme to its extreme, in such a way that it is no longer humorous but grotesque. The three most powerful people in the Kingdom of Women desire and pursue Tripitaka: the empress, the prime minister, and the princess. They fight with each other and treat Tripitaka as a sexual object. Several female demons also join the battle. As Yan Liang observes, *The Land of Many Perfumes* and the other three films in this series are darker and more sinister than the Ming dynasty novel and "present a bleak picture of both the demon and the human world" (1293). Liang connects this bleak image with Hong Kong's precarious situation between several political regimes. Such an interpretation ignores the thematic implications, from the gender perspective, behind this fierce female competition.

For the most part, *The Land of Many Perfumes* follows the farcical mode initiated by the variety drama, and its depiction of women's active sexual desire is more titillating than subversive. The brutal female competition over one male character reinforces the desirability of the opposite sex and thus gender stereotypes. We may be reminded of Terry's words from Charlotte Perkins Gilman's *Herland* (1915), where he assumes the citizens of Herland "would fight among themselves," since "women always do. We mustn't look to find any sort of order and organization" (10). Nevertheless, the male character in *The Land of Many Perfumes*, Tripitaka, is objectified and almost becomes a victim of rape. He endures sexual harassment and attempts at seduction and does his best to protect his virginity. All these situations put him in a position resembling that of the average woman in a patriarchal society. In the end, the court officials of this kingdom blame the empress for neglecting her responsibilities as ruler because of her infatuation with Tripitaka, and they launch a military rebellion. This plot is a travesty of the traditional trope of the "dangerous beauty," as the concubine Daji mentioned previously. Like Helen of Troy, beautiful women in ancient Chinese history were often scapegoats for public criticism in the event of an empire's collapse. In this film, Tripitaka is positioned as a woman would be in traditional Chinese society, and this reversal reveals the irrationality of treating women merely as sexual objects and scapegoats.

Another option chosen in later adaptations is to romanticize the relationship between Tripitaka and the empress, thereby transforming this religious allegory into a secular tale of doomed love. This tendency began with the mainland TV series adaptation of *Journey to the West*. Released in 1986, the two-season series was highly influential in the 1980s and afterward, and is considered a canonical work. It has been rerun almost every year and has become a nostalgic symbol of the childhood of the post-80s generations in China. The plot of this live-action adaptation focuses on the recurrent episodes of adventure in the Ming novel, and its length provides the scope to elaborate on every micro adventure. Episode sixteen details the story line of the Kingdom of Women from chapters 53 and 54 of the original novel. In the confrontation scene between Tripitaka and the empress, camera shots and moves emphasize Tripitaka's wavering and fluttering through highlighting eye contact. At first he dares not look directly at the empress, and later, when his gaze finally falls on her, he cannot move his eyes away. Tripitaka refuses the empress's courtship verbally, but his facial expressions and body language indicate the opposite. His words, "If there is a next life . . . ," also reveal his true feelings. The departure scene is portrayed as sentimental and heartbreaking, with a tearful empress and a cheerless Tripitaka. A theme song, "A Maiden's Love" ["Nüer qing"], is inserted into this episode, and its sad and beautiful melody and lyrics render this episode an almost-love-story between a Tang monk and a female monarch. This 1986 version is highly regarded by the audience for its innovative adaptation of a familiar story, and this episode about unfulfilled love strikes a chord with a generation who choose individual happiness over religious salvation.

A fuller romance between the monk and the empress has been realized in the film *The Monkey King 3: Kingdom of Women* (*Xiyou Ji zhi nüer guo*, 2018) directed by Hong Kong director Cheang Pou-Soi. Since 2010, China's bustling film industry has experienced a boom of fantasy blockbusters based on classical literary novels and tales, and Cheang Pou-Soi's *The Monkey King* trilogy (2014, 2016, and 2018) is representative. In this third film, the empress and Tripitaka fall in love at first sight, and both face a dilemma: whether or not to forsake duty for love. For Tripitaka, although he would love to stay in the kingdom and live happily ever after with the empress, he is obligated to complete his religious quest to collect the Buddha's scriptures. The empress tries to leave her country and embarks on the journey with Tripitaka, only to discover that the people of her land are petrified without her. It is no longer only Tripitaka who experiences an ordeal and has to make a choice; the empress, also, must choose between personal happiness and collective wellbeing. The film ends with Tripitaka's insight that "love for a person or the world is clearly the same," which can be viewed as a secularized interpretation of the lack of discrimination between altruistic and universal compassion (in the Buddhist concept) and personal eros.

The secularization of *Journey to the West* is not exceptional, especially among contemporary adaptations; Jeffrey Lau's *A Chinese Odyssey* (*Dahua xiyou*, 1995) is the most prominent example of this. Lau's film embodies both the carnivalization and romanticization strategies, by adding several new female characters and putting Sun Wukong's love stories at the center (Zeng, "Adaptation as an Open Process" 190). This tendency is echoed in Stephen Chow's new adaptation (codirected with Derek Kwok), *Journey to the West: Conquering the Demons* (*Xiyou xiangmo pian*, 2013), which creates a love story between a young Tripitaka before tonsure and a female exorcist. Transforming the religious pilgrim narrative into a romantic story is a natural development in a post-Enlightenment and secular age, when the pursuit of individual happiness through love and marriage is legitimated. But both *A Chinese Odyssey* and *Journey to the West: Conquering the Demons* are stories told from the perspective of their male protagonists.

For the first time, *The Monkey King 3: Kingdom of Women* tells the familiar story from the perspective of the empress. Previous adaptations have integrated romantic elements into the religious allegory and portrayed Tripitaka as a more humane character with worldly desires; however, the encounter with the empress is still a trial for him, and what matters is his choice. In the penultimate scene of *The Monkey King 3: Kingdom of Women*, Bodhisattva advises Tripitaka to follow his heart in his choice between loving one person and loving all sentient beings. She declares that if Tripitaka can put on his cassock again, then he can resume the journey to the West. No matter how Tripitaka and Sun Wukong try, the cassock constantly falls, suggesting that Tripitaka's love for the empress outweighs his faithful adherence to duty.

The finale of this film positions the empress as the focus, as it is she who makes the final decision. Motivated by altruism, she decides to relinquish this love and she buttons Tripitaka's cassock. She tells Tripitaka that she had a dream. In this dream, she and Tripitaka marry and grow old together, with Tripitaka resuming secular life and growing his hair long. But she observes that Tripitaka is not genuinely happy, indicating he cannot totally forget his religious quest. In a later scene of the finale, depicting the citizens of the Kingdom of Women drowning in the river because of a flood summoned by the villain River God, the empress sees Tripitaka praying to Buddha to save the drowning people and witnesses a miracle. Her dream and witnessing the miracle urge her to rethink their relationship, and she decides to sacrifice her love for the common good. Thus, this film portrays the transformation of the empress from a solipsistic love-smitten girl into a responsible and altruistic heroine, and her character arc eclipses even that of Tripitaka.

It may be seen as a timely choice for *The Monkey King 3: Kingdom of Women* to present a women-centered narrative, given the momentum and publicity that the feminist movement has gathered in recent decades. Around the same time that the film was produced, the category "big heroine drama" appeared in the Chinese media landscape, referring to television dramas that center on a female protagonist and focus on her life story, which is often set against the background of ancient China (Ying Zhang 212). Cheang's film follows the same trend of giving a voice to neglected female characters from history and literature.

The film also endeavors to dismantle the gender stereotype in its several subplots. For example, it elaborates on the parthenogenesis motif from the original novel. Parthenogenesis is a method of reproduction without fertilization by sperm. As the Ming novel *Journey to the West* tells us, women in this all-female kingdom become pregnant by drinking water from the Child-and-Mother River. In the novel, Tripitaka and Pigsy accidentally drink the water and become pregnant. Wukong takes pains to fetch water from the Abortion Stream to terminate their pregnancies. This plot ridicules the embarrassment men feel in female roles and expresses a comic horror. In contrast, the film renders this plot in a more serious and sentimental way. Tripitaka feels affection toward his unborn child and decides to give birth to the child and raise her. Wukong forces him to drink the Abortion Stream water against his will. This plot change deessentializes the link between femininity and maternity.[3] Another subplot features an unrequited lesbian romance between the madam preceptor of the Kingdom of Women and an androgynous river god (played

---

3. Male pregnancy is not entirely absent in Chinese supernatural literature. For example, the tale "Male Pregnancy" ("Nan shengzi" in Pu, 1034–35) from *Liaozhai* features a male concubine of an official who gives birth to two children. In the fantasy film *Monster Hunt* (*Zhuoyao ji*, 2015) directed by Raman Hui, the little monster Huba is given birth to by a male character, Song Tianyin, who loves cooking and sewing and shows anti-stereotypical characteristics. All these non-normative childbirths among gay, lesbian, or asexual subjects present various distortions of the familiar heterosexual childbirth motif.

by an actress, but with a male upper body), with an audacious scene depicting their almost touching lips. Nevertheless, unlike Larissa Lai's *Salt Fish Girl*, which gives a deeper reconfiguration of themes of parthenogenesis and lesbian romance, the film touches on these themes without further exploration.

Chinese literary imaginings of a matriarchal world defined by a reversal of power roles are more abundant than those of the female-only society, and they provide insights into how the matriarchal society comprising two sexes has been reimagined to reflect the constructiveness of gender roles and stereotypes. The following section will present two representative matriarchal romances published online, in order to analyze the complexity and the contradictions behind their reimagining of femininity and masculinity.

The Reversal Paradigm

In Li Ruzhen's *Flowers in the Mirror*, the Kingdom of Women is transformed from the single-sex domain of *Journey to the West* into a society with reversed gender roles. Li's innovation becomes the foundation for *nüzun*, a subgenre of Chinese online popular romance: matriarchal fictions set in a society comprising both sexes but ruled by women. The earliest *nüzun* fiction appeared around 2006, nearly ten years after the germination of Chinese online literature. The *nüzun* subgenre continued trending from 2006, with its popularity starting to decline in 2012.

Feng Yiqing notes that, according to the setting of its matriarchal society, *nüzun* fiction can be divided into three categories: completely reversed, partially reversed, and futuristic (34). The first two groups anchor their narratives in an imaginary feudal dynastic past, while novels from the third group are set in a near or far future. Jeffrey C. Kinkley observes that unlike Western speculative fictions, which usually imagine a dystopia embodied in stories of future technology and societies, in Chinese narratives the preference is to meld historical fables with the dystopian novel (ix). This Chinese preference explains why the first two groups make up the large majority of *nüzun* fiction. Among these pseudodynastic historical novels, the distinction between complete and partial reversal lies in their handling of the matriarchal system. Completely reversed novels turn power relationships between the sexes upside down mechanically, with biological traits also reversed. In these novels, women are taller and physically stronger than men and it is the males who give birth. Women have the right to be educated and work in the government and army, and enjoy polygamous marriages (with multiple male partners) and the patronage of (male) prostitutes, but men are deprived of these rights and are reduced to sexual and childbearing objects. Partial reversal novels present a relatively realist picture, with the biological features of men and women remaining unchanged. Pregnancy still belongs to the female sex. But the imagined societies of these novels are matriarchal on the social and cultural levels. The crucial difference between these two story modes lies in which sex is delegated to give birth. The futuristic novels resolve this issue by anticipating technologic advancement. In their imaginings, in vitro fertilization and artificial wombs disengage pregnancy and childbirth from the human body, and thus this process is not limited to one particular sex. The futurist matriarchal society is founded on women's superior physical and intellectual power, achieved through mutation during the evolutionary process.

Essentialism Revisited

As mentioned, which sex is allocated to give birth determines whether a novel belongs to the completely reversed or the partially reversed group of *nüzun* fiction, an issue that is important to the authors and readers. Chinese online literature is famous for its close interaction between readers and writers and its community-building atmosphere. During the development of the subgenre of *nüzun*, the completely reversed mode gradually became mainstream and overshadowed its more realist counterparts. Researchers such as Feng Yiqing lament readers' narrow understanding of female superiority, with the most extreme one as the most appreciated by the readers (43). Observations from online literature websites show that if a novel tags itself as *nüzun* but portrays women as being the ones who give birth, some readers feel disappointed and dissatisfied, to the extent that they will abandon the novel and direct hostile comments to its author. The overwhelming popularity of the completely reversed *nüzun* mode is attributable to its taking the reversal to its extremes, its escapism, and its retaliatory nature. Some female readers find these narratives fulfill their fantasy of female empowerment (Jin Feng 98). I will use an example of this type of narrative to illustrate its charm and its pitfalls in envisaging an absolutely sexually inverted world.

Flowers of Four Seasons: Reborn in the Kingdom of Women (*Sishi Huakai zhi Huanhun Nüer Guo*, hereafter *SSHK*, 2006–27) is generally viewed as the first online *nüzun* novel, and its plot fits into the completely reversed mode. *SSHK* was written by a female author under the pseudonym Gongteng Shenxiu, and was originally posted in 2006 in installments on the website *Jinjiang*, before being published in a series of three print novels in 2007. The protagonist is a plain-looking modern girl who dies in an accident and is then reborn as Ruizhu, the younger sister of the empress in an ancient matriarchal world. Coming from a patriarchal modern world, she experiences a transitory cultural shock and then adapts smoothly to the new system. The major section of this novel revolves around Ruizhu's romantic relationship with several male concubines and prostitutes, not without explicit sexual depictions. Such a narrative parodies polygamous marriage and the patronage of prostitutes enjoyed by men in ancient China. The novel ends with the heroine's "success at establishing and heading a happy domicile including one or more male sexual partners" (Jin Feng 85).

The matriarchal setting of *SSHK* is an overall reversal of the Chinese feudal patriarchal system, as the women are taller and physically stronger, while men are physically and psychologically weaker. Women have the right to be educated and work in the public sphere; men are deprived of these rights and are confined to domestic realms, trying their best to maintain their beauty and competing with each other for the favor of powerful women. Physical beauty and chastity are crucial to males, and men also experience childbirth and breastfeeding.

SSHK is also one of the first pioneers of the trope of male pregnancy in *nüzun* fiction. The mechanics of male pregnancy in *SSHK* are a bizarre fusion of human heterosexual sex and botanical processes. Men must eat a fruit named *qiongguo* before sexual intercourse with women. If the conception is successful, the man's chest will grow a red lump with the fetus inside. After three months, the fetus will grow out of the chest and must be grafted into the *qiongguo* tree. When the fetus has developed into a fully formed baby, the fruit of the tree is cut open and the infant is taken out.[4] Since in the patriarchal culture females have all too often been viewed reductively in terms of

---

4. Infant-shaped fruit born from the tree is a trope that appeared in *Journey to the West* (chapter 24). This chapter describes a rare type of ginseng fruit, whose shape resembles newborn infants, and people can achieve immortality by eating it.

fertility, which is closely connected to nature, Gongteng Shenxiu's invention of a hybrid reproductive system combining the human and the tree reinforces this connection between the fertile sex and nature. However, transmuting the man's chest into a uterus-like organ mocks what used to be a symbol of virility, and it becomes instead a symbol of chastity and fertility. The series also depicts males breastfeeding following labor (chapter 178), although in an erotic style.

The power relationships between the two sexes are turned upside down in *SSHK*, and its defamiliarization of presumed normalcy pushes readers to engage critically with many sexist arguments in the real world, which otherwise remain unnoticed. However, men in the world of *SSHK* are victims of sexism, because they are smaller, physically weaker, and childbearing. Such a simple reversal of the biological traits of the sexes re-essentializes the repressed, physically weaker, and childbearing sex, thereby confirming biological determinism. Readers are able to experience retaliatory pleasure by identifying with Ruizhu and vicariously acting as the holders of power. The radical feminist potential of *SSHK*, in my opinion, lies not in its reversal of normative gender roles but in its explicit descriptions of sex from a female perspective.

Female Sexual Subjectivity

Many sections of *SSHK*, such as depicting coitus between Ruizhu and her male partners, could be viewed as pornographic writing, insofar as gesture and procedure are described in graphic detail.[5] Although *SSHK* creates a new biological system to transfer gestation from the female to the male body, the sexual intercourse still follows the normal biological mode with the male penetrating the female. In patriarchal culture, the prevailing understanding of sexual penetration is inherently inimical to women's subjectivity (Ziv 101). This view is challenged by the inner chamber scenes portraying Ruizhu as agentive and subjective during sexual interaction.

Amalia Ziv notes that there are three constituents to sexual subjectivity—sexual identity, sexual desire, and sexual agency—and that "the dominant constructions of sexual desire and sexual agency" are in conflict with female sexuality (16). However, *SSHK*'s depiction of sexual activity portrays Ruizhu's

---

5. See, for example, chapters 52, 55, and 70. These pornographic sections have been deleted in the print version, but remain accessible online, https://www.sto.cx/book-163950-37.html.

sexual desire and agency in an affirmative way. First, Ruizhu experiences herself "as a desiring subject and as one whose desires are not merely reactive but self-originated" (Ziv 16), and she expresses her desire boldly. Second, Ruizhu possesses sexual agency, "a capacity not only to identify one's desires but also to act upon them" (Ziv 16). Ruizhu plays the dominant and active role during foreplay and sexual activities, assuming riding positions for most of the time. The ultimate goal of these sexual activities is satisfaction for Ruizhu, rather than male orgasm and ejaculation. Often, during the course of these sexual activities, her male partners have attained orgasm while Ruizhu has not. In these situations, coitus continues until Ruizhu calls it quits. Although Ruizhu's attitude and position during sexual acts can be viewed as a kind of mirroring of the male role in traditional heterosexual relations, the descriptions of her corporeal pleasure and reactions belong unmistakably to the female body. In this sense, *SSHK* is liberating in that it is pornography by women and for women.

Pornography used to be viewed as harmful to female subjectivity because of its subordination and objectification of women. However, feminist critiques of the anti-porn claims argue that "pornographic discourse is recuperable for women and for a feminist agenda" (Ziv 6). The sexual scenes of *SSHK* are empowering in their appropriation of the discourse of pornography. The author creates a space where women can express sexual desire freely and aggressively. This depiction has inevitably come under the scrutiny of China's cultural gatekeepers. The original online version of *SSHK* has been blocked by the website *Jinjiang*, since the Chinese government has forbidden pornographic content on the internet since 2014 (Yang and Xu, "The Love that Dare Not Speak"; Jacobs). In the printed version of *SSHK*, all of the sexually explicit content has been expunged, but the full version of this novel remains obtainable online in archived files.

Reclaiming the Public

Unlike *SSHK* and the novels that imitate it, another group of *nüzun* novels turns its focus away from the activities of inner chambers and pivots on women's ascent to power in the public arena. These novels generally imagine a more realist matriarchal society, with the biological features of women remaining unchanged. *A Song of Mountains and Rivers* (*Shan He Fu*, hereafter *SHF*, 2006–9) written by Zhao Tongying is representative of this trend.

In traditional Confucian culture, the distinction between men and women manifests through the disparity between the realms of *nei* and *wai* (Rosenlee 70). The literal meaning of *nei* (inner) and *wai* (outer) denotes specific structure, but in the metaphorical sense the terms are often equated with two conflicting spheres—family/private and state/public. Women are allocated to the *nei* realm and take responsibility for household management, acquiring the domestic skills of weaving, spinning and embroidering, food preparation, and so on. Men belong to *wai*, a realm of classical learning and political skills. Education and officialdom are exclusively male privileges, and women are not allowed to acquire social honors in the realm of *wai*. For example, the imperial civil service examination excludes the participation of women, even those who are literate and educated.

This group of *nüzun* fiction, represented by *SHF*, is attempting to challenge the normative gender-based division of labor grounded in Confucian culture. Ruizhu, in *SSHK*, declares that she has no interest in political struggle and state affairs, even though she is a member of the royal family. She indulges herself in the inner quarters, occupied by her concubines. The heroines of *SHF* are by no means Ruizhu-like—they are prime ministers, generals, and royal heiresses, endeavoring to build a powerful and prosperous nation. Rewriting the dynastic history of feudal China to feature women in positions of explicit social and political authority challenges the Confucian tradition, which views women in power as a serious transgression, and has ramifications for current gender politics.

However, the author of *SHF* does not idealize female government. In her gallery of female characters, just and wise rulers and officials coexist with fatuous and unqualified ones, and benevolent duchesses and gentlewomen are juxtaposed with cold-hearted schemers and backstabbers. There is no singular protagonist, like Ruizhu in *SSHK*, whose central position is beyond doubt. In its million-word content *SHF* presents at least three leading female characters and dozens of supporting ones. The main story arc depicts the long and arduous journey of a deposed crown princess, Jialan, to reclaim the throne with the help of her capable counsellor, Zhao. The complicated love-hate relationship between the counsellor Zhao and an eminent officer, Shuiying, also takes center stage. Women's homosocial activities and their military and political achievements are meticulously illustrated. In contrast, their (mostly heterosexual) romantic and family lives are included but are not given prominence. The novel also briefly touches on lesbian relationships, though in a negative way.

In line with the realist portrait of female rule, neither idealizing nor ridiculing it, *SHF* also imagines a matriarchal society that is less hostile and repressive to men than that in *SSHK*. The author designs a system that is fundamentally matrilineal, but allows men's partial involvement in education and public affairs. Its cultural belief generally follows the principle that "women are superior to men," but acknowledges a small number of men who are exceptional. The novel introduces a family in which the wife and husband both have successful careers as high officials, but the wife acts as the head of the family, and she has a male concubine to take care of household work. Polygamy is prevalent among women, but the requirement for male chastity is relaxed, indicating that men are not viewed solely as sexual objects but are granted a certain level of subjectivity. Correspondingly, *SHF* returns the child-bearing function to women. For the author, the fertility of women is a strength rather than a weakness, although this idea is rebuked by some readers. Overall, this novel envisages a not-so-radical version of a gender role–reversed world. Unlike the completely reversed novels such as *SSHK*, which can be regarded as vengeance from the wronged sex, *SHF* imagines a feminist utopia that aspires to an egalitarian future.

As a potential feminist rewriting of the dominant historical narrative, *SHF* asks "what if history were a herstory," and challenges canonical historiographical tradition. In this rewriting, the gender of rulers and officials has been reversed, but their governing method and statecraft remain the same. In the Confucian ideal, the moral commitment of upright and strong leaders brings about prosperity and national unity. It also imagines and constructs a concentric world, with China at the center, with the barbarian tribes submitting to a central authority. The illustration in *SHF* of the imagined state's affairs and its relationship with neighboring countries generally conforms to this picture, indicating a sense of cultural superiority, and emulating the military expansion of China. For example, the deposed crown princess, Jialan, reclaims her authority and fame largely through her military achievement, after repelling several barbarian invasions. In another *nüzun* novel, *Tai Ping* (2007), the eponymous heroine is an heiress of a military family that has defended its country against nomadic peoples for generations. Inheriting the bravery and martialism of her bloodline, Tai Ping conquers a neighboring barbarian country and slaughters its people. The novel justifies this brutal action by claiming that this ethnic extinction can guarantee a peaceful border for many years and is thus beneficial to the lives of the commoners of the country. However, this "end justifies the means" message is firmly grounded on the ideological positioning of ethnic and cultural nationalism. Online *nüzun* novels rarely cast a critical eye on Sinocentrism and imperial hubris. These novels describe wise and capable female rulers who stick to Confucian ideals of benevolent governance and are concerned with the lives and livelihoods of even the poorest commoners. However, the setting of these alternative history narratives in a feudal past inevitably rearticulates the imperial discourse of Chinese superiority.

Conclusion

A literary genre like myths, for its ancientness and profound impact on the sense of history, religion, philosophy, and psychology for the people in their community, is a significant component of the cultural capital as well as the collective unconscious. Some parts of Chinese mythology are empty signifiers without any moral implication, but more scripts are concerned with building a standard model of social behavior for their audience, with rigid assumptions about the differences between the two sexes, between selfhood and others, and between freedom and authority. The innovative usage of familiar schemas and scripts from mythical texts in contemporary narratives can dismantle this rigid system, and thus enlighten readers to the critical reception of myths and their ideologies.

The existence of multiple versions of Nüwa story and the interpretive gap left by the obscure and archaic expressions endows the image of Nüwa with flexibility and freedom. Similarly, the script of the Kingdom of Women also opens many possibilities for later adaptations to interrogate the gender ideology deeply ingrained in Confucianism. Many of its modern and contemporary successors reveal both the advantages and the shortcomings in the literary imaginings of a matriarchal society. As Clare Bradford et al. observe, concerning the female-centered community portrayed in Jean Ure's postapocalyptic fiction *Come Lucky April* (1992), through the author's deployment of the strategy of estrangement to describe a community in which power relationships between the sexes are turned upside down, readers are positioned to recognize the sexist argument but also experience it as unfamiliar, and "are thus enabled to take a distanced, but fresh view of the ideas involved, engaging critically both with the imagined world of the community and with the real world of the reader and the author" (124). However, such a construction of a female-dominated society is still based on binary oppositions but does not interrogate them. Anne Cranny-Francis, in her examination of feminist fantasy featuring role-reversal, also notes that "the problem with this kind of role-reversal is that it does not challenge the nature of the role itself," but, she argues, these stories "were useful as ground-breaking exercises," which can raise the consciousness (84). Maybe these role-reversal imaginations are merely the first step toward breaking through the old rules of male dominance, and what is still waiting to be imagined is a society in which both sexes are treated as equal and are allowed to achieve their full potentials.

4

Chinese Folklore for Modern Times

FEMINIST REVISIONS OF "THE LEGEND OF THE WHITE SNAKE"

The previous chapter examined the transformation of mythological materials in contemporary fantasy. Another genre that is intimately attached to myths and is also constantly adapted is folklore. Folktales function as a form of cultural heritage in contemporary society and offer models for interpreting experience in everyday practice, but the beliefs and values conveyed by many folktales are ingrained in a patriarchal discourse. Thus, the models they offer are often challenged by the modern prominence given to women's perspectives. This chapter applies an intertextual analysis in a broad cultural context by exploring how the White Snake story has been transformed to cater to the modern progressive attitudes on gender and sex. By focusing on the modern adaptations of the White Snake legend by female authors—Hong Kong author Li Bihua's novel, *Green Snake* (1986), Chinese American writer Yan Geling's novella, "White Snake" (1999), and two online novels—this chapter examines how contemporary female authors incorporate and adapt old folktales in their separate narratives. By adapting the well-known folktale through female voices, these novels challenge the inherited literary and cultural tradition, interrogate and question its gendered discourse defined by the heteronormative patriarchal family structure, and suggest ways in which nonnormative sexuality and gender roles can be imagined and practiced by female members of society.

Folk literature is a rich resource for contemporary writers, but it occupies a particularly paradoxical position in the adaptation process. On the one hand, folktales act as a form of "coded communication in which important cultural values and lessons are guarded and kept in the possession of the society" (Giskin 124). On the other hand, these important cultural values and lessons are not eternal and universal but contingent upon certain social and historical contexts, and may lose currency and be at odds with modern progressive attitudes about issues such as gender, identity, and individuality. Meaning, subjectivity, and sociality, as Stephens and McCallum insist, "are represented through and as endemically gendered structures" (*Retelling Stories* 205). A simple comparison between behaviors and roles displayed by the different sexes in folktales could easily prove the accuracy of such an argument, in which male characters are active seekers and adventurers and also the unshakable center of narration while female characters are assigned to passive or caring roles and even function as rewards for ideal male models.

Moreover, important cultural values and lessons, including issues of right and wrong, good and evil, marriage, and family life, are supposedly embodying culturally specific meanings. A good example is the different status of the Cinderella story in Western and Eastern cultures. The Cinderella script is one of the canonical Western fairy tales that has been retold numerous times. In contrast, the Chinese story of Ye Xian, a supposedly much earlier version of a story about an innocent persecuted heroine, first recorded in a Tang compilation, draws little attention from premodern Chinese writers and storytellers, and it is seldom retold and rarely reprinted in multiple classical and vernacular story anthologies. Recent interest in the Ye Xian story is largely a result of Western influence, as the new adaptations are initiated by Chinese American authors Ai-Ling Louie and Ed Young (1982). Through a comparison with the Western Cinderella, the Chinese rediscovered Ye Xian from obscure ancient records. One reason for the lack of interest in the Ye Xian story in premodern Chinese folk literature seems to be its dubious origin. The story seems to belong to a minority ethnic group inhabiting a region in southwest China and Annam (now Guangxi and North Vietnam, respectively), either the Viet or Yueh (Ting, *The Cinderella Cycle* 40) or the Zhuang (Beauchamp 447). The majority of literati and professional storytellers in ancient China are unsurprisingly Han Chinese, and they show little interest in a story whose protagonist is a young ethnic girl. The deeper reason for the lack of interest, I would argue, lies in the gendered structures so ubiquitous in ancient Chinese society that are grounded on patriarchal Confucianism, for the myth of "rags to riches" is mostly reserved for the male members in society, and the story of a typical poor Cinderlad who ascends to high social status with the help of an otherworldly wife is retold ceaselessly. When it comes to women's social ascent, there are tales about a virtuous courtesan who becomes the wife of an official, as illustrated by the Tang tale "The Biography of Li Wa" ("Liwa zhuan," in Zhang Youhe 103–19), or the wife who remains loyal in poverty, as illustrated by Gao Ming's renowned play *Pipa ji* [*Tale of the Pipa*]. These tales extol aspects of women's virtue such as filial piety, marital fidelity, and self-sacrifice, but the social ascent of these women is dependent on their husband's achievements. The case of Cinderella and its absence in ancient China aptly illustrates the cultural and gender specificity behind the so-called universal lessons and values embodied in folktales.

Apart from ideological conflict, another challenge for modern writers who wish to adapt folktales lies in their conventionalized form, especially the formulaic beginnings and endings, the stereotypical characters, and the repetitive actions and motifs, which "tend to reinforce existing metanarratives and so make it difficult to reshape the stories without recourse to more drastic processes of revision, such as parody, metafiction, or frame-breaking" (Stephens and McCallum, *Retelling Stories* 201). Folk literature is also dynamic in its close relationship with oral storytelling traditions, which are usually performed in interactive ways. There is not a singular and fixed version of a story because it has been altered every time it has been told. Maggie Ann Bowers sees in the modern writers' employment of oral storytelling a potential to resist interpretive closure, for the multiple versions of one story give readers access to different material that encourages responses that are complex and contradictory, and thus emphasize "the possibility of expressing multiple perspectives in the text" (85). Retold texts that fit with her argument must self-consciously point to the many different versions of their pre-texts, and thus allow room for conflicting and complementary interpretive perspectives. This chapter is concerned with feminist revision of one particular tale type that is deeply ingrained with a conservative gender paradigm: the interspecies romance script as represented by "The Legend of the White Snake." I explore four novels written by contemporary female authors as a sample to analyze the narrative strategies used by these authors, including multiple narrators, parody, frame-breaking, self-conscious juxtaposition of multiple versions, and generic ambiguity, to dismantle the patriarchal ideology inculcated in the folklore.

These adaptations from female authors correspond to the Western feminist revisions of classical fairy tales by authors such as Angela Carter and Margaret Atwood. Altogether they introduce female voices to patriarchal scripts.[1] The study of feminist adaptation of Chinese folklore, as an interactive dialogue between studies of folklore and studies of contemporary women's writing, contributes to the academic examination of folk and fairy tales through a feminist perspective.

The Interspecies Romance and the White Snake Script

In China, as in many other cultures around the world, the history of folktales and storytelling is long and flourishing, but one distinct feature of Chinese storytelling is that the oral tradition and the literary tradition have always closely intertwined (Jing Li 194). Therefore, works from the literati, written in either the classic language or the vernacular language, become an abundant resource in tracing the development of Chinese folktales. Most folktales and their written records exist in many retellings and thus encompass multiple variations. Modern and contemporary adaptations of these folktales usually draw on a shared skeleton of plot sequences instead of a specific pre-text, and blend with many homologous tales. Therefore, in the discussion of adaptations, it is more proper to use script from cognitive narratology to address a certain folktale pre-text. A script may be represented by a pattern of action sequences, or by a single action sequence within a larger pattern (Sung-Ae Lee, "The Fairy-Tale Film" 208). One of the most prevalent folktale scripts in China is the cross-species romance, especially the marriage between a mortal man and an otherworldly woman. The basic components of this script include the metamorphosis of the otherworldly maiden, the encounter and marriage between her and a human male, and their eventual separation. These core sequences connect variants of a tale and create a

---

1. The European fairy tale canon contains tales predominantly written or edited by men, including "Cinderella," "Little Red Riding Hood," "Rapunzel," "Sleeping Beauty," and "Snow White and the Seven Dwarfs," with the exception of "Beauty and the Beast," whose canonical version was penned by Jeanne-Marie Leprince de Beaumont (Koehler, Wagner, Duggan, and Dula 1).

network as identified by Donald Haase, a "web of multiple texts in dialogue with each other" ("Hypertextual Gutenberg" 223).

Chinese tales on interspecies romance correspond roughly with the famous motif of the Swan Maiden in Europe. In the Aarne-Thompson-Uther index of folktales, this group of tale-types, numbered from 400 to 459 as "supernatural or enchanted wife (husband) or other relatives," includes a wide range of subtypes and variations. Since the index is "constructed according to tales important to Western Cultures," and "the inclusion of Eastern tales depends on whether they are versions of Western tales" (Gutierrez, "Metamorphosis" 25), the Eurocentric preoccupation in this influential index renders it an inappropriate way to organize global tales. Many efforts are made, however, to broaden the scope of this index. Nai Tung Ting's *A Type Index of Chinese Folktales* tries to show the comment elements between the Chinese folktale tradition and its European counterpart, based on the Aarne-Thompson tale-type system. Ting identifies four Chinese subtypes of the Aarne-Thompson 400, of which the most representative tale is "The Cowherd and the Weaver Girl" as subtype 400A. Although the heroine in "The Cowherd and the Weaver Girl" is a celestial goddess, other subtypes also include the heroine as a bird, snail, goose, and fox. Additionally, Ting identified "The Legend of the White Snake" as the Chinese version of Aarne-Thompson 411: the king and the lamia (*A Type Index* 72). Therefore, both "The Cowherd and the Weaver Girl" and "The Legend of the White Snake" could be viewed as variations of the interspecies romance script.

In her study of the Swan Maiden story type, Barbara Fass Leavy acutely observes that the tale is "only deceptively romantic," and its power resides "not in a love story but in its depiction of a fierce marital struggle" (33), where the power struggle between woman and man ends when the swan maiden is forced into domesticity by a mortal man, suggesting her loss of agency. In East Asian versions of the Swan Maiden motif, the maidens usually go willingly, and even gladly, with the men in an understanding of mutual need (Gutierrez, "Metamorphosis" 34), and seldom do they want to part with their husbands and return to their natural homeland. This softened and domesticated figure contrasts with their more wild and unruly Western sisters such as the Selkies from Celtic and Scandinavian folklore. Influenced by the romantic depiction of water spirits in Friedrich de la Motte Fouqué's *Undine* (1811), Hans Christian Andersen also produces a docile otherworldly maiden who willingly surrenders herself to the normative society of humans. Combined with the willingness of the otherworldly maiden to integrate into human society, the Chinese script is inclined to blend with Andersen's mermaid script.

According to Wilt L. Idema, all of the "four great folk legends" in China, including "The Cowherd and the Weaver Girl" and "The Legend of the White Snake" are stories about failed relations, whereby modern interpretations of these folktales argue that the interspecies marriage is doomed because of the evil patriarchal system ("Old Tales" 38). Idema argues that this modern reading tends to oversimplify the complicated negotiation within the evolution of these tales. A more nuanced examination of these tales and their contemporary adaptations is needed with a special focus on the changed and unchanged parts of the script, and the thematic significance behind these new or retained forms. Modern readers would hope to choose an authentic version among folktale variations that reflect their modern interpretation, and their "discussions seem to be based on the unspoken assumption that all premodern versions basically reiterate the same story, and that any variations are minor and of no great significance," which is far from true (Idema, "Old Tales" 38). There is never a fixed and authentic version of "The Cowherd and the Weaver Girl" or "The Legend of the White Snake," and the versions on which contemporary adaptations are based are commonly not the earliest or most detailed ones but a syncretic script. As Idema explains, "the earliest extant premodern versions of these Chinese tales and legends are no less varied and multiform than their modern adaptations," and we could not "assume that these stories embodied a single, unchanging, essential meaning" (*The White Snake* vii). Modern opinions on "The Cowherd and the Weaver Girl" and "The Legend of the White Snake" may regard them as similar because both are tales of a doomed romance between a mortal man and an alien woman, but the two tales in their premodern forms are far from a stereotypical love story. "The Cowherd and the Weaver Girl" is known as a tale of filial piety in ancient China (Idema, "Old Tales" 36; Gutierrez, "Metamorphosis" 34). The Jade Emperor is so impressed by a man named Dong Yong and his filial piety toward his father that he sends down an immortal maiden to help him pay off his debts by her supernatural weaving skills.

"The Legend of the White Snake" has a much more complicated and mutating history and thematic significance. The earlier versions of this script—the Tang tale "Li Huang" and the Song *huaben* version "The Story of the Three

Pagodas in West Lake" ("Xihu santa ji")—both depict the white snake spirit as a malevolent seductress. After a sexual encounter with the white snake disguised as a beautiful woman, a young man, Li Huang, dies horribly with only a skull and a puddle of water left behind. The male protagonist, Xi Xuanzan, in the Song *huaben* version nearly dies at the hands of a carnivorous serpent woman, who regularly changes male partners by killing the old one once she is attracted to a new one. Xi Xuanzan's uncle, who is a Daoist priest, subdues the serpent spirit and her two companions (black bone chicken and otter) and locks them at the center of West Lake with three pagodas on top. In these two versions of White Snake the heroines are not only unruly seductresses but also merciless perpetrators.

Feng Menglong's vernacular story, "Madam White Is Kept Forever under the Thunder Peak Tower" ("Bainiangzi yongzhen leifeng ta"), included in his *Stories to Caution the World* (*Jingshi tongyan*) collection (1624), is one of the first versions that depict White Snake from a sympathetic perspective, but the cruelty and fierceness of the animal spirit still linger in this much-tamed White Snake. Feng's tale also introduces a new character, Qingqing (also known as Little Green, who is a green fish spirit), as White Snake's maid. Disguised as a beautiful widow, Madam White seduces a poor scholar, Xu Xuan, and marries him. She tries to enrich Xu Xuan through her supernatural power, but the stolen silver and clothes turn Xu Xuan into a crime suspect. After White Snake's nonhuman identity is exposed, a terrified Xu Xuan wants to leave her. But Madam White threatens him and forces him to stay with her, otherwise she will summon a flood to destroy the city. The story ends with a powerful monk, Fai Hai, saving Xu's life and coercing the two spirits to go under the Leifeng Pagoda in West Lake. Up to now, White Snake has embodied the lustful nature of female sexuality and the destructive power of the nonhuman animal. The monk Fa Hai, like the Daoist priest in the Song *huaben* version, is a righteous defender of social norms and the natural order.

Subsequently, the legend went through a major transformation during the Qing dynasty insomuch as new versions turn White Snake from a powerful she-demon to a good wife and caring mother (Liang Luo, "The White Snake" 87). Qing operatic versions of this story unfold as follows. After years of Taoist cultivation, a white snake spirit transforms into a beautiful young woman named Bai Suzhen. She falls in love with a poor scholar, Xu Xian, and the couple quickly marry. Suzhen accidentally drinks some realgar wine and reveals her true form to Xu Xian. At the sight of a giant snake, the young scholar is frightened to death. White Snake thus steals a magic herb to bring her husband back to life. The monk Fa Hai takes Xu Xian to the Jinshan Temple to separate the couple, since he believes the marriage between human and nonhuman violates the heavenly order. To rescue her husband, White Snake and Little Green flood the temple and the nearby town. Ultimately, using a magic alms bowl, the monk subdues a pregnant White Snake and imprisons her in Leifeng Pagoda on the banks of West Lake in the city of Hangzhou. As Idema remarks, the birth of the son between White Snake and Xu Xian is a new creation by the theatrical actors in the eighteenth century, "catering to the conventional desire of a happy ending" (*The White Snake* xvii). In these popular opera versions, the hybrid son passes the examinations as top-of-the-list and sees his mother liberated from the pagoda. In this case, the birth of children, especially male, legitimates the status of a nonhuman wife in human society. Ann Louise Huss views the change from the Tang to the Qing version of the same script as a change in the "intellectual definition of sexual morality," and she argues that the elevation of the White Snake from a monstrous seductress to a domesticated wife reflects a revision and reinterpretation of the informing morality from the perspective of the self (189). Her opinion generalizes this change to cater to all members of society and overlooks the implication it has for female identity. The taming and domestication of a female monster ultimately marks the demolition of the power and autonomy of the female subject.

More generally, there may be a gradual change in the images of Chinese animal women. Earlier records of such tales often depict them as wild and even cruel, and their temporal domestication often ends in the return to their natural world. Several bizarre tales of beast/woman transformation from the fifth-century *Garden of the Strange* (*Yiyuan*) and eighth-century *Records of Gathering Anomalies* (*Jiyi ji*) depict dangerous and unruly otherworldly women (Hui Luo 100–111). One tale ends with the woman not only transforming back into a tiger but also mercilessly devouring both her human husband and their son. Hui Luo observes that during the genre evolution from *zhiguai* to *chuanqi*, a process of "humanization and domestication" occurred: "the awe-inspiring beast/human hybrids were gradually depopulated from the genre, and tamer variants, such as ghosts and fox-spirits, became the more standard characters in later tales" (130). In the narratives from later centuries, with the Confucian patriarchal system strengthening its grip on Chinese society, the otherworldly women become tamed and domesticated. The evolution of "The Legend of the White Snake" fits within this pattern, with the earlier fierce and unruly White Snake turning into a docile and ideal wife and mother in the Qing versions. In this process, the monstrous and animal nature of these female beings—an embodiment of their female sexuality and fertility—is downplayed and controlled under the new socio-symbolic order. If later authors want to free female subjectivity from this patriarchal repression, they must return to the wild and unruly snake as the source of empowering and creative energy.

The White Snake script is likely to have a mythic origin, since it is closely associated with a water schema (Chia-Ju Chang 8). Feng Menglong's version starts with an encounter between White Snake and a human male, Xu Xuan, by the West Lake on a rainy day. In the final battle between the white and green snakes and the monk Fa Hai, the snakes summon a flood to destroy the temple where Fa Hai lives. Both water and woman are the embodiment of *yin* power in the traditional Daoist cosmic system, and in this sense, the serpent figure also relates to the ancient Goddess Nüwa examined in the previous chapter, who in some mythological writings is depicted as a figure with a female head and a serpent body.[2] Credited with the feat of the creation of human beings, Nüwa used to be "a positive and even savior-like image among the Chinese," but her image experienced "a great degradation during China's societal transition from matriarchy to patriarchy after the Han dynasty" (Zifeng Zhao 293). The taming of the ferocious snake-woman and the degradation of a serpentine goddess reflect a motivation that impels male authors.

The goddess Nüwa is the mythological archetype for the folkloric White Snake, as the embodiment of both the dangerous and the glamorous aspects of female sexuality and fertility. Later adaptations of the White Snake script split this female archetype in two, with White Snake as the domesticized and model wife and Green Snake as the wild and dangerous femme fatale. The

2. Similarly, Alan L. Miller argues that Japanese version of the swan maiden tale type may have a mythological and religious origin: "In Japan the sacred weaver takes on cosmic, even cosmogonic dimensions in the mythic figure of Amaterasu. In the folktales a more humble and even domestic scene is portrayed, but the vision of the mysterious, even magical power of creator still is strongly preserved in these more popular narrative forms" (81).

bifurcation initiates the disempowerment of the ancient goddess as well as female subjectivity, but the bifurcation and doubling of femininity also hold the potential to depict female subjectivity and sexuality as porous, plural, and dynamic. Leavy argues that the Swan Maiden's encounter with her mortal mate "thematically links the war between the sexes with the controversial subject of female bonding" (40), and to put female bonding as a theme in the Swan Maiden tale presupposes that it is a woman's story (43), instead of a story of male plight and adventure. The integration of Green Snake into the White Snake script exemplifies Leavy's proposition, for it displaces the narrative focus from the mating plot and creates an oscillation between female solidarity and male dominance.

A folkloric script is only a skeleton; "The Legend of the White Snake" began as a tale of demonic seduction, and then other elements were added to give it flesh and substance (Whalen Lai 53). One of the primary ways adaptations elaborate a script is through expansion, such as adding new characters, subplots, and background stories to the simple script. In the White Snake script, Little Green (*xiaoqing*), also known as Green Snake, is a result of a script expansion. She does not appear as the supporting character in this script until the Ming version (1624), but once she is introduced, in some regional versions, she "loomed so large in importance as to eclipse nearly all the other characters" (Shang 319). In some Qing theatrical scripts, Green Snake appears on stage first as a male spirit, and initiates a combat with White Snake. Defeated by White Snake, he willingly transforms into a female to act as White Snake's maid.

More provocatively, the addition of Little Green to this script—whose core plot is the romance between human and nonhuman—successfully transforms an originally heterosexual tale into a story exploring female companionship and homosexual desire. Her androgynous origin in theater also evinces a potential to disrupt the romance between White Snake and Xu Xian. The looming emergence of Little Green over White Snake's male love interest is largely a creation of contemporary female writers. As Liang Luo argues in her genealogy of myriad adaptations of the White Snake script, "unlike previous texts and visual representations created by men, these female-authored texts made possible the emergence of alternative voices and interpretations of transgressive female sexuality, especially those not fitting the heterosexual norms" ("The White Snake" 98). Hong Kong author Li Bihua's novel *Green Snake*

(*Qingshe*, 1986), Chinese American writer Yan Geling's novella "White Snake" ("Baishe," 1999), and two online authors' popular renditions of this folklore are representatives of this female-voiced retelling of the snake story, and all four works engage in the shift from normative heterosexual love to alternative possibilities of female desire and subjectivity. In what follows, my analysis of the four novels will primarily focus on two essential narrative strategies that successfully challenge the latent patriarchal discourse inherent in traditional folklore: the intertextual connection with previous literary and cultural texts, and the storytelling by female characters as focalizer and narrator. Each White Snake adaptation I examine here has developed a narrative strategy that precludes any straightforward replication of the pre-text. These narratives are thus multivocal and polyphonic in their dialogue with old texts and ideologies.

Green Snake: The Fluid Desiring Subject

Li Bihua is well acknowledged for her "fascination with the materials of past literature" (Chow 73), including folklore, legends, and classical literary books. *Green Snake* (1986) is one of her many adaptations of literary materials from the past. This novel and its renowned cinematic adaptation by Hark Tsui (1993) are the earliest experiments in transforming a heterosexual romance script into a multifarious exploration of both female and male sexuality.

Green Snake approaches the familiar folkloric script of White Snake in a critical and reflective way. It makes Green Snake the protagonist of the story, unlike Ming and Qing vernacular and operatic versions, which foreground White Snake. In this contemporary adaptation, White Snake is lured to the human world by its symbolic order and civilization, while Green Snake retains her wild and unrestrained animalistic instinct. Although both are in the liminal state of in-between human and nonhuman, White Snake nevertheless shows more affinity with the human world through her admiration of elite culture such as poems and calligraphy, through her marriage with her human husband, Xu Xian, and through her voluntary subordination to the gender roles defined by Confucian principles. In contrast, Green Snake retains many serpentine attributes in her swaying way of walking, in her fondness for dancing and pleasure, and in her emotional dependence on her sister—the only kindred she has in the human realm.

The divergent paths chosen by the two snakes are illustrated in an early scene in which they peer down from the roof of a brothel. Green Snake is fascinated by the dancing girls and cannot resist coming down and joining the dancing group, and she turns out to be the best among them, since "is there a woman's waist suppler than a snake's?" (Li, *Qingshe* 19) Meanwhile, White Snake is attracted by the publishing house next door to the brothel, where she finds a poem recited by Xu Xian and falls in love with both the poem and the young male apprentice. As Jen-Hao Hsu's interpretation of this scene from Tsui's film shows, Green Snake's "downfall into the pleasure house indicates her propensity for the 'unethical' and her tendency to fall back into the non-human" (13), while White Snake is presumably closer to the human world. The unethical tendency is further reinforced in Li's change to the theft plot. In Feng Menglong's 1624 version, it is White Snake who uses her supernatural power to steal silver from the government to benefit her lover, and Li innovatively transfers this crime to Green Snake in her novel. Zifeng Zhao views theft as a crime similar to the function of cannibalism in the earlier vernacular version of this script, which is the characteristic of an evil monster that deserves imprisonment (298). Therefore, by transferring the crime committed by White Snake to Green Snake, Li purifies White Snake and reifies Green Snake's monstrous and immoral side. Green Snake's seduction of Xu Xian, her brother-in-law, and their adultery not only reinforces her immorality but also sabotages the once-ideal heterosexual romance between White Snake and Xu Xian.

Paradoxically, the monstrosity endows Green Snake with more agency and freedom than White Snake, and the difference between them functions to "expose the structural limitations of human ethics and challenge the legitimacy of the superhuman sovereign" (Hsu 13). Green Snake steals the heart of Xu Xian from her sister, and even intimidates the authoritarian monk, Fa Hai, with her daring desire for him, and he spares her from the same destiny of imprisonment as White Snake and runs away. Green Snake's desire moves freely among her sister, Xu Xian, and Fa Hai, without fixing on one point. As Alvin Ka Hin Wong argues, Li's representation of "the constant fluctuation of Ching [Green]'s multiple sexual subjectivities and her unstable object choices actually trouble the cosmological hierarchy of gender that originally structures Feng's text in the Ming dynasty," which "polarizes femininity as either heterosexually alluring or demonically destructive," and substitutes a storyworld "where desire has no orderly flow, where whatever sexual transgression can be possible, and where a perverse utopia of subversion seems too powerful to be true" (143–44).

Apart from the Legend of White Snake, which is the dominant pre-text of Li's adaptation, Green Snake alludes to many other Western and Chinese literary tropes and conventions in either covert or explicit ways, including Christian mythology and Eileen Chang's novella "Red Rose, White Rose" ("Hongmeigui yu baimeigui," 1944). In Li's novel, Green Snake and her sister, White Snake, spend hundreds of years of their lives in a state of chaos and nondistinction, since they are animal spirits who are born out of natural essence and enjoy immortality. Green Snake tells readers that "my biggest happiness is sleeping after eating, eating after sleeping, unchanged for five hundred years" (8). A male god disguised as an old man interrupts the two snakes' Edenic life by tricking them into eating some magic dumplings, just as the serpent tricks Adam and Eve into eating the forbidden fruit. The dumplings make White Snake realize her boredom when it comes to having only a female companion, and she starts to desire a heterosexual romance. Although Green Snake feels aggrieved, she nevertheless follows her sister's path to venture into the human world. Here, Li blends the forbidden fruit motif from Christian mythology with the Chinese folkloric script. In both the biblical pre-text and Li's adaptation, the eating of the forbidden fruit marks the inauguration of the patriarchal order. Li's novel depicts a moment when the heterosexual norm invades and erodes the paradise of female companionship; this parallels the punishment for Eve's disobedience, which initiates male authority over the female. This blending works to make explicit the latent sexism in the pre-texts, and thus opens the path to invalidating it.

In the ending, Green Snake's narration sufficiently summarizes the theme of her story with the famous metaphoric description inherited from Eileen Chang, the iconic modern female author who serves as a forerunner and model for Li Bihua. Chang opens her "Red Rose, White Rose" with two such paragraphs:

> There were two women in Zhenbao's life: one he called his white rose, the other his red rose. One was a spotless wife, the other a passionate mistress. Isn't that just how the average man describes a chaste widow's devotion to her husband's memory—as spotless, and passionate too?
>
> Maybe every man has had two such women—at least two. Marry a red rose and eventually she'll be a mosquito-blood streak smeared on the wall, while the

white one is "moonlight in front of your bed." Marry a white rose, and before long she'll be a grain of sticky rice that's gotten stuck to your clothes; the red one, by then, is a scarlet beauty mark just over your heart. (1)

Li revises Chang's famous passage from "Red Rose, White Rose":

Every man wishes to have two women in his life: White Snake and Green Snake, who can simultaneously and alternatively decorate his bleak destiny. It's just that when he gets the White Snake, she gradually becomes the pale ash that is left at the side of the red door, while the Green Snake is the crisp and alluring new leaf on the tip of the tree. By the time he gets the Green Snake, she nonetheless becomes an aging herb left in the cabinets, while the White Snake turns into the tenderly fluttering first snow that he waited so long to spot.

Every woman wishes to have two men in her life: Xu Xian and Fa Hai. Yes, Fa Hai is the gold-plated figure of a god that you have tried every means to get a smile from. You spent your whole life waiting for him to show a tender and encouraging demeanor, and you worship him even more. Xu Xian is the beautiful boy who can hold your hand and paint the eyebrows patiently for you and who can speak the sweetest words to warm your heart. But once you have had him, you start to realize none of his words are genuine and none of his gestures are tough. But once Fa Hai has surrendered to you, you start to hate him for his lack of consideration and indifference. (Li, *Qingshe* 123–24)

The additional second paragraph is essential to Li's parody and inversion of the objectification of woman presented in the metaphor of two roses. Her narration gives voice to female desire and the erotic imagination of men, and her juxtaposition of these two kinds of desire by the opposite sexes asserts a more dialogic and communal mode of discourse without objectification of any side. Both male and female are simultaneously and alternatively changing between the object and subject, and the stereotypical ending of heterosexual romance, "living happily ever after," is ruthlessly ridiculed by her sarcastic description of what happened after. The White Snake folklore and Eileen Chang's "Red Rose, White Rose" are culturally specific pre-texts that might not be recognizable for all readers, but the script of heterosexual romance and love triangle belongs to a universal story prototype. In her appropriation of these either specific or universal scripts, Li engages critically with the gendered discourse implicated in these pre-texts.

Apart from critical intertextual allusions, the subversive potential of *Green Snake* is also realized by its female-voiced narration. Li puts the narrative focus on Green Snake—the marginalized supporting character in Feng Meng-long's vernacular story from the Ming dynasty—as from the outset the novel is presented as the first-person narration of Green Snake: "I am one thousand and three hundred years old this year" (*Qingshe* 3). The story is told entirely from the perspective of Green Snake, in such a way that the novel could be interpreted as an autobiography. But the narration of Green Snake is innately multivocal, with a temporal separation of eight hundred years, wherein her recollection of a youthful memory is automatically formed by two perspectives: a much wiser and more mature Green Snake and her younger and more innocent self.

Through her active storytelling and manipulative narrative voice, Green Snake becomes a freely desiring subject. As the primary focalizer and narrator, Green Snake employs a mischievously manipulative voice to frame her story, which endows her with subjective agency. At the beginning, she embarks on a teasing dialogue with the implied reader: "I forgot to tell you that I was a snake" (Li, *Qingshe* 4). Her subversive power is also realized by her challenging of the authenticity of male authors' storytelling. Later in the novel, she calls into question the faithfulness of previous versions of her story written by male authors:

> In the Ming dynasty, there was a guy named Feng Menglong who included [our story] in a collection titled *Stories to Caution the World*. He even gave it a name, calling it "Madam White is Kept Forever under the Thunder Peak Tower." When I looked through it though, alas . . . none of it was as I remembered. He had covered up the ridiculous truth. The wind and rain of sorrow and jealousy, the entanglements between the four of us, none were dealt with in his book. I was not satisfied. (Li, *Qingshe* 125)

This metafictional section criticizes the previous tales as unfaithful to the truth and instead insists that her telling is the authentic one. In other words, Li's Green Snake authenticates her female voice by dispensing with the official male narratives; however, her accusation that the stories written by others are unreliable also "calls her own narrative attempt to question" (Gan 27). She may be the protagonist of her own story, but she is also the other in the love story of White Snake and Xu Xian, and her description of their relationship is not without imagination, exaggeration, and distortion. Green Snake's manipulative first-person narration does not have more credibility than Feng's Ming version since they are both fabricated stories. By pointing out truth, this paragraph simultaneously reinforces and dismantles the authenticity of her own narration.

Green Snake's narration is thus inspired by previous male narratives and at the same time tries to flout them. Her personal storytelling confronts the official historical discourse of China: "No one can write the story of others. This is China. No records handed down by Chinese people are the truth of their protagonists" (Li, *Qingshe* 125). Li's adaptation uses the personal discourse of female subjectivity to counter the official discourse of historical totality. The distrust of historical discourse is further manifested by the ending of the novel, in which Green Snake witnesses the brutality of the Cultural Revolution in 1970s China. In such a way, Li's adaptation resonates with Yan Geling's "White Snake" (1999). As another female author's revision of the same folkloric script, Yan's novella similarly employs female desire and subjectivity to dismantle the historical totality and brutality represented by the Cultural Revolution.

"White Snake": Queering Heterosexual Romance

Yan Geling's novella, "White Snake" (1999), is located within the backdrop of the Cultural Revolution, and thus in a realistic and historical discourse. But Yan introduces a metaphorical and allegorical layer to this otherwise realistic fiction with her metafictive narrative form, which blurs the boundary between performers and the performed. Sun Likun, once a dancer renowned for her stage performance as White Snake and now a political prisoner, continually identifies herself as White Snake and interprets her life experience through the folktale plot:

> She felt as if he had come to rescue her, taking measures that were completely unfathomable to her, *similar to Green Snake's saving White Snake in the magic-herb-stealing episode.* Yet she couldn't penetrate this young man's aloofness

and politeness to discover his true mission. Sometimes she felt as if this storeroom stuffed with scenery had organized itself into a play and the wiry young man had become a character in it. (Yan 38)[3]

In Sun Likun's narration, the old storeroom in which she is imprisoned by the Red Guards becomes the stage of a play where she and the mysterious young inspector are characters. She is undoubtedly White Snake, but the status of the young man is ambiguous and cannot be neatly assigned to a fixed character from the White Snake script. In this passage, Sun compares him to Green Snake, who comes to rescue her when she is in danger. In an earlier scene when they first meet, Sun's narration links him also with Xu Xian: "she realized that she was standing by the backdrop of Broken Bridge from *The Legend of White Snake*. The light gray stone of the bridge had become permeated with its dismal history" (Yan, *White Snake and Other Stories* 19). In the folklore, the Broken Bridge is supposedly the place where the White Snake and Xu Xian meet and fall in love. The ambiguous identity of this young man reaches its climax when he takes Sun from her prison to a hotel room, and the truth is finally unveiled, that "he" is actually a cross-dressing female fan who since her childhood has been obsessed with Sun's dance.

The female fan, Xu (with the same pronunciation as the legendary figure Xu Xian), ten years younger than Sun, is a gender-troubled girl from a prestigious family, and also interprets her reality through a folkloric lens. Her infatuation with Sun and her charming dance routine awaken an awareness of her sexual difference at puberty, and she identifies with the androgynous Green Snake from the theatrical version to emancipate her transgender desire. In a diary, she recalls when she was twelve years old and first watched Sun's performance:

Onstage they had just performed up to the part where White Snake and Green Snake start their battle. Green Snake tries to woo White Snake, and they are determined to test each other in battle. If Green Snake wins, White Snake will

---

3. The excerpts from "White Snake" are translated by Lawrence A. Walker, with modification. As Liang Luo ("Writing Green Snake" 30) observes, Walker's translation omits an important sentence from the Chinese original: "similar to Green Snake's saving White Snake in the magic-herb-stealing episode." Without this sentence, the intertextual link to the folklore is obscured.

marry him, and if White Snake wins, Green Snake will become a female and serve White Snake all her life. Green Snake is defeated, and as soon as the stage lights go dark, then light up again, he has already become a female. After becoming a female, Green Snake is so loyal and brave, so attentive toward White Snake even in the smallest matters. What if he had not become a female? Wouldn't White Snake then have avoided having anything to do with that idiot Xu Xian? I really can't stand Xu Xian! If it hadn't been for him, White Snake would not have suffered such tribulations. If it hadn't been for that detestable Xu Xian, White Snake and Green Snake certainly would have been very happy together. (Yan, *White Snake and Other Stories* 29)

The teenage Xu's description of the battle scene between Green Snake and White Snake overtly refers to the Sichuan Opera tradition, whose trademark is using one male actor and one female actress to alternate in the role of Green Snake (Tang 57). Her interpretation of the story, "What if he had not become a female," enacts what Bonnie Zimmerman identifies as the what-if moment in heterotexts for queer readers: "when the lesbian reader refuses to assent anymore to the heterosexual imperative; a point in the narrative labyrinth where she simply cuts a hole and follows her own path" (139). Her hatred of Xu Xian and her fantasy of the "very happy together" two snakes display her creative ability to change and rewrite the familiar story for her purpose.

Guided by her strong identification with the operatic "loyal and brave" Green Snake, Xu starts to realize her body is "inherently androgynous," and this realization "opened a strange and wondrous door" for her, "a door that led to unlimited possibilities" (Yan, *White Snake and Other Stories* 36). Like Green Snake in the Sichuan Opera, Xu first appeared as a male to court Sun the White Snake, and their relationship is inevitably based on hierarchical heterosexual romance. In the Sichuan Opera version, the two snakes embark on a battle, with two outcomes, each of which is grounded in the hierarchical relations of husband/wife and master/servant. Similarly, Xu as a young male investigator, develops a condescending relationship with Sun as a female prisoner. "He" is civilized, elegant, and in a politically higher status, while Sun is almost illiterate, has lost all her past glory, and is an anti-revolutionary prisoner. The strong obsession that Sun develops with Xu during the investigation, not unlike the obsession of the Little Mermaid with the Prince, is deeply ingrained in her self-considered inferiority: "how could she ever deserve a man like this?" for she now "had no past and no future, just a lot of years and a pile of political offenses" (Yan, *White Snake and Other Stories* 40). In Sun's view, Xu is superior and out of her reach, and it is impossible that this unbalanced relationship could end positively. Sun becomes mentally unbalanced after she realizes Xu's true gender.

Once Xu reassumes her real gender as a female and replaces her male pseudonym, Xu Qunshan (*shan*, as a mountain), with her born female name, Xu Qunshan (*shan*, as coral), a more therapeutic and egalitarian relationship between them can develop. Xu constantly comes to the psychiatric hospital to visit Sun, and Sun starts to view her as Shanshan, instead of as male imposter Xu Qunshan. A genuine half-sisterly, half-sexual bonding between them starts to form. Sun feels she "truly did love Shanshan," because "Shanshan was the only ray of sunshine in her life, a ray full of dust, but also full of warmth" (Yan, *White Snake and Other Stories* 56). The dusty yet warm sunshine replaces the perfect and flawless image of the young investigator who finally wins the heart of White Snake. In this sense, although cross-dressing as a male has enabled Xu to come close to the imprisoned Sun, it is her female sensitivity and tenderness that lies at the core of their intersubjective relationship.

Yan's novella is remarkably ambitious and complicated in its treatment of the narrative voice, which employs three interrelated yet conflicting voices to tell the same story: the official accounts, the popular accounts, and the untold story. The official accounts are a series of reports that provide Sun's biographical information in a typical revolutionary Mao style. The narrator of the popular accounts is reminiscent of the omniscient storyteller in traditional vernacular stories, whose tone resembles gossip and hearsay, with repeated phrases such as "they say" and "actually." The popular accounts, however, relate all of the events but with no access to the inner thoughts of the characters. The untold story, in contrast, is told separately from Sun's perspective as a third-person focalizer and from Xu's perspective in her first-person diary. In this version, readers are granted access to the emotional and mental aspects of the two female characters. Both the hypocritical official accounts and the gossipy popular accounts are narrated through the discourse of males, whereas only the untold section is a real self-expression of the heroines. Unlike Li Bihua, Yan does not denounce the two public accounts as false, and her untold story does not claim to be true and authentic; instead, the juxtaposition of the three versions asserts the multivocal nature of any narration, and their complementariness and contradiction allow space for conflicting interpretations. This narrative strategy for destabilizing a traditional script accords with Alicia Ostriker's argument "[that] vital myths are paradoxically both public and private, that they encode both consent to and dissent from existing power structures, and that they have at all times a potential for being interpreted both officially and subversively" (*Feminist Revision* 28). The White Snake script is such an indeterminate and porous story, and revisionist adaptations of this script by female authors create open space for accommodating multiple interpretations and ideological implications.

Female revisionist adaptations not only engage in an intertextual dialogue with the traditional folklore but also supplement and interact with each other in their thematic concerns and narrative skills. The subtle homosexual undercurrent in Li's *Green Snake* indicated by Green Snake's covert desire for her sister, White Snake, has been made explicit in Yan's "White Snake," in which Xu Qunshan (Shanshan) as Green Snake has replaced Xu Xian to become the love interest of Sun as White Snake. This lesbian desire could not, however, be realized in China after the Cultural Revolution, a society that still "regulates its people's concept about a 'normal' marriage and supervises its people's 'unhealthy/abnormal' sexual lives" (Tsai 141). At the end of Yan's novella, Shanshan marries a man in an attempt to hide her unconventional sexuality, and whether she maintains her relationship with Sun remains ambiguous. This repressed lesbian desire has been fully realized in online female authors' novels, which entirely discard the heterosexual convention and embrace a radical queer identity.

Story of the Golden Bowl and Mahoraga: Grassroots Imaginations of Homosexual Snakes

Unlike Li and Yan, who are prestigious authors not lacking in literary fame and academic attention, online amateur writers actively fabricate their adaptations of the White Snake story with more freedom and enthusiasm. As Ling Yang and Yanrui Xu observe, "the low threshold of online publishing and the relative freedom of cyberspace combine to provide a unique opportunity for young Chinese women to express their desires and aspirations in a supportive community" ("Queer Texts" 133). These grassroots creations may seem coarse by the standard of highbrow literature, but they boldly experiment with prior texts and different genres, and freely express the authors' nonmainstream and transgressive attitudes toward sexual identities and orientations. I have chosen two novels posted online to illustrate the imaginative recapitulations of Chinese traditional folklore by grassroots authors in the new millennium. Each of them inherits the basic character prototype of the White Snake script, but radically reorients the story into new directions and forms.

Among the various modern and contemporary adaptations of the White Snake script, Li Bihua's *Green Snake* (1986) and Hark Tsui's cinematic version of this novel (1993) are remarkably influential. Li's unconventional rewriting of the legend is saturated with a homoerotic undercurrent, and Tsui's film gives such subtext a vivid visual display. Both the novel and the film are thus celebrated as a cult canon. On the other side, the most influential mainstream adaptation of this folklore is Taiwan's TV series *The New Legend of Madame White Snake* (*Xin bainiangzi chuanqi*, 1992). This 50-episode TV series was broadcast in Taiwan, Hong Kong, and mainland China, and became a TV classic among Sinophone audiences. Like the Disney animated versions of European fairy tales, this television drama became the most familiar rendition of "The Legend of the White Snake" for most Chinese people. Based on two Qing dynasty novelized versions of this tale, *The New Legend of Madame White Snake* constitutes a rather faithful adaptation of its original texts, and unfolds a family-friendly romance featuring the star-crossed love between White Snake and Xu Xian. The latter half of this series focuses on the story of their son, Xu Shilin. Although the television drama generally asserts a rather conservative opinion on gender and sexual roles by foregrounding heterosexual romance and mother-son bonding, the casting choice infuses a queer aura into this series, for it assigns an actress to perform Xu Xian via cross-dressing. Li Bihua's *Green Snake* and the 1992 Taiwan TV series exert a profound influence on later writers who are interested in rewriting the well-known legend.

Fakeyang's *Mahoraga* (*Mohuluojia*, 2009) and Bai Yushi's *Story of the Golden Bowl* (*Jinbo Ji*, 2013)[4] are web-based serialized fiction written by amateur authors under pseudonyms, and these two narratives draw on the aforementioned two adaptations to the extent that they are viewed as fan fiction of

---

4. Both have been removed and deleted from their original posting website, *Jinjiang*, and they can be accessed via online archived websites. The year given refers to their original posting date.

either *Green Snake* or *The New Legend of Madame White Snake*. To borrow the terms from fandom studies, "The Legend of the White Snake" as folklore is the canon, whereas *Green Snake* and *The New Legend of Madame White Snake* are two early fanon (fan canon), and *Mahoraga* and *Story of the Golden Bowl* are later works derivative of both the canon and the fanon. But neither remains faithful to its predecessors.

Story of the Golden Bowl is a GL fan fiction of the White Snake script. Girls' love (GL) is a genre of online literature that depicts romantic and sexual relationships between female characters, and it includes both original GL novels and GL fan fiction. The latter is known as femslash (female slash or f/f slash) in Anglophone fan culture. Correspondingly, boys' love (BL), borrowed from Japanese terms, refers to narratives about male homosexual relationships. Ling Yang and Hongwei Bao observe that compared to the proliferation of the BL genre, "GL is relevantly marginalized in mainland China's fanfic communities, a fact evident in fewer fan productions, smaller readership and a paucity of scholarly attention" (844). GL novels nevertheless occupy a niche market. As an openly coming out lesbian, the author Bai Yushi adds the tag GL to her title *Story of the Golden Bowl* when posting online to target specific readership, and she transforms the familiar folklore into a GL novel with explicit same-sex intimacy and sexual practices between White Snake and Green Snake.

Story of the Golden Bowl[5] inherits many side characters and detailed events from *The New Legend of Madame White Snake*, but its central theme is the lesbian romance that Li's *Green Snake* briefly touches yet with no deeper exploration. In this novel, sincere romantic love is born between two female snake spirits, the older Bai Suzhen (White Snake) and the younger Little Green (Green Snake). Bai Suzhen has to marry Xu Xian to repay her karmic debt. In their previous lives, Xu Xian was a shepherd boy who saved Suzhen in her animal shape from being captured by a butcher. Suzhen has no affection for Xu Xian, and the marriage is torturous for her since her heart belongs to Little Green. The conflict between genuine affection and moral obligation troubles White Snake. According to Li Fengmao (221), to repay a debt of gratitude, in Chinese culture, bespeaks a sense of righteousness, which is driven by an ethical code of conduct. Paying off a debt of gratitude also benefits religious

---

5. The bowl referenced in the title is the magic alms bowl Fa Hai used to subdue demons. In 1943, Tian Han, a Chinese drama activist and playwright, turned the White Snake story into a Chinese opera, naming it *Jinbo Ji* (*Story of the Golden Bowl*).

cultivation. Romantic love and sexual attraction between the two snake spirits, in contrast, are not germinated from moral principles. Xu Xian becomes suspicious about the extreme intimate relationship between his wife, Suzhen, and her maid, Little Green, and he accidentally discovers the sexual relationship between the two women. When Little Green is severely wounded, Suzhen sets out to Southern Pole Star Palace to find a way to rescue her, which is a plot twist based on the traditional magic-herb-stealing episode. During Suzhen's absence, lecherous Xu Xian tries to rape the bedridden Little Green. Xu Xian views the attempted rape as natural and ethical since the Confucian patriarchal family structure grants the husband ownership over his wife as well as the household maids. Similarly, he also turns a blind eye to the homosexual relationship between Suzhen and Little Green, and feels unthreatened as long as Suzhen fulfills her obligations as his wife. In ancient China, female same-sex activities were generally rendered invisible, not because they were suppressed but because they were fully integrated into the lifestyles of ancient Chinese societies, and they are sanctioned only under the policing eyes of a patriarchal and heterosexual marriage (Ho; Laura H. Wu). Xu Xian's tolerance affirms this lesbian invisibility in premodern China. In *Story of the Golden Bowl*, Xu Xian may act as a traditional Confucian intellectual; however, Suzhen and Little Green are by no means obedient wives and concubines as depicted by male authors in Ming and Qing literature. They are literary characters created by a contemporary female author, who projects her modern awareness of sexual identity and sexual orientation onto ancient characters. The attempted rape deeply irritates both Suzhen and Little Green, and they swear to kill Xu Xian for revenge. Xu Xian escapes and seeks refuge in the temple where Fa Hai presides. Thus, the destructive flood summoned by the two spirits is not to rescue Xu Xian from Fa Hai, as the old tale goes, but to kill him. Furious, Little Green finally kills Xu Xian, and Suzhen is imprisoned under the pagoda as a punishment. In summary, *Story of the Golden Bowl* bends and twists basic plots from old materials to fabricate a brand new story of lesbian romance, which also challenges the ideal harmonious polygynous marriage craved by premodern male authors.

The egalitarian lesbian relationship constructed in *Story of the Golden Bowl* not only interrogates the heterosexual romance, moreover, but it also counters the vertical hierarchical division between the highest heaven (gods and buddas), the middle ground earth (humans), and the lowest flora and fauna (animal spirits). As stressed earlier, in East Asian versions of the Swan Maiden motif, the maidens usually go willingly and even gladly with the men, and do not want to come back to their natural world. Alien women's longing for incorporation into the human realm by marrying a mortal man is largely created by male authors to voice their fantasy, which reinforces male-centered and anthropocentric values. In the novel, the first time Little Green expresses her passion to Suzhen happens to be under the water. The confession is followed by intimate caresses and kissing between them. The author describes the scene in figurative language:

> Except for hugs and kisses, they didn't have any extra action, and they slowly sank, while their black hair was entangled together, wrapping their bodies, and their green and white clothes floated slowly. Groups of fish shuttled through their hair and clothes, ignoring the scene as if they had embraced each other like this from the moment the world was born, and it won't end until the sea is dead.
>
> At this moment, they are not in the human realm, not in heaven, but only in each other's dreams. (Chapter 16)

Discarding heavenly order and human ethics, this image of two females hugging and sinking under the water highlights their close connection with nature. The end of the novel discloses that Suzhen is actually the reincarnation of the goddess Nüwa, and she is released from the pagoda. As immortals, Suzhen and Little Green retreat into the wilderness and live happily ever after. Such a closure further dismantles the tripartite hierarchy of gods-humans-animal spirits, and rewrites the conventional happy ending of heterosexual romance into a queer love story.

If Bai Yushi's *Story of the Golden Bowl* flaunts homoeroticism and female sexuality unapologetically, *Mahoraga* (*Mohuluojia*, 2009)[6] spotlights the androgynism signified in the character of Green Snake. Written by a female author under the pseudonym of Fakeyang, *Mahoraga* is chiefly circulated and admired among readers of BL novels, since it consists of various male homosexual plots. The novel presents Green Snake as the embodiment of destructive power and

---

6. Mahoraga, which is transliterated as Mohuluojia in Chinese, refers to a race of deities in Hinduism and Buddhism, who are often depicted as anthropomorphic beings with serpentine bodies from the waist down. A song from Tsui Hark's film *Green Snake* (1993) is titled "Mahoraga."

androgynous sexuality, who, as a first-rate beauty, changes arbitrarily between male and female bodies to seduce and manipulate others. The main story line delineates the epic battle between Green Snake and Amoghapāśa, who in this novel is equated with Avalokiteśvara, also known as bodhisattva Guanyin in Chinese Buddhism. Amoghapāśa, as the guardian bodhisattva of humankind, tries her best to redeem their sins and prolong their existence. Green Snake, as a rebellious and powerful demon, is determined to destroy the human world to save White Snake, the only kindred he/she cares about and loves. Amoghapāśa, as the representation of religious and ethical authority, cautions against the illusion of carnal desire. Green Snake, by contrast, is the epitome and champion of lust and sexual pleasure. In the end, Green Snake loses the battle due to the betrayal of White Snake, who unexpectedly allies with the authoritarian side. But Green Snake, like Lucifer in Milton's *Paradise Lost*, is illustrated as an attractive and intriguing antihero to whom readers are drawn and with whom they sympathize.

Through the voice of Green Snake, the novel expresses its rebellion against religious authority and puritanical morality. In tandem with this iconoclastic spirit, the novel also includes several incestuous and homosexual relationships among its male characters. In his male snake form, Green Snake and White Snake give birth to a snake son named Xueqing. Xueqing and Green Snake, in both their male human forms, indulge in homosexual intercourse, during which their serpent bodies frequently appear. Xueqing later falls in love with his half-brother Shilin, who is the hybrid son of White Snake and Xu Xian. The incestuous same-sex romance between fathers and sons and between brothers (by either blood or adoption) abounds in Chinese BL fiction. Yanrui Xu and Ling Yang's study suggests incest plots in BL "concern not only light-hearted sexual fantasy but also imaginary compensation for the lack of pure love in parent-child relationships, as well as an implicit social critique of the authoritarian parenting/governing style" (33). Therefore, as an unorthodox adaptation, *Mahoraga*, in its praise of incest and male homosexuality, confronts the heteronormativity and religious authority embedded in the traditional White Snake story.

By employing first-person narration and polyphonic strategy, Li Bihua's *Green Snake* and Yan Geling's "White Snake" distance themselves from the conventionalized narrative form of folklore. At the more popular end of the spectrum of literature, *Story of the Golden Bowl* and *Mahoraga* follow the tradition of Chinese vernacular novels to use omniscient narrative perspectives. However, *Story of the Golden Bowl* inserts several inner monologues of Suzhen and Little Green into its narrative that function similarly to arias sung by female characters in Qing dynasty dramas. Charged with sensual passions and carnal cravings, these inner monologues grant readers access to the mental landscapes of the two heroines. *Mahoraga*, on the other hand, employs an omniscient narrator whose narrative voice is strikingly vague and elusive, full of foreshadowing and echoing, as well as exquisite metaphors and literary and religious allusions. Like its protagonist Green Snake, whose actions are always unpredictable, this enigmatic narrative style precludes a straightforward interpretation and arouses shock and wonder from readers at every plot twist and turn. Both novels create characters for whom readers feel sympathy, and transform a didactic tale aiming to caution against the danger of immoral desire to melodramas exploring complicated and various queer sexual relationships.

Conclusion

Revisionist adaptations of the White Snake script by female authors create open space for accommodating multiple interpretations and ideological implications. All of these novels under examination draw widely and cross-culturally from quintessential interspecies romance scripts such as "The Legend of the White Snake" and "The Little Mermaid" and their manipulation and conscious dialogue with these folktales simultaneously preserve story elements from the past while seeking ways to challenge the dominant patriarchy ideology.

This chapter gives a nuanced examination of folktales and their contemporary adaptations with a special focus on the changed and unchanged parts of the script, and the thematic significance behind these new or retained forms. Adrienne Rich defines revisionary writing as "an act of looking back, of seeing with fresh eyes, of entering an old text from a new critical direction" (18). The critical adaptations of the White Snake script by female authors such as Li Bihua, Yan Geling, and online writers not only emancipate the female characters from their prewritten scripts and destiny but also emancipate them from the monolithic understanding of gender roles and sexual orientations encoded in traditional patriarchal stories. Through the queering of a folktale canon of heterosexual romance such as "The Legend of the White Snake," these revisionary novels depart from the familiar stories and imagine alternative scenarios that interrogate the socially and culturally defined attitudes toward gender and sexualities prescribed by the dominant discourse and create new pathways for nonnormative female subjectivities.

5

The Visible and Invisible Ghost

THE METAMORPHOSIS OF THE STRANGE TALES FROM *LIAOZHAI*

The previous chapter examined the revisionist transformation of a folkloric script of interspecies romance. This script not only appears frequently in the folk and vernacular tradition but also remains a recurrent trope of Chinese elite literature, in which an amorous female ghost or fox spirit features prominently as the love interest of a male scholar within strange tales written in classical Chinese language. The focus of this chapter is cinematic and literary adaptations of the strange tales (hereafter *zhiguai*, that is, "records of the strange") that involve ghosts, with particular attention to the ghost-mortal romance script epitomized by the tales of the Qing dynasty author Pu Songling. As noted in chapter 2, Chinese narratives with supernatural themes first appear in the form of short stories and anecdotes written in classical language, commonly acknowledged as the genre of *zhiguai*. Therefore, strange tales are a notable component of a Chinese fantastic literary tradition and could be viewed as a premodern forebear of modern Chinese fantasy literature.

This chapter continues the thematic exploration of the previous chapter and focuses on the power relationship between male and female. It begins with a survey of multiple cultural implications behind the ghost image in China and then gives a short introduction to Pu Songling's work, *Strange Tales from Liaozhai* (*Liaozhai Zhiyi*, 1766, hereafter *Liaozhai*). After disclosing the conservative gender ideology inherent in his iconic tales, the main sections of this chapter carry out a textual analysis of different depictions of ghosts in contemporary Chinese fantasy novels and films. The ideologies represented by Pu's tales are grounded on the assumption that "ghosts are inferior to human beings in the natural and moral order of things, just as daughters are less valuable than sons" (Zeitlin, *The Phantom Heroine* 17). Through an in-depth analysis of several cinematic and animated adaptations of Pu's tales, this chapter explores the polysemic metamorphosis of the female ghost character and the thematic implications for changing ideas of gender norms and female subjectivity.

The Cultural Significance of Ghosts

Ghosts, spirits, and specters, as the undead souls who still haunt the living world, have been the focus of both oral and written narratives across many cultures throughout history. As Maria del Pilar Blanco and Esther Peeren argue, the representational and sociocultural functions, meaning, and effects of spectral beings have been "as manifold as their shapes—or non-shapes, as the case may be—and extend far beyond the rituals, traditions, ghost stories, folktales, and urban legends they populate" (1). Ghosts could be understood literally, as a revenant in many religious beliefs, or metaphorically, as the "disturbing forms of otherness" in gender, race, ethnicity, sexuality, and class (3). Either as an actuality or as a conceptual metaphor, ghosts are rich in their cultural representations and ideological implications.

A commonplace explanation of the ghost image in literature and culture is psychological, in that ghosts are seen as a metaphor for the discord and conflict of emotions in people's hearts. However, another interpretive perspective is social and historical rather than psychological, in that the ghost as a symbol of otherness represents the marginalized members of society. These two approaches, the psychological and sociohistorical, are not mutually exclusive. Instead, they could be combined to provide a more nuanced interpretation of the recurrent ghost stories in literature and films. The psychological trauma of a person allegorically reflects the political and socioeconomic failing of the society. As Avery Gordon argues, "the ghost is not simply a dead or a missing person, but a social figure, and investigating it can lead to that dense site where history and subjectivity make social life" (8).

According to Anthony Yu, the Chinese character for ghost—*gui* and its various cognates—represents "only one concept within a bountiful vocabulary of the spirit world." It closely relates to terms such as *shen* (god, deity), *ling* (spirit, soul), *yao* (monster, fiend), *guai* (strange, anomalous), and *mo* (demon, goblin, ogre) (398–99). From this wide range of spiritual vocabulary, two most prominent connotations of *gui* could be selected, one literal and the other figurative. If combined with the character for spirit or soul, *hun*, then the word *guihun* refers to the ghost, the spirit of a person who is already dead, who does not necessarily have to be evil and malicious. This meaning corresponds with ghost in the English semantic field, especially in its literal understanding, "an apparition of a dead person which is believed to appear or become manifest to the living, typically as a nebulous image" (OED). Although not necessarily evil, *gui* as the returning dead still evoke disturbing feelings in perceivers, since they represent the obscure and numinous underworld. The figurative usage of the Chinese *gui* is commonly associated with the character for evil, *mo*, and the word *mogui* signifies a devil or a demon. *Gui* as a ghost is a more neutral term, while *gui* as a devil is clearly tinted with negative connotations.

The existence of ghosts as dead spirits who linger on in the living world was a popular conception in premodern China and formed a continuum with ancient practices of placating spirits and honoring the souls of departed ancestors. There is no clear demarcation between everyday physical existence and the afterlife in Chinese popular or folk religion, which is characterized by its syncretic, pragmatic, and utilitarian traits (Yao and Zhao 196). Lacking the transcendence of Christianity, the imagination of the afterlife in China is secular and realistic, with the veneration of the dead often taking the form of burning paper money and paper houses and cars to guarantee the deceased has a comfortable afterlife. In some regions of China, ghost marriages are arranged by parents for their prematurely dead sons and daughters. This custom is depicted in contemporary writer Wang Anyi's short story "Match Made in Heaven" ("Tianxian Pei," 1998), in which the ghost bride, a modern revolutionary heroine, was attributed posthumously with a mythical and local image "burdened with all the obsolete beliefs, rituals, and superstitions" (Ban Wang 620). Even though the modern communist state sets up historical materialism as its official ideology, many Chinese people continue to embrace a spiritualism grounded in folk beliefs, including the belief in ghosts and an afterlife. As the village head in Wang Anyi's short story manifests, "he had received a proper education and was, after all, a Materialist. But then he thought, maybe Idealism is the best way forward—Idealism can comfort the soul, and no matter what happens, there will always be something there"

(26). Therefore, the belief and disbelief surrounding ghostly beings becomes a contested space upon which the struggle between the past and the present and between traditional spiritualism and modern rationalism takes place.

The ghost as a conceptual metaphor signifies groups suppressed and silenced by the dominant discourse. The Chinese language imbues many terms relating to ghosts with derogatory implications, and social members who are figuratively labeled as *gui* may be subject to severe discrimination and even physical violence from the mainstream. Firstly, a tendency to link females with ghosts is particularly prevalent in Chinese folk religion and is based on the Daoist *yin-yang* paradigm. *Yin* represents "women, darkness, passivity, and often sickness and death." *Yang*, in contrast, stands for "men, light, activity, and life force" (Moskowitz 206–7). It is logical, then, to connect females with ghosts since they are both embodiments of *yin* power. In traditional Daoist bedchamber manuals, men were warned that ejaculation would deplete their life energy, their *yang* power (Van Gulik 78), and the fear of losing one's life force through sexual activity is intensified when the partner is not only a female but also a ghost. Another explanation for the recurrence of female revenants is the Confucian ritual code. "The demise of a young unmarried woman by definition disrupted the patrilineal, patrilocal structure of the normative Chinese kinship system," since "not truly belonging to her natal family, she had no proper burial place, and without a husband and children, she had no one obligated to look after her posthumous worship" (Zeitlin, *The Phantom Heroine* 11). Therefore, the ghost naturally becomes a symbol for female members in a patriarchal society.

Secondly, the word *gui* sometimes refers to children, as manifested in the word "little ghost" (*xiaogui*), which is an expression addressing children with affection yet a slight rebuke (Ken-fang Lee 112). Foreigners or political enemies who threaten the rule of the imperial authority and political descendants are also commonly branded as ghost/demon. For example, both China and Japan tend to label foreigners, especially foreign forces that threaten the governance of the nation, as *gui* or *oni*. In this usage, *gui* is better understood as demons or devils rather than dead spirits. In Medieval Japan, when a being was beyond the reach of the emperor's control or was considered to be an enemy of the establishment, it often came to be designated as *oni*. During World War II, Japanese also applied the image of *oni* to describe the leaders of the Allied forces (Reider 138, 147). Similarly, *guizi* is a Chinese

slang term for foreigners, which is used to express racist hate and depreca-
tion. During the Boxer Rebellion (1899–1901), the term *yang guizi* (Western
devils) was used to refer to the Western colonists. In and after World War II,
riben guizi (Japanese devils) was regularly used as a hate expression of anti-
Japanese sentiment in China. Not only foreigners but also political dissidents
are branded as pejorative *gui*. During the Cultural Revolution, the idiom *niugui sheshen* (ox-headed demons and serpent gods) was a sobriquet bestowed
on the "right-wing" writers and intellectuals. Etymologically this idiom has
no pejorative meaning. Instead, it is an aesthetic appraisal. It first appears in
the preface written by Tang poet Du Mu (803–52) to the posthumous poetry
collection of another Tang poet, Li He (790–816). Du Mu uses this phrase as
a metaphor to describe Li He's wild imagination. Pu Songling, in turn, uses
this allusion in his own preface to his *Liaozhai* tales, thus placing himself
in the tradition of literary genius. The derogatory meaning of this idiom
during the Cultural Revolution may derive from the hostile attitude toward
feudal superstition in Mao's Communist China. Therefore, as Hui Luo points
out, "the denunciation of ghosts also meant the symbolic execution" of political
dissidents, and the symbolic violence was "turned into physical violence during
those tumultuous years" (227–28). Females, children, foreigners, and political
dissidents—that is, anyone who prefers a lifestyle, habits, and customs that
differ from the social norm—risk being branded a ghost or a monster. For
Haiyan Lee, "these modern ghost stories often incorporate the occult into the
everyday lifeworld of the city dweller, thereby pointing to the fragility of modern rationality and undermining the confidence of secular modernity" (59).
Thus, the representations of ghosts in cultural artifacts become the battlefield
where dominant ideology and resistant ideology encounter and contend.

The Gothic and the Uncanny in West and East

Two literary concepts are related to ghost stories in the West, the Gothic and
the uncanny. Literary ghost stories emerged as a major genre at the end of the
eighteenth century through the medium of Gothic novels, such as works by
Ann Radcliffe and Horace Walpole.

Chinese traditional tales, dramas, and novels that include ghost characters are broad and myriad, and the scope and depth of this tradition go far

beyond any particular work. Out of a practical consideration, therefore, for this chapter I have chosen *Liaozhai* tales from Pu Songling as representative pre-texts for later adaptations. After its numerous textual transformations into films and TV series in today's China, *Liaozhai* has become almost synonymous with, and lent its name to, the genre of ghost stories (You 85). For example, translations of ghost stories from Montague Rhodes James (1862–1936) are included in a series called "Foreign *Liaozhai*" published by the People's Literature Publishing House in 2016. In the same series one can also find work by H. P. Lovecraft and Sheridan Le Fanu. *Liaozhai* as an indigenous local literary tradition has become a catchall term for ghost stories, the Gothic novel, and horror fantasy from the English world.

Psychoanalysis, especially Freud's theory of the uncanny, has more often than any other theory been applied to interpret the appeal of the Gothic novels. As a countercultural reaction to the dominant cultural logic of rationalism in the Enlightenment, Gothic novels provide a tool for expressing the repressed fear and desire that lurks in the subconscious for everyone, that unknowable and unreasonable fear of death, speculates Heidegger, or of castration, speculates Freud (Trites 162). Freud's "uncanny" refers to something that is familiar yet frightening, that "arouses dread and creeping horror" (Freud 219), such as inanimate objects coming to life, blinding, doubles, déjà vu, coincidences, the immediate granting of wishes, the return of the dead, spirits and ghosts, dismemberment, and live burial (219–52). In Pu Songling's collection, many tales arouse this kind of uncanny feeling. For example, "Living Dead" ("Shibian," *Strange Tales from a Chinese Studio* 10–15) tells a story about a female corpse who stands up, walks toward the travelers, breathes into their faces, and causes their death. In "A Certain Man in Zhucheng" ("Zhucheng moujia," *Strange Tales from Liaozhai* [translated by Sondergard] 679–82), a man is killed by bandits, but his head is still slightly connected with his neck. He miraculously recovers from this deadly wound and lives another ten years until one day he laughs too much at a friend's joke and his head falls off and he dies. The family of this man sues his friend for the cause of the death. These two rather grotesque and macabre tales are not typical of the majority of Pu's works, but even in these explicitly uncanny works, Pu tries to naturalize and moralize these uncanny elements to mitigate the effects of fear. The comment from Historian of the Strange, who is the avatar of the author, upon "A Certain Man in Zhucheng" is that if a joke could cause a head to fall, it is a marvelous and unprecedented joke. And the friend who accidentally causes the man's death is perhaps in debt to him in their previous incarnations. In this comment there is no amazement about the sudden death and the strange head but only praise for the witty rhetoric of jokes and a religious rationalization of the accident. Therefore, even though Pu describes many subjects that fall within categories of the Freudian uncanny, these descriptions do not necessarily, and indeed rarely, "involve feelings of fear, horror, or dread" (Zeitlin, *Historian of the Strange* 222 n.15). Pu's primary purpose is not to arouse fear in his readers but to elicit moral lessons.

Of the three categories offered by Todorov, the uncanny (consciously differentiated from Freud's), the fantastic, and the marvelous, the fantastic is most similar to Pu's writings. For Todorov, at the end of a fantastic story, the reader must "opt for one solution or the other" after the experience of hesitation (41). For example, to read Henry James's *The Turn of the Screw* (1898) as a fantastic novella, the reader must decide whether the governess is mad and hallucinating or she truly sees ghosts. However, as Judith Zeitlin's comparative analysis between *The Turn of the Screw* (1898) and "Scholar Chu" ("Chusheng," Pu, *Strange Tales from Liaozhai* [translated by Sondergard] 1518–25) demonstrates, Todorov's fantastic does not precisely cover the aesthetic nuance of Pu's records of the strange, since "the strange often results when things are paradoxically affirmed and denied at the same time. In other words, the boundary between the strange and the normal is never fixed but is constantly altered, blurred, erased, multiplied, or redefined" (Zeitlin, *Historian of the Strange* 7). Therefore, "the expectation that the reader must inexorably choose between a supernatural cause or a rational solution is entirely absent," since it is the "complementary rather than oppositional relationship" between the normal and the strange, between reality and imagination, that distinguishes *Liaozhai* and Todorov's fantastic (Zeitlin, *Historian of the Strange* 10).

Todorov's structural categories require the reader to choose between two mutually exclusive entities, the uncanny *or* the marvelous, but tales from *Liaozhai* are simultaneously uncanny *and* marvelous. This paradoxical characteristic reflects the Chinese principle *maodun* (spear-shield) proposed by Eugene Eoyang. Referring to a fable about an "impenetrable shield" and an "invincible spear," the concept is based on paraconsistent or "four-cornered logic," as opposed to binary logic (Gutierrez, *Mixed Magic* 24). This concept allows both dualities to be true, for one to be true and the other false, or for both to be false (Eoyang 115–26). Such a logic allows readers a more inclusive attitude toward the supernatural and the abnormal. What is significant in this concept is not whether an instance is true or false but what has been reflected behind such an instance.

Freudian psychoanalysis provides useful insights for the Chinese ghost stories tradition since many of Pu's tales are sexual fantasies of a male intellectual. A typical scenario would be when a beautiful and talented female ghost or fox spirit comes to the young male's place at night to offer sexual congress. However, to use Freud alone to explain Chinese ghost stories is not enough. The repression comes not only from repressed sexual desire but also from institutional alienation. It is widely agreed that Pu devotes his energies to supernatural story writing out of a contempt toward the official examination system. He had failed many times and then he gave up and turned away from the only legitimate and promising career for a male intellectual in feudal society. Therefore, the work is also a diatribe against the failings of his age: corruption in official career and examination systems, ruthlessness of the rich and the privileged, and hypocritical behavior. I suggest the most significant contribution of *Liaozhai* lies in its depiction of the life and trouble of lower-class members in his society: peasants, merchants, poor intellectuals, and so forth. We can see the toil and suffering of German farmers and workers in the Grimms' fairy tales and other oral folklore, and the reflection in these tales of the most urgent concerns of the poor—for enough food, for a secure place to stay, for a solution to the impact of sudden shifts between social classes. Similarly, we could see also the most pressing wish of the Chinese poor fulfilled in Pu's stories: parents whose children die dream that their sons and daughters come back to life from the underworld, and poor intellectuals dream of a beautiful female as a partner and high achievements in an official career.

The ideology of Pu's collection, in a nutshell, accords with his time. Though his fantastic writings give an alternative voice to orthodox Confucianism, which disavows the discussion of ghosts and spirits, his works are still informed by the moral protocols of Confucian beliefs. He criticizes corruption in the bureaucratic system, but still yearns for high achievement in the imperial examination system and a high official position. He partially expunges the misogyny of Confucian culture by depicting various charming and talented female ghosts and fox spirits, but still positions them strictly within a phallocentric hierarchy.

The power struggle and negotiation between masculinity and femininity is the thematic concern of a group of adaptations based on the script of ghost-mortal romance. In this group of texts, the ghost works as a metaphor for repressed members in the society, and the ghost-mortal relationship becomes isomorphic with female-male relationship. The best adaptations provide storyworlds in which their relationship is based not on hegemony and repression but on cooperation and dialogue.

The Absence of Horror-Inducing Ghosts in Contemporary Fiction and Films

Anthony Yu identifies three categories of ghost fiction in Chinese classic literature, the ghostly apologue (stories dealing with belief in or skepticism about the existence of ghosts), stories featuring the avenging ghost, and stories featuring the amorous ghost (403, 415, and 423). He does not limit his sources to *Liaozhai* but refers to a broader scope of works ranging from the Six Dynasties to the eighteenth century. Robert Campany distinguishes naturalistic and moral relations between the living and the dead in Six Dynasties *zhiguai*, and he observes that the moral discourse dominates the early medieval *zhiguai* stories, and that this reflects how "new kinds of moral, social, ritual, and emotional ties were being forged across both the boundary separating life from death and that separating kin from stranger" (18). In later adaptations, where the ghostly apologue is combined with stories of the avenging ghost, or with moralizing stories of karmic retribution and revenge, the horror aesthetics akin to the naturalistic mode are necessarily downplayed. In parallel with Yu's typology, two types of ghost image can be discerned in *Liaozhai* tales, and these two types correspond to two prior literary genres in the history of strange writings. Lydia Chiang identifies a group of ghost figures that are grotesque, dangerous, and deadly and that exemplify a kind of "horror aesthetics." This type of ghost is depicted in tales belonging to the *zhiguai* style, which are short, anecdotal, and terse in the description (Chiang 123–25), but the horror-inducing type is overshadowed by a gallery of beautiful and sensual ghosts. This second type, the romantic ghost, is feminine, sexual, and enchanting and features more in longer tales in *chuanqi* style, which is more elaborately fabricated and polished. These two types should have spawned two branches of adaptation, ghost horror and ghost romance, but the ghost horror genre is always outnumbered and overshadowed by its more sentimental alternative. There are two reasons for this difference.

Historically, by virtue of the moralizing strategies employed by Pu and other writers, the horror aspect of ghosts is always deemphasized and normalized. As Zeitlin observes, the Chinese literary ghost tradition is "singularly uninterested in horror or suspense," but rather exemplifies the tendency to "displace fear back on the specter, whose timidity and loneliness as an abject creature arouse instead feelings of pity and tenderness" (*The Phantom Heroine* 3). Another reason why ghost horror is unpopular in Chinese adaptation is due to the state's censorship in contemporary cultural productions, especially with regard to films.[1] Perhaps because ghost belief is ubiquitous in premodern Chinese folk religion, and it closely relates to many practices viewed as barbarous and absurd from a modern enlightened view, the mainland socialist state extols an official ideology that eschews spiritual existence. In this ghost censorship promoted by the state, film and visual representations are subject to more severe impact than verbal works because films, especially commercial genres, enjoy a broad audience base, and vivid visual representation of spectral entities might leave a stronger mental impact on the viewer. Therefore, films on ghost subjects, especially depicting horror-inducing ghosts, are generally banned in contemporary China. In contrast, television series, theatrical performance, and novels are relatively free in their expression of ghostly beings.

The ghost has been an essential trope in horror cinema, and in the contemporary culture industry there has been a revival of ghost figures in Asian horror films produced in Japan, South Korea, and other Southeast Asian countries. However, the ghost as a trope is discernibly absent in contemporary Chinese horror films; their ostensible existence can only be legitimated by an ultimate rational explanation, such as sociopathology, hallucination, or drugs. The replacement of ghosts with the sociopathic or psychological diseases is one of the many strategies adapters utilize to avoid censorship. Another common method is to change female ghosts into female fox spirits, another supernatural being that resembles ghosts in many ways but is less politically fraught.

---

1. The process of alternative permission and prohibition placed by the state on ghost figures on the big screen is complicated. For detailed delineations, see Li Zeng, "Horror Returns" and Laikwan Pang, "The State Against Ghosts."

A recent popular method is to replace ghosts with tropes from science fiction such as mutants or extraterrestrials.[2]

The disguising and absence of horror-inducing ghosts in contemporary adaptations proves to be an intriguing case to study the tug-of-war between tradition and modernity, religion and science, politics and economy, and censorship and market in China in the new century. As Laikwan Pang's insightful research shows, the reason behind the state's anti-superstition film policy is twofold. First, it is the literal meaning of ghosts that a modern socialist state tries to eschew since folk beliefs about ghosts are so ingrained in the daily life of Chinese people since the distant past. Second, the rich allegorical potential of ghost images "might be encoded and decoded in ways over which the state has no control" (461). Horror-inducing ghosts are inclined to be vengeful, and usually victims of injustice in their lives. Their return and haunting implicitly criticizes the failure of legal investigation. As Patrick Hogan remarks, societies tend to "develop representations of justice that . . . [favor] official modes of criminal investigation and punishment and . . . [disfavor] individual initiatives outside the control of the state" (225). Therefore, to make vengeful ghosts disappear from the screen is also to make the repressed members in society invisible, to avoid the reflection of social malaise and injustice. Consequently, the ghost is rendered either as domesticated and sexual, as featured in fantasy romance, or as childlike and cute, as featured in children's fantasy. The grotesque and horror-inducing possibility is seldom realized.

Gendered Ghosts: The Ghost-Mortal Romance Script and Its Depiction of Female Subjectivity

Two tales in *Liaozhai*, both featuring female ghost images, represent, respectively, horror in *zhiguai* style and romance in *chuanqi* style. Both tales follow a similar narrative sequence: seduction, sexual union, revelation, and return. This ghost-mortal romance script and its variation are particularly illuminating in their implications for romantic intersubjectivity and the gender norms on which they are based.

---

2. The 2018 online drama *Guardian* (*Zhenhun*) transforms the ghosts from its source novel into aliens. See Cathy Yue Wang, "Officially Sanctioned Adaptation."

The first, "Painted Skin" ["Huapi"] (Pu, ["Huapi"] *Strange Stories from a Chinese Studio* 76–84), is a chilling story about an encounter between a young intellectual, Wang, and a beautiful girl. The girl claims she has been forced to marry a wealthy landlord as a concubine but receives abuse from his jealous wife. Enchanted by her beauty, Wang offers her refuge and secretly shares a bed with her. A Daoist priest informs Wang that he has been bewitched. Startled, Wang returns to his place, looks through the window, and sees a nightmarish scene, "a hideous devil, with a green face and jagged teeth like a saw, spreading a human skin upon the bed and painting it with a paintbrush. The devil then threw aside the brush, and giving the skin a shake out, just as you would a coat, threw it over its shoulders, when, lo! it was the girl" (Pu, *Strange Stories from a Chinese Studio* 79). The latter part of the story focuses on the subjugation of the devil by the priest. The devil tears Wang's heart out of his breast, and Wang's wife, Chen, brings him back to life at the price of being humiliated by a beggar. The comment provided by Pu under his sobriquet Historian of the Strange underlines the moral allegory in this story: "Heaven's Way has its inexorable justice," since "her husband has fallen prey to lust," then the wife, Chen, has to suffer (Pu, *Strange Tales from a Chinese Studio* 521). As Hui Luo remarks, "a typical piece of moral didacticism that denounces sexual promiscuity, extols faithfulness, and endorses belief in karma and retribution" could be inferred from this comment (119). Although the tale plays with the theme of double identity, whereby a beautiful human skin is a surface that covers a hideous demon, it does not give information about the identity of this lady-devil figure. However, a grotesque impression of her is conveyed by "giving the skin a shake out" before wearing it and "tearing Wang's heart out of his breast." The minimalist description is in typical *zhiguai* style, and readers' emotional reaction toward the tale is aroused more by their active imagination based on limited textual cues than by vivid and detailed description.

Unlike the anonymous demon in "Painted Skin," the titular heroine of the tale "Nie Xiaoqian" (titled "The Magic Sword and The Magic Bag" by Minford, Pu, *Strange Tales from a Chinese Studio* 168–79) is a beautiful ghost with memories of her lifetime. She dies at eighteen and is improperly buried, and therefore becomes a wandering ghost. The ghost Xiaoqian (literally, Little Beauty) is forced by a yaksha-demon to seduce and kill male victims until she meets the righteous intellectual Ning Caichen, who refuses her seduction.

Xiaoqian asks Ning to "take my bones back home with you, and give them a decent burial" (173). With the help of Yan Chixia, a swordsman with unusual power, Ning defeats the yaksha-demon and gives Xiaoqian's bones a proper burial as promised. The freed ghost Xiaoqian offers to be a maid of the Ning family out of gratitude. She fulfills expectations of filial piety as she takes upon herself the household chores, and gains the affection of Ning's mother. After Ning's wife dies of a disease, Xiaoqian marries Ning as a ghost wife and she gives birth to a male child, who becomes an eminent scholar afterward.

"Painted Skin" and "Nie Xiaoqian" are similar stories but with apparent differences. To borrow the tropes from Sandra Gilbert and Susan Gubar, the pure and innocent Xiaoqian is like "an angel in the house" while the demon in "Painted Skin" is the evil witch, both generated by male authors (17). The ghostly image of Xiaoqian embodies the angel image described by Gilbert and Gubar, "slim, pale, passive beings whose charms eerily recalled the snowy, porcelain immobility of the dead" (25). At the wedding feast of Ning and Xiaoqian, guests were struck speechless by Xiaoqian's beauty. In their eyes "she was a goddess, not a ghost" (Pu, *Strange Tales from a Chinese Studio* 178, translation modified). In this parallel of goddess and ghost, we see that the image of Xiaoqian is modeled on the ideal female in male fantasy, who is beautiful, filial, and talented (we are told that Xiaoqian is "a talented painter of plum-blossom and orchids" [178]). The diverging endings of the two tales also indicate that genuine attachment is promoted over pure lust. Wang's lust causes his doom, while Ning is rewarded for his righteousness and faithfulness. In a way, "Painted Skin" is a cautionary tale about the danger of uncontrolled lust, in which a misogynistic attitude is loosely disguised in the horrifying description of the demon, while "Nie Xiaoqian" is fundamentally a male narcissist dream of an ideal partner, successful career, and promising offspring.

The two represent apparently different depictions of the ghost image, but these two images of angel and witch are ultimately the same construction generated by male authority in patriarchal ideology. The angel in the house in "Painted Skin" is Wang's virtuous and enduring wife, while the monster in "Nie Xiaoqian" is the yaksha-demon who, disguised as an old woman "in a long faded red gown, silver comb in hair, humped-backed and feeble-looking" (Pu, *Strange Tales from a Chinese Studio* 169, translation modified), forces Xiaoqian to seduce and kill men for her. In both tales, the powerful female monsters are wiped out, order is restored, and the obedient and domesticated angels are rewarded. Pu's tales are, after all, not too far away from the Grimms' tale of "Little Snow White" as discussed by Gilbert and Gubar.

Gilbert and Gubar's "paradigmatic polarities of angel and monster" (76) provide an effective analytic framework within which to embark on a discussion of female otherness in a literary tradition that has been dominated by male authors. For Gilbert and Gubar, the twin images of angel and monster present obstacles for female writers, and a woman writer "must examine, assimilate, and transcend the extreme images of angel and monster which male authors have generated for her" (17). Angel and monster, as well as similar tropes, including fairy, spirit, ghost, and witch, may serve as metaphors in Gilbert and Gubar's feminist critique, but, in fantastic narratives, they are nevertheless given a literal existence. If we view the angel in the house as the idealized female partner originating from the male fantasy of desire, and the monster as an embodiment of the fear and anxiety of a male confronted with female autonomy, then the gradual removal of wicked and unruly female monsters from Chinese traditional narratives reflects the rigid patriarchal protocol of Confucian ideology that had an incalculable impact on traditional Chinese society and culture. As discussed in the previous chapter, the evolution of "The Legend of the White Snake" from Tang to Qing dynasties showcases how otherworldly women become tamed and domesticated. Similarly, ghosts historically have been designated as "demonic agents capable of causing disease and death" (Zeitlin, *The Phantom Heroine* 15), but female specters, with their intensive "physical weakness and shyness," shifted from frightening to frightened during the late Ming and Qing dynasties (*The Phantom Heroine* 27). During this transition from frightening to frightened, female conformity and docility were induced and the feelings of fear and anxiety invoked by these alien women were purposely turned into desire. The strangeness and danger of these alien women were thereby tamed and controlled.

"Painted Skin" and "Nie Xiaoqian" as tales about ghost-mortal romance are among the most often adapted tales from Pu's collections. However, as various adaptations of these iconic tales illustrate, the boundary between the female monster and the angel is usually porous, and the figures interchangeable. As Zeitlin comments on the visual representations of female ghosts, "the superlativeness of both beauty and ugliness" reinforces the fact that "these seemingly opposite visual qualities are fungible, two sides of the same thing" (*The Phantom Heroine* 28). In later adaptations in fiction and film, the anonymous and powerful female monster in "Painted Skin" is significantly unpopular, and it is the beautiful and domesticated Xiaoqian that wins people's hearts. A common strategy is to change the *zhiguai*-like "Painted Skin" into a romantic *chuanqi*, and to transform the female demon into another Xiaoqian.

Among the four film adaptations of "Painted Skin" from the 1960s to the present, only Bao Fang's *The Painted Skin* (*Hua pi*, 1966) gives a faithful representation of the original text and hence became an iconic horror cinema forerunner in both Hong Kong and mainland China.[3] The other three cinematic versions of this story are all transformed into sensationalist melodramas. King Hu's 1992 *Painted Skin* (*Hua pi zhi yinyang fawang*) gives the anonymous female ghost a name, Feng (Maple), and a background story. During her life she was a beautiful opera singer and killed by a powerful male demon king. Enslaved by the demon, Feng is forced to seduce intellectual Wang. Here we see an evident influence of the prototypical script of Xiaoqian blended with "Painted Skin." In the latter part of Hu's film, the evil demon king comes to the earth, possesses Wang's body, and tries to violently rape Wang's wife. Now the victim in the original tale turns out to be the terrifying perpetrator. Where a female doppelgänger is transformed into something between an adorable and attractive girl and a powerful and hideous monster in Pu's original tale, here this doppelgänger is transformed into the male character in Hu's film.

A total reversal of the relationship between male-victim and female-perpetrator is not unusual among adaptations of "Painted Skin." In the 2005 TV series adaptation of *Liaozhai*, the section presenting "Painted Skin" (six episodes) also features the intellectual Wang as the real demon who causes the tragedy of the female victim. Mei Sanniang (Plum, the third daughter)[4] is a talented and beautiful courtesan, who engages in a love relationship with a poor intellectual, Wang. Wang ruthlessly kills their baby and burns Mei Sanniang to death in order to marry another lady whose father occupies a high official position. Mei turns into a ghost and exacts revenge on now

---

3. It is rumored that when Bao Fang's *Painted Skin* was screened in mainland China in the 1980s, it caused great terror in audiences. It was said an old lady was scared to death. This film was subsequently banned in Mainland China. See Hui Luo, 252–55.

4. The name Mei (plum) might be inspired by Bao Fang's 1966 *Painted Skin*, whose female monster is disguised as a beautiful girl named Mei Niang. Here we see an example of palimpsestuous intertextuality, in which a later adaptation alludes not only to the original text but also to intervening adaptations.

high-ranking Wang. Her hideous face under the human skin is the result of her merciless death by burning at her ex-lover's hands. Both King Hu's *Painted Skin* and the 2005 TV series version transform the female monster into a sympathy-arousing victim. Now the grotesquery and terror do not stem from the monstrous-feminine but from predatory masculinity. However, by placing blame on male heartlessness and cruelty, these two adaptations rest on the sentimental aspects of the sad destiny of women in the face of human weakness without fundamentally questioning the Confucian patriarchal society that plays a significant role in the miserable fate of female members. These two adaptations are trapped in the sentimental melodrama, which only touches the surface of the problem while failing to probe its depths.

Gordon Chan's *Painted Skin* (*Hua pi*, 2008) is in many aspects an innovative adaptation of "Painted Skin." This mainland China-Hong Kong coproduced big-budget blockbuster is an action-romance with delicately designed mise-en-scènes and CGI special effects, and with only a slight touch of horror. Unlike the previous adaptations, which highlight the simple dichotomy between female and male or good and evil, Chan's *Painted Skin* proves to be a complicated exploration of the power struggle between masculinity and femininity in a modern sense. Li Zeng views it as an allegory of marriage and family crisis in contemporary China that revolves around "the confrontation between a seductress and a homemaker," with the male protagonist the victim of "this women's war" ("*Painted Skin*" 230). This polygynist theme seems highly conservative from a gender politics perspective, and its ultimate glorification of "true love conquers all" also signifies an unpromising message. However, with a more comprehensive analysis, especially of its intertextual relationships with other *Liaozhai*-inspired works and the ghostlore tradition, this genre-blended film provides a more subtle and nuanced demonstration of female agency and subjectivity in modern times, even disguised in a historical and fantastic vein. Its demonstration of multiple female figures provides an alternative possibility to the traditional virtuous housekeeping wife. And its destabilization of masculine hegemony also manifests a paradigm shift in the configuration of gendered subjectivity in the postmodern Chinese context.

Chan's painted-skin demon is a blending of ghost and fox spirit schemas. Xiao Wei is a fox spirit disguised as a beautiful girl, who needs to eat human hearts to keep her shape. The shift from female ghost to fox spirit, as I mentioned earlier, is to avoid the censorship in mainland China of ghost figures on the screen. Moreover, as Sung-Ae Lee notes, "adaptations of folktales are more often based on scripts than specific recorded versions, and those scripts may draw core schemas from several related or similar folktales" ("Lost in Liminal Space" 139 n.2). The ghost-mortal romantic script and fox spirit-mortal romantic script are isomorphic in plot, and thus rendered interchangeable. This substitution of fox spirit as the heroine instead of ghost is practical and adroit. The cannibal habit of eating hearts is a remnant of the horror-inducing ghost from the pre-text. However, Xiao Wei's cannibalism and brutality are depicted in only a few scenes, and her must-do heart-eating is repulsive even for herself. Even early in the film, it is evident that her monstrous identity is at odds with her disguised human identity.

All three main female characters in Chan's adaptation are ambiguous and boundary-crossing. Instead of being utterly evil, as in Pu's tale, Xiao Wei is a combination of "malicious ghost and amorous ghost," both "a fetishized object of the male gaze and a woman with strong agency who dominates every scene in which she appears" (Zeng, "Painted Skin" 223). Calculating and manipulative, she puts on a masquerade of conventional femininity to fool the men around her. She constantly shifts between her submissive masquerade and her vicious monstrosity. Although this fluid feminine identity challenges fixed gender roles and thus resists the conventional representation of femininity under patriarchal order, she is finally defined by her yearning for the position of a human wife and her ultimate self-sacrificial action. As a human-fox hybrid, the image of Xiao Wei inevitably exhibits animal features. In the latter part of the film, her vulpine ears stand out and her hair turns white like fur. After giving up her cultivated essence, she appears in her true form as a white fox in the final scene. The image of the little white fox is quite poignant, since she has been pushed back to observe the human world from the margin. The film closes with the fox and her shape-shifting lizard companion back in the desert—even further marginalized. The desert echoes with the pre-credit sequences as the place where Xiao Wei comes from. Such a closure indicates her failure to achieve integration into the human realm.

Therefore, as Li Zeng argues, this film continues the narrative of "the containment of the monstrous-feminine and the affirmation of women's traditional virtues" ("Painted Skin" 225). Wang's wife, Pei Rong, is also a more complicated character than the virtuous housewife stereotype. She is observant and resourceful, so that after she has deduced that her husband is perhaps seduced by a nonhuman monster, she goes out of the house and seeks help from her ex-suitor. A third female character is the cross-dressing demon hunter Xia Bing. Her existence shows a break away from the dichotomous gender roles of angelic wife and monstrous seductress. The exorcists in *Liaozhai* and many adaptations are primarily Buddhist monks, Daoist priests, and mysterious swordsmen, all of whom are male. For the first time, the Eastern Dr. Van Helsing role could be played by a female character, and she is empowered by her cross-dressing.

Although this film is arguably a quasi-feminist narrative in its depiction of three active female characters, the agentic desiring Xiao Wei, the discerning and fearless Pei Rong, and the cross-dressing demon hunter Xia Bing, the subversive potentials of all three are undermined by the thematic closure, in which Xiao Wei and Pei Rong both choose self-sacrifice for their beloved male. The only exception is perhaps Xia Bing, whose romantic relationship with Pang Yong is developed upon a common cause and indicates a more equal relationship between the two sexes. This quasi-feminist feature marks the complicated negotiation of progressive and conservative gender ideology in the contemporary Chinese context. On the one hand, the society and culture recognizes the rising of female economic power, sexual autonomy, and intellectual capacity; on the other hand, the threatened patriarchal order tries to control this newly awakening feminist pulse and reaffirm the traditional gender order.

The depiction of male characters in Chan's adaptation also fits with this paradoxical attitude. Despite his transformation from an intellectual to an army general, Wang is deliberately portrayed as soft and feminine, played by the handsome yet not macho actor Chen Kun, who is famous for his performance as beautiful androgynous characters. In the diegesis of this film, Xiao Wei is the object of the gaze of the male characters; however, throughout the diegesis it is Wang who becomes the object of both Xiao Wei's and female audiences' gaze. In a sequence in which Wang dreams of making love with Xiao Wei (01:11:14–01:12:45), he explicitly wears feminine makeup, long loose hair, and a silky outfit, which implies an androgynous encounter (Pang 473). The sex scene may be understood as a self-conscious cliché that aims to draw the attention of avid moviegoers, but it is also suggestive of a complicated power negotiation between the two sexes. The camera first gives a full shot of Wang walking toward the audience, and then changes to a medium shot to display his feminine outfit. He walks toward the lake, where Xiao Wei emerges from under the water. In a shot-reverse-shot sequence depicting the encounter between these two characters, Wang is framed with a medium close-up shot while Xiao Wei appears in an extreme close-up shot of her eyes. The emphasis on Xiao Wei's eyes makes the androgynous Wang the object of her erotic gaze. A close-up of a woman's eyes normally implies access to her inner being, but this shot-reverse-shot frame asserts she is the agent of the gaze, not its object. This sequence is another aspect of how the scene plays with convention. The following sex scene portrays Xiao Wei and Wang as almost indistinguishable, seen from a distance, and the line between subject and object, male and female, and initiative and passive is dissolved. The erotic objectification of Wang through costume, makeup, and camera shot in this sequence could be seen as a fan service to the female audience, in which sensual pleasure comes from the female gaze at the beautiful yet not threatening male body.

The elevation of traditional femininity over powerful female agency manifested by the film's closure also privileges an altruistic over a solipsistic ideology, a humanistic over a multicultural ideology. Just as the romantic love for the prince from Andersen's "The Little Mermaid" is mingled with the mermaid's longing for mortality and a Christian soul, Xiao Wei's eager desire to become Mrs. Wang is also not only sexual desire for a handsome man but also a yearning for mortality and humanity, for inclusion in the normative human society. Confronting Xiao Wei, Pei Rong asserts, "you know nothing about love." Underpinning this phrase is the accusation that her way of love is monstrous because she solipsistically satisfies her desire with no regard for the well-being of others. Xiao Wei finally learns the way of altruistic love when she gives up her cultivated essence to bring Wang and Pei Rong back to life. Taming the female monster parallels civilizing the barbarous foreign.[5] Therefore, the self-sacrifice committed by Xiao Wei has multiple symbolic

---

5. In the pre-credit sequence, Xiao Wei is rescued from a barbarian tribe in the desert by Wang and his Han Chinese army. Pu's original tale does not specify the historical background, but Chan sets his adaptation in the Han dynasty, according to the period mise-en-scène, costumes, and customs. The Han dynasty is famous for its border conflict with nomadic tribes, most significantly Xiongnu. Andy Willis contends that this film is set during the Yuan dynasty (21). No explicit cues designate its historical background, and any guess is arguably possible. Both the Han and the Yuan dynasties are characterized by their tense ethnic and racial conflicts.

meanings, including the triumph of the male over the female, the center over the periphery, and culture over nature. Xiao Wei as a *yao* (monster), a female, and an outsider receives triple abjection, since "one kind of difference becomes another as the normative categories of gender, sexuality, national identity, and ethnicity slide together like imbricated circles of a Venn diagram" (Cohen 11). As Jeffrey Jerome Cohen explains, monsters are "difference made flesh" (7), and "fear of the monster is really a kind of desire" (16). Although they always dangerously entice, if monsters "threaten to overstep these boundaries, to destroy or deconstruct the thin walls of category and culture" (17), as in Xiao Wei's desire to change places with Mrs. Wang, they must be controlled and terminated to restore order.

The outcome of several adaptations of "Painted Skin," as my analysis shows, is that the female ghost/demon is returned to the underground/animal world where she belongs, and the social order of the human world is restored. Whether she is threatening or sympathetic, her irruption into the ordinary world will ultimately be brought to an end because of the failure of the romantic intersubjective relationship with a mortal man. In the most recent adaptation, *Painted Skin: Resurrection (Hua pi II zhuansheng shu,* 2012), the monster Xiao Wei finally finds a way to be accepted by human society, through combining with a human princess both in soul and in flesh. For the first time acceptance is achieved not by heterosexual romance but through female friendship and companionship. A number of sequences show the promise of lesbian encounters, especially when the two female characters change skins and thus identity during the bath, even though the sanctity of heteronormativity is ultimately preserved (Pugsley 53). The multiple adaptations of "Painted Skin" thus prove to be a contested space upon which is grounded a struggle between rising female autonomy and conservative gender politics.

The Transformative Power of the Carnivalesque in Animation Adaptation

"Nie Xiaoqian," as another tale about ghost-mortal romance, has also been adapted several times. In 1960, the renowned Hong Kong film studio the Shaw Brothers first adapted the story of Nie Xiaoqian into a film called *The Enchanting Shadow (Qian nü you hun).* Directed by Li Han-hsiang, this film remains roughly faithful to the original tale, and employs an elegant and poetic style. Situating the story in the turmoil of the transition period from the Ming dynasty to the Qing dynasty, the film is more realistic than fantastic (Hongjian Wang 143). Twenty-seven years later, director Ching Siu-tung and producer Tsui Hark readapted this famous tale into *A Chinese Ghost Story*, and its Chinese title, *Qian nü you hun*, is identical to that of the 1960 film. It was an instant box office triumph in Hong Kong, winning both commercial and critical acclaim. Unlike its predecessor, which is historically solid, the 1987 adaptation purposefully obfuscates the historical context and sets the story in a vaguely premodern past. According to Hongjian Wang, the 1987 film turns a serious, moralistic, and patriotic story (Li Han-hsiang's version) into a comedy that "is combined with erotic romance, action-packed martial arts, gross-out horror, cultural parody, and social satire" (145). The conflict between progressive and conservative gender paradigms observed in the adaptation web of "Painted Skin" is also extant in the adaptations of "Nie Xiaoqian." For Marc L. Moskowitz, *A Chinese Ghost Story* (1987) conveys paradoxical messages on gender roles, "in the midst of portrayals of such surprisingly strong, assertive, and capable women, coexisting themes of normative heterosexuality and patriarchal order have been restored" (217). In 2011, Wilson Yip made another cinematic adaptation of "Nie Xiaoqian," and it was also titled *A Chinese Ghost Story*. This live-action version explicitly pays homage to Ching and Tsui's now-classic adaptation, reproducing the same theme song and same tree demon (an innovation in the Ching and Tsui version). Sarah Woodland sees Yip's movie as a remake of the 1987 canon. However, restrained by the mainland's censorship on ghosts in the screen, Yip changed Xiaoqian from a female ghost to a fox spirit, as in Gordon Chan's *Painted Skin* (2008).

Ten years after the release of Ching and Tsui's live-action adaptation, the animation remake *A Chinese Ghost Story: The Tsui Hark Animation* (directed by Andrew Chan) (hereafter *Xiaoqian*) appeared. This time Tsui Hark worked as the screenwriter rather than the producer. This animation was not a financial success and remains a relatively lesser-known film (Macdonald, *Animation in China* 191). Targeting a younger audience, *Xiaoqian* is not a simple transmedia remake of the live-action version that deletes explicit sexual and violent scenes; it is a more exquisite rendition of the story employing the same cast of characters. Moreover, by employing a carnivalesque strategy, Tsui's animation version displays the transformative power of laughter and humor in a text. Thus it offers a more liberating message about gender politics than do other adaptations of ghost-mortal romance scripts that target an adult audience.

In many ways, *Xiaoqian* resembles Hayao Miyazaki's *Spirited Away* (2001), especially in their depictions of the relationship of Ning/Xiaoqian and Chihiro/Haku as romantic and companionable. In the English-language version of *Spirited Away*, the relationship between Chihiro and Haku is called love, but for Cristina Bacchilega and John Rieder, this is not romance, since it "lacks the sexual overtones of other anime." Rather, their connection "energizes dynamics of care, respect, and responsibility which can be restorative" (39). Similarly, Xiaoqian in the animation is deprived of the amorous aspect of the original text and previous adaptations, and her relationship with Ning is no longer an erotic male fantasy but it becomes a mutual supporting friendship in a modern sense. Ning, a poor and heartbroken young man who has just been dumped by his snobbish ex-girlfriend, experiences bizarre adventures in a ghost city and comes of age through his relationship with the ghost Xiaoqian. Xiaoqian, on the other hand, is a sassy female ghost who holds an unrequited love toward Black Mountain Monster and is employed by the tree demon to seduce mortal men for their essence. The flawed intersubjective relationships among the inhabitants of the ghost city are reminiscent of the social illness of contemporary Hong Kong, in that both men and women are obsessed with vanity and peers compete fiercely for limited resources. Xiaoqian's ex-lover Black Mountain Monster is a rock star consumed by vanity and narcissism. The hilarious sequence of his concert in the ghost festival is an obvious parody of the Cantonese pop stars' concerts. Similarly, the tree demon Grandma who reminds the audience of Miyazaki's Yubaba is also obsessed with maintaining her youth and beauty at the price of killing innocent males for their essence. The ghost city in this animation is truly a metaphoric space for Hong Kong: as Sean Macdonald observes, the landscape of the ghost city is "ironically localized in the commercial district of Mong Kok, Hong Kong, the location of Sinocenter, which is a large mall of several stories of small shops that caters to fans of anime, manga, computer games, music, and fan culture in general" (*Animation in China* 192). Lost in the self-centeredness produced by the rapid development of capitalism and consumerism, these antagonists inhabiting the ghost city exhibit the director's sharp critique of the materialism and toxicity of contemporary Hong Kong society.

Produced in 1997, the same year Hong Kong was returned to mainland China after British colonial rule, the film also represents the liminal space of the ghost city, between the living and the dead, as a symbol of Hong Kong's ambiguous cultural identity. The continual threats received by the ghost city from powerful ghostbusters such as Buddhist monks and Daoist priests are also symbolic of the vulnerable autonomy of Hong Kong in the face of the superpower nations of China and the United Kingdom. Xiaoqian, as a local inhabit, at first refuses to leave her hometown and does not desire rebirth as a human. It is only after she has been exposed to the selfishness of her ex-lover and the cannibal nature of her grandma that she decides to leave and seek a new beginning. As a human who accidentally intrudes into the ghost city, Ning manifests a nonhegemonic tendency to assimilate with the local rather than striving to conquer it. He is initially fascinated by the extravagant flamboyance of this ghost city and then attracted to the beautiful Xiaoqian. His willingness to be consumed by the tree demon for Xiaoqian shows his openness to becoming an other, a ghost. More intriguing is the denouement, in which the attempt by the protagonists to become reincarnated fails. Xiaoqian remains a ghost and Ning a human, but they form a genuine caring relationship in spite of their difference.

The Qing short story written by Pu ends with Xiaoqian's "reintegration into the human community" (Yu 428). After Xiaoqian comes into Ning's family, she gradually loses her ghostliness and becomes more human-like: "at first Xiaoqian ate and drank nothing, but after six months had passed, she gradually began to take a little thin congee. Little by Little, mother and son became extremely attached to her, and they would never have it mentioned in the house that she was a ghost. Indeed, strangers were unable to distinguish anything ghostly about her" (Pu, *Strange Tales from a Chinese Studio* 177, translation modified). The loss of her ghostliness in Pu's closure signifies the hegemony of the human world over ghost subjectivity. In contrast, the live-action film adaptations of "Nie Xiaoqian" close with the separation of Ning and Xiaoqian, for humans and ghosts ultimately belong to different realms. This ending in separation reinforces the impossibility of coexistence and hybridity between the marginalized domain and the dominant domain. The animated version is unique in its depiction of a dialogical relationship derived from mutual acceptance and reciprocal support without the dominance of one discourse over another.

Two sequences in *Xiaoqian* are explicitly carnivalesque. In his analysis of the carnivalesque in children's literature, John Stephens identifies this mode in books that "create roles for child characters which interrogate the normal subject positions created for children within socially dominant ideological frames" (*Language and Ideology* 120). Mikhail Bakhtin, whose *Rabelais and His World* is a key source for the concept of the carnivalesque, suggests that the carnival has a transgressive characteristic, which "in mocking and symbolically inverting hierarchical social structures, has the potential to critique and subvert the institutions that maintain those social structures" (McCallum 86). In Ning's first encounter with Xiaoqian in the ghost city, the culturally hierarchical relationships of male over female and human over ghost, which are so prominent in the earlier versions of the script, are effectively eliminated. In the midst of a sequence that features a dazzling parade of ghosts, Ning is intoxicated by the central figure, Xiaoqian, who sits in a sedan chair. The following sequence, accompanied by a musical song, captures the moment when Ning falls in love with Xiaoqian. The shots make Xiaoqian the more central and powerful character by first making Ning shrink and then capturing these scenes from a low angle. The tiny-sized Ning leaps over peach flowers surrounding Xiaoqian, who is confident and smiling. In the contrast between a gigantic Xiaoqian and toy-like Ning, the power relationship between female and male is turned upside down, effecting what Stephens describes as a type of interrogative text "which examines and inverts a social ideological paradigm" (*Language and Ideology* 139). Although Xiaoqian is the object of Ning's male gaze, her manipulation of the flowers and the visual contrast between their figures clearly shows her strong subjectivity. This sequence also foreshadows a later interrogative scene when the traditional gender order is reaffirmed during the concert performance of Black Mountain Monster: Xiaoqian is here represented as a small figure who dances on the shoulder and within the hair of the huge monster. The episode, however, satirizes vainglorious masculinity, first in Black Mountain's narcissistic song ("Let me always love myself, Only I am worthy of my love") and then in his violent rage when Xiaoqian damages his hair. He is appropriately destroyed in a battle with the ghostbusters.

Ning is an outsider who not only loses his power at the sight of beautiful Xiaoqian but also loses his privilege as a human when he becomes an other in a city full of ghosts. Just as Chihiro is accused of exuding a human stench in Miyazaki's bizarre bathhouse, Ning also comes under threat as a human in a restaurant whose staff and customers are all ghosts, while the meal served consists of human flesh. In a standard ghost-mortal romance script from Pu's tales, it is usually ghosts who desperately want to become human again, since they are viewed as inferior and incomplete in their subjectivity. Female ghosts try to gain legitimacy as human through sexual intercourse with mortal men, while male ghosts win back their place in the living world by their good virtues such as integrity and filial piety. The implicit hierarchy in such a paradigm asserts that men are associated with the mind and women with the body. This point is illustrated by the scene in *Painted Skin* when Wang refuses Xiao Wei a sexual role as wife or concubine and she retorts that she is thus rendered useless. However, in the ghost city depicted by the animation, the normal hierarchy is reversed and Ning must rely on help from Xiaoqian to survive in a world that is hostile to a human being.

Another carnivalesque sequence happens at the end when the Buddhist concept of reincarnation is materialized in animated visual form. Various weird looking ghosts are going through the gate of reincarnation, as well as the film's human ghostbusters. Through the long tunnel-like gate, all characters experience physical infantilization, including the three human ghost hunters. Their body size and facial features are retrograded, as all adults are turning back into children and then babies. In this sequence, the hierarchical relationship between adult and children is again distorted, most strikingly illustrated by the infantilization of the three hunter figures. Previously the two monks and the priest Yan are powerful and authoritative figures who are capable of demolishing ghosts. However, in the carnival gate of reincarnation they are turned into vulnerable babies. The rivalry between the Daoist priest Yan and the two monks is also ridiculed, since as the three are jostling together they pass through the gate and are reborn as triplet siblings. This scene is truly a "world-upside-down," in which "the oppressive structures of everyday life are overturned" (Stam 92). This visual materialization of reincarnation also mocks the rigid morality within this Buddhist concept. In the traditional understanding of karmic retribution, the new life form inevitably reflects the virtue of the dead person. People who commit sins during their life turn into animals in their afterlife as punishment, while people who are kind and virtuous are rewarded by being born into a rich family. These themes are not uncommon in Pu's tales, including "Past Lives" ("Sansheng," Pu, *Strange Tales from a Chinese Studio* 98–101) and "Sheep Skin" ("Mougong," Pu, *Strange Tales from a Chinese Studio* 206–8). However, in the animation's carnivalesque scene of reincarnation, all the debts and orders are replaced by an egalitarian jollification. Subversive pleasure is produced from this denouement, for it undermines narrow-minded dichotomies of good and evil, human and ghost, and adult and child.

Young audience members may particularly enjoy the reincarnation of Ning's dog, Solid Gold. He has been transformed into a cat through the gate, but retains his memories of life as a dog, barks, and generally behaves as a dog. This is not just an extended joke, however, but communicates major thematic significance. When in the closing moments he appears with a fish he has caught, the film affirms behavioral hybridity. In blurring species categories, the film represents identity as fluid and unfixed, and therefore encourages the cross-boundary romance between human Ning and ghost Xiaoqian. They are accidentally kicked out of the reincarnation gate and happily retain their previous forms and memories. In other words, the ghost Xiaoqian does not need to become a human to qualify as Ning's partner. The film moves toward closure with the cascading laughter of Ning, who rejoices in his reunion with Xiaoqian. The laughter is a final affirmation of the carnivalesque characteristic of this film. The laughter does not represent the cliché ending of "happily ever after" of many fairy tales; instead, it comes from the subversive pleasure. The laughing Ning is viewed as insane and crazy and is pitied by other human characters, which indicates that conventional decorum is not fully annihilated. However, the reassuring laughter is, after all, "the form of a free and critical consciousness that mocks dogmatism and fanaticism" (Stam 87).

As an adaptation of the ghost-mortal romance script in *Liaozhai* for a younger audience, *Xiaoqian* employs its carnivalesque aesthetics to send the most liberating message on issues of gender, power, and childhood. The several cinematic adaptations of "Painted Skin" and "Nie Xiaoqian," although trying to update old tales by advanced visual technology and modernized character-ization, are still trapped by the haunting patriarchal ideology. The animation *Xiaoqian* successfully disables the ingrained hierarchical relationship of human over ghost, male over female, and adult over child by employing a carniva-lesque strategy both in visual representation and in content. The happily-ever-after ending does not dismantle its progressive potential, for it is a mutually respective relationship with both Ning's humanity and soft masculinity and

Xiaoqian's ghostliness and powerful femininity unsacrificed. Their intersubjectivity is a genuine hybrid without any form of hegemony and homogenization.

Conclusion

This chapter examined how the metaphor of the ghost has been deployed in contemporary Chinese fantasy novels and films to represent women as marginalized figures. In their *Spectralities Reader*, Blanco and Peeren contend that the ghost as a conceptual metaphor "remains a figure of unruliness pointing to the tangibly ambiguous," and "its own status as discourse or epistemology is never stable, as the ghost also questions the formation of knowledge itself and specifically invokes what is placed outside it, excluded from perception" (9). The lack of monstrous and vengeful ghosts in contemporary Chinese cinema reflects the state's anxiety toward not only its disturbing and traumatic past but also its current rapid development and injustice. Since revenging ghosts have usually been wronged when they were alive, their vengeance thus calls into question the functionality of the legal system, the welfare facilities, and social justice.

The pseudofeminist depiction of amorous female ghosts in adaptations of the ghost-mortal romance script signals the conflict between wakening female autonomy and pervasive gender norms. In the classic tale, the female ghost is the production of male fantasy, and her arduous quest to be integrated into the human realm mirrors the status and the lived experience of women in a society primarily dominated by male authority. This patriarchal ideology is seldom subverted thoroughly in contemporary adaptations.

My reading of the ghost figure focuses on its dynamic intertextual relations with literary predecessors and cultural context. In Chinese society, age-old conventional burdens manifested in various traditional stories still restrain and inhibit the realization of agency and fuller development of its marginalized members. Subversive and innovative adaptations that diverge from a familiar script have the potential to encourage a more critical and reflective understanding of many traditional stories and their implicit cultural attitudes regarding gender, monstrosity, and childhood. The following chapter will continue to explore how the young members of the society accommodate and survive in an adult-controlled world, and how this intergenerational conflict prompted by age differences is entangled with sectional imbalance based on gender.

6

Disappearing Fairies and Ghosts

FEMALE AND CHILD CHARACTERS AS OTHERS IN
CONTEMPORARY CHINESE CHILDREN'S FANTASY

Depicted either as fairies, ghosts, or other forms of alien creatures, other-worldly female figures are pervasive throughout Chinese literary history, and find a way of re-entering contemporary Chinese fantasy narratives. Rania Huntington identifies four nonhuman creatures in Chinese supernatural literature in a roughly descending order of *shen* (gods), *hsien* [*xian*] (immortals, fairies), *kuei* [*gui*] (ghosts), and *yao* (spirits, monsters) ("The Supernatural" 112–14). The prototypical way these alien women interact with the human world is through romance with male mortals. Through heterosexual romance and marriage, they try to be incorporated into the normative family structure of the human realm. The previous two chapters focused on the contemporary adaptations of the interspecies romance script, as represented by "The Legend of the White Snake" and classical ghost tales from *Liaozhai*. "The Legend of the White Snake" depicts the marriage between man and snake spirit, whereas *Liaozhai* tales feature ghost-human romance.

Adding a hybrid child into the interspecies romance script changes the familiar romantic tale into a family narrative. Such a shift enriches the thematic concerns of retellings of traditional folktales, in addition to the feminist questioning discussed in the previous chapters; it also addresses the unequal power relationship between parent and child in contemporary China. The parent-child relationship in ancient China was always shaped by "a natural pecking order of superior-inferior relationships," and this hierarchical system within the family also enabled "political indoctrination and moral cultivation" in a broader sense (Bi, Fang, and Bradford 36). Moreover, in dealing with the two power relationships between male and female, adult and child, the repressive mechanisms used by the male and the adult are similar. Intersectional feminism reminds us that "different aspects of power asymmetries work together to affect the individual's abilities" (Palo and Manderstedt 129). To avoid an analysis that treats such elements as "disparate forces," we should keep in mind that they "are actually mutually dependent and co-constitutive" (Cole n.p.). An intersectional approach will allow us to see the interconnections between patriarchal ideology, parental authority, and anthropocentrism, to see how the otherworldly characters are subject to a triple rejection, being simultaneously female, nonhuman, and nonadult.

Situated within the changing economic and political contexts of China's modernization and globalization, children's fantasy novels prove to be apt vehicles for exploring the plights and challenges that women and girls face in the new millennium in China. This chapter provides an intersectional feminist critique of two contemporary Chinese children's fantasy novels, *My Mother Is a Fairy* (*Wo de Mama shi Jingling*) (1998) by Chen Danyan and *Jiujiu from the Ghost Mansion* (*Laizi gui zhuangyuan de Jiujiu*) (2010) by Tang Tang (the pen name of Tang Hongying) and examines the marginalization and silencing of the otherworld female/child characters in these narratives. It focuses on how they construct the hybrid child's subjectivity and how they adapt old literary tropes and conventions from multicultural sources. These two novels are found to construct a binary opposition between the fantastic-female-child and the rational-male-adult, with the latter dominating the female and the child by repressing their propensity for imagination and fantasy. However, although these fantasy novels might seem to conform to the ideological status quo in terms of the patriarchal family structure, they also have a subversive edge in the way that the binary opposition between male and female is transgressed. Such novels point to the formation of a new kind of intersubjective relationship that is based on understanding and tolerance rather than rejection and dominance.

Chinese Contemporary Children's Fantasy through a Gender Lens

While scholars have fruitfully turned to feminist criticism in order to examine Chinese children's literature, the focus of these investigations has generally been on realistic fiction. Jiahua Zhang uses Qin Wenjun's school story series to discuss the contest between essentialism and constructionism and the gendered depiction of femininity and masculinity in Qin's characters (48–55). Qiao Yigang and Wang Shuainai provide a comprehensive literature review of scholarly works that employ feminist theories to analyze Chinese children's literature (17–29); Lisa Chu Shen's two studies focus on the queer possibilities of anti-stereotypical transgressive figures, such as tomboys and effeminate boys, in several realist children's fictional works ("Femininity and Gender" 278–96; "The Effeminate Boy" 63–81). When children's fantasy books have been considered, they are usually treated in one of two ways: either to examine the distinctive generic characteristics of these works, in contrast to those of realist fiction, or to ponder the effectiveness of fantasy in promoting children's imaginations. More serious ideological concerns, such as those of gender, class, and ethnicity, tend to be neglected (Zhu and He; You). It would therefore be fruitful if there were more dialogue between feminist criticism and Chinese fantasy fiction, for, as Lucy Armitt notes, "the fantastic is starting to play an increasingly powerful metaphorical role in the development of feminist criticism and theory in general" (6). Fantasy literature could then be approached with a view to exploring how it discusses important contemporary problems, such as gender equality, in a more nuanced and subtle way.

My Mother Is a Fairy and *Jiujiu from the Ghost Mansion* are two representative children's fantasy novels from contemporary China. They deploy, respectively, the figures of the fairy and the ghost to explore issues of alterity, femininity, and subjectivity through their female and child protagonists. The two novels share many thematic and generic features. Both novels have female children as their protagonists, which sets them apart from male-centered children's fantasy novels produced by other Chinese authors, such as Peng Yi, whose protagonists are mostly boys, and whose narratives follow the traditional mode of a quest story, being action-driven and full of adventure. Female characters in Peng's works are generally peripheral and passive. In his novel *The Crazy Green Hedgehog* (*Fengkuang lü ciwei*, 1996), for example, the male protagonist's friend and love interest, Xueying, is depicted as fragile and in need of male protection. In contrast, the male protagonist himself, Xia, is repeatedly identified as strong, tough, and unyielding. This novel is therefore explicit in situating a patriarchal model of masculinity and femininity at the heart of modern Chinese fantasy literature for children.

Against this trend, in Chinese children's fantasy that contains female protagonists, we find that the familiar quest and adventure plots have been transformed into everyday, domestic melodramas. Yin Jianling's *The Crying Fairy* (*Kuqi Jingling*, 1999) provides one such example, sharing many of the characteristics of Chen's *My Mother Is a Fairy*. The former depicts the maturation of a young girl, Mili, which occurs with the assistance of a fairy named Dingdong. The biggest challenge faced by Mili, then, is not from mythic monsters, as in Peng's novels, but the family crisis of divorce. So, unlike boys in novels by male writers, who come of age by defeating monstrous villains from a mythical past, in works by female writers, such as Yin Jianling and Chen Danyan, the female protagonists mature by accepting the inevitable loss of family members. The narrative pattern characteristic of the female fantasy bildungsroman, then, conforms to that depicted by Elizabeth Abel et al., where, instead of "active accommodation, rebellion, or withdrawal" there is, "inner concentration" (8). While Peng's male characters actively seek and fight, their female counterparts think and receive. However, this does not mean that the gender ideology of Chinese children's fantasy is always regressive, as forms of subversion can be achieved through an innovative adaptation of old tales and the conscious manipulation of female character focalization.

The novels of Chen and Tang provide two good examples, demonstrating not only the way that women and girls are represented in literary texts but also the plights and challenges such characters face in the new millennium in China, where they find themselves trapped in a gender bind. On the one hand, the competitive economic environment demands that women be financially and psychologically independent; on the other hand, the official rhetoric still requires the individual to "defer to the collective social will" (Jackson, Liu, and Woo 16). The Confucian ideal that requires women to take responsibility for domestic duties and embrace a sacrificial position is still largely at work. Women thus find themselves torn between their rising economic independence and their traditionally dependent position. Children and adolescents, too, especially the generation who grew up under the one-child policy (1979–2016), share with women the risks and opportunities present in a postsocialist China. Although the younger generation generally enjoys ample material resources and attention, it is nevertheless restricted by the demands of obedience and conformity to parents and society.

The Hybrid Child

It is not uncommon for folktales about interspecies romance to include the role of the hybrid child, as the Celtic folktale about the Selkie wife and its adaptations demonstrate. Moreover, the hybrid child of a human/nonhuman couple will face an ineluctable predicament that relates either to parental separation or to his or her own existential crisis as a product of hybridity and alterity. In more recent animated adaptations of this script—such as Tomm Moore's *Song of the Sea* (2014), which is a retelling of the Irish Selkie tale, and Hosoda Mamoru's *Wolf Children* (2012), a gender-reversed version of the script, in which the father is a werewolf and the mother is a human—the theme has shifted so that the emphasis is now on the hybrid identity of the children and their need to choose between the other world and the human one.

Usually, the marriage between a nonhuman wife and a mortal man is forced, and in such cases the offspring of their relationship works as a further step to coerce the otherworldly female into the patriarchal family structure, as she becomes trapped by the irreconcilability of self-autonomy with family duty. However, as stressed earlier, in East Asian versions of the Swan Maiden motif, the maidens usually go willingly and even gladly with the men, and do not want to come back to their natural world. In these cases, the birth of children, especially males, legitimates the status of the nonhuman wives in society. The incompatibility between free will and family responsibility imaged in the Western Swan Maiden tales is largely absent in these East Asian versions. In contrast, the nonhuman wives have to reluctantly separate from their beloved husbands and sons because of some external religious forces, and their reunion with family members turns out to be a satisfactory happy ending for the masses.

Despite their apparent differences, in examples from both the West and the East, the relationship between the hybrid children and their otherworldly mothers plays an essential role in both the formation of the child's identity and the mother' agency. In his analysis of two picture books that retell the Selkie wife story, Stephens argues that the animal mother's quest for freedom and happiness is often in conflict with her children's requirements, and "to perceive that the mother has an independent being and to let her go is to achieve a sense of object/person permanence which marks the child's maturation beyond an egocentric relationship with the world" (*Language and Ideology* 63). As my Chinese textual example shows, to accept the departure of the mother is indeed represented as a sign of the child's transformation from egocentric to altruistic being, but the process is much more complicated due to the weak agency exemplified by the mother figure, and the narrative closure is less satisfying in its depiction of a mother who leaves unwillingly and a freed father.

Chen Danyan's novel, *My Mother Is a Fairy* (1998), is a story whose protagonist is the hybrid daughter of a human father and a fairy mother.[1] Miaomiao, as a hybrid daughter, is entirely humanized, but her oscillation between the conflicting emotional positions posed by the different worlds of her parents is at the heart of the novel. As the only child of a middle-class family (with a surgeon father and an artist mother), the protagonist, Chen Miaomiao, lives a carefree and happy life until the day she discovers, first, that her mother is a fairy from another world and, second, that her parents have decided to divorce. Her initial reaction upon discovering her mother's identity as a nonhuman is one of fear. She is also angry at her parents' decision to separate and indulges in self-pity. However, following a series of conversations with her fairy mother, Miaomiao comes to understand that her mother's love for her is unchanging, regardless of her form. After several failed attempts to reunite her parents, Miaomiao also realizes that a failed relationship cannot be repaired by others. The novel ends with Miaomiao gaining in maturity, moving beyond her solipsistic subject position, and learning to accept three things: the otherness of her mother, the dissolution of her family, and loss. She is thus equipped to accompany her father to see, sadly but peacefully, the fairy mother return to her own realm.

In Miaomiao's case, she matures out of a solipsistic subjectivity into one that is more altruistic. Confronted with her mother's identity as a fairy and her father's wish for a divorce, Miaomiao initially reacts in a self-centered way. Later on, after several conversations with other characters, Miaomiao starts to reflect on her own position and view what is happening to her from the

---

1. There is an abridged English translation of the novel by J. J. Jiang and published by Better Link Press in 2006. I use Jiang's translation as a reference point for my analysis, with some modification. Jiang's translation uses the past tense, but it is necessary to keep in mind that the Chinese language has no obvious tense signs, such as changes in the verb form. It is also worth noting that the abridged translation does not include any of the photo illustrations that are featured in the original novel.

perspectives of others. Their internal, psychological states are captured mainly through conversations, and such dialogic activities enable readers to appreciate the contrasting and often conflicted subjectivities. Thus the supernatural, fantastic subjectivity of the mother contrasts sharply with the rational and scientific subjectivity of the father.

The different careers of Miaomiao's father and mother also support oppositional constructs of gender through their engagement with the unemotional/emotional, rational/intuitive divisions between masculinity and femininity. Her father is a surgeon, "supporting Mom and me by cutting people open with a scalpel" (Chen, *My Mother Is a Fairy* 9). "Support" means he is the breadwinner in the family, and "cutting" suggests a sense of aggression and violence. By contrast, her mother works as a freelance illustrator, an artist. Their different personalities are also sharply differentiated. In comparison with her father, who is serious, cold, and grim, her mother is sensitive, caring, and childish. The latter often talks in a funny and childish way, but her husband forbids her imaginary talk. As a result, she can express herself freely only when the father is not watching. As this sequence indicates, she is subject to his authority:

> She floated over where Dad was still fast asleep. Looking closely at his face, she grimaced. She would never do that if Dad were awake. But he continued in his deep sleep, unaware of what was going on.
>
> I laughed at the scene.
>
> Then Mom kissed Dad on his face and began to mimic Dad, closing her eyes as though intoxicated. She would never have dared to do that had he been awake. I burst into a fit of laughter. (Chen, *My Mother Is a Fairy* 30–31)

Comments like, "she would never do that [make a funny face] if Dad were awake" (Chen, *My Mother Is a Fairy* 30–31), which are repeated, emphasize the intimidating power the father has over the mother. In fact, the relationship between the father and mother is similar to the relationship between children and traditional parents. Her silence represents that she has been deprived of her voice and subjectivity. She has been further "othered," since she is from another species, another world.

The supremacy of the father echoes the pervasive rationalism of Chinese culture. Since Marxism was established as the official state ideology, the prevailing worldview in contemporary China has been one that leaves little room for traditional superstitious beliefs or foreign forms of spiritual existence. As a hybrid mixture of superstition and spirituality, "the fairy mother" in Chen's narrative is marginalized and finally expelled. In the following conversation between Miaomiao and her father, Miaomiao simultaneously recognizes and challenges his rationalist way of thinking:

> "Your mother can't really change what she is," he told me. "So I am the one who had to adapt. I am a surgeon working in a scientific environment where people don't believe in fairies. Of course, I was taken aback to learn that your mother was a fairy. *My whole world almost collapsed. Unlike you, I could not accept the existence of fairies so easily.* I almost fainted at this fact.
>
> "I read a lot of books about the subject, almost all psychological, Jung's books, and Stephen King's novels. Why? I wanted to accept this reality. I wanted science to help me accept it. Parapsychology talks about the existence of the soul, but it says nothing about feelings transposed to someone else. There is more to this than just flying around in the sky. You don't understand yet.
>
> "I am sad, *I can tell you, Chen Miaomiao, if a man is sad, then he is really sad."*
>
> *"So you say the sadness of women is not real?" I asked.*
>
> *Dad said, "It is real too. But women get sad easily, and that makes the sadness less noticeable. Maybe my judgment is not scientific."*
>
> *I said, "If a woman is sad, the sadness is real too."*
>
> *Dad nodded,* "I have thought that it's not right for me to make the whole family so sad. So, I tried to love your Mom again. But it turned out that I couldn't do it. Love is very strange. If there's a person whom you cannot even touch, you can't really love that person, *no matter how important, how nice the person is.* That's it. It is just like you cannot eat capsicum." (Chen, *My Mother Is a Fairy* 95–96)[2]

In this excerpt, the father's scientific mindset prevents him from accepting the existence of a supernatural being, even though he makes a great effort. His love has also dissipated as a result of his wife's alien identity. Although he admits that his opinion might not be correct, he still interprets the situation from a scientific perspective, by comparing the doomed relationship with a child's dietary preferences or allergies. This analogy obscures the hegemonic

---

2. In this and the following excerpts, I use italics to identify sentences that have been omitted from Jiang's English version. The translations in italics are mine.

nature of his rationalism. Correspondingly, his view that women easily become sad reinforces the artificial binarisms of emotional/unemotional and intuitive/ rational, with the former qualities, thanks to patriarchy, being associated with femininity and dissociated from masculinity. In contrast, Miaomiao easily accepts the existence of fairies because her mind is imaginatively open; moreover, in confirming the reality of women's sadness, she also implicitly debunks stereotypical opinions about women's sentimentality. As is evident from this exchange, the reader is placed in an active, interpretive position, able to see both perspectives. Such an openness to experience is confirmed by the author in her afterword, where she notes that "It is impossible for a child to try and save the fundamentally flawed marriage of her parents, but in the busy streets of Shanghai, it is possible for fairies to pass by the KFC on Huaihai Zhong Lu and sit on the trolley bus line."[3] Her assertion about the possibility of fairy existence is embedded alongside liberating messages about the importance of the imagination to young readers, which is something at odds with the rational and utilitarian attitude promoted within the Chinese education system and, more broadly, within the whole of Chinese society.

The pragmatic goals of this society, as advanced by teachers, are to urge students to work harder and play less, to achieve more and conform to the rules, with an emphasis on their scores and intellectual achievements, but at the possible expense of their mental health and well-being. It is no coincidence, then, that the subplot of the narrative features Miaomiao's school life in the primary school, where pupils are contending for a place at the best high school. As Miaomiao reflects:

> *This exam was very important.* Those who failed the exam would not attend a good high school, and then would have little chance of entering a good university. Without education in a good university, one could hardly find a good job, which in return would mean a poor life and hardships. I didn't want a poor life and hardships, so I had to study harder. (Chen, *My Mother Is a Fairy* 40)

This shows the extent to which Miaomiao's mind has been shaped by the prevailing utilitarian ideology. Its profit-oriented logic leaves no room for

---

3. These sentences are from Chen's Afterword for the new edition of her novel, included in the 2014 Chinese version, but omitted from Jiang's English version.

the children to be playful and imaginative. Miaomiao's parents reluctantly subscribe to this doctrine, with her fairy mother showing more sympathy for her daughter trapped in this rigid system:

> "If I really mess up the exam, what will happen?" I asked, *because now, it was of the greatest concern to me.*
>
> Mom replied, "You have a heart filled with feelings and emotions, which is the most precious thing in the world. If you pass the exam, that's good. If you fail, it won't be too bad."
>
> "But others won't look at it this way," I said. I don't look at it this way, either. Feelings are nothing. Everyone has them. We needed more than that to have a good life.
>
> Reading my thoughts, Mom whispered, "You humans just want too much."
> (Chen, *My Mother Is a Fairy* 70)

Miaomiao's contempt for feelings and her emphasis on the importance of material abundance is clearly influenced by the larger cultural and social context, since "others won't look at it this way," making conformity to the majority the predictable outcome. The mother's response, though, expresses contempt for the commercial greed of contemporary life. In an earlier scene, she has already made explicit her views on humans' conformity: "In here, everyone wants to be the same as everyone else. Even if you have to pretend, you must act like the others" (Chen, *My Mother Is a Fairy* 48). However, since she is a powerless and silenced subject, she can do little, in practical terms, to challenge the dominant ideology. Instead, the mother chooses to use her supernatural ability to give her daughter a flying trip as a way to transcend the hustle and bustle of modern life with its utilitarian profit-driven society.

In this novel, the fairy mother is capable of flying as well as summoning a pair of blue flowers as her eyes that could fly and see things happening a thousand miles away. Miaomiao, as a hybrid daughter of two different species, two different worlds, does not inherit any of her mother's supernatural powers, which include flying and clairvoyance. She is one hundred percent physically human, which signifies the earthly power over the otherworldly, the male power over the female. However, although she did not inherit the magic power of seeing with flying eyes, she has her own way of seeing. If photography can be considered another way of seeing, a more active and creative way of seeing, or in Susan Sontag's words, "an ethics of seeing" (3), then Miaomiao is capable not only of witnessing but also of recording the fantastic events that occur inside her family, inside her mother, which contrast with her father's reluctance to accept and see his nonhuman wife. The novel ends with the fairy mother's return to her own realm, which means that the fantastic elements are expelled and ordinary reality is restored. However, the manner of the fairy mother's disappearance aligns the novel with much other children's fantasy fiction, which, Sarah Gilead argues, reveals the fictionality of common sense reality at their closure: "instead of restoring or inverting conventional orders of significance, the return may function as the point at which the text most dramatically turns on itself to reveal its duplicities and discords" (289). At the end of the novel, when the mother returns to her fairy world, Miaomiao gives her the photos as a farewell gift:

> I looked at Mom's moonlit face. She looked tired but very pretty. I handed her an envelope. It contained photos that I had taken: dusk at the Route 49 bus stop, our sitting room, and various family pictures. I hoped they would remind her of the days in Shanghai, the days she was with us before she went back to her fairy world. (Chen, *My Mother Is a Fairy* 141)

In this paragraph, Miaomiao's photography gives her the ability to crystallize the memories she has shared with her mother. Her reflections also demonstrate that she is capable, at last, of empathetically understanding her mother and her decision to leave. Her mother does not take the photos away; instead, she marks each photo with a blue flower and then gives them back to Miaomiao, to let Miaomiao remember "a childhood with a fairy mother" (Chen 143). This exchange of gifts between mother and daughter is a gesture that functions to empower them both. The photos created by each of them (taken by the daughter and marked by the mother), including elements from realistic Shanghai (the bus stop, the sitting room) and the fantastic world (blue flowers), become a liminal bridge that brings together two different worlds.[4]

---

4. Chen's novel also has a metafictional aspect since the photos taken by Miaomiao as described in the diegesis are displayed as the illustrations of the novel in its Chinese original version, which are actually photos taken by Chen's ten-year-old daughter, Sunny Chen (Chen Taiyang). This strategy further obscures the boundaries between realism and fantasy and fiction and nonfiction.

The phrase "a childhood with a fairy mother" indicates a period during which the young protagonist has been able to develop an interconnection with the fantastic fairy world. This interconnection with another world and its alternative ideology allows her to experience a genuinely intersubjective relationship with her mother, and also implicitly functions to undermine the dominant rational, utilitarian ideology of modern China.

The Adopted Ghost Child

In the interspecies marriage script examined in the previous chapter, alien women usually represent repressed and marginalized femininity in a patriarchal society. In a family story involving a ghost child, the ghost character similarly becomes a metaphor for children in the adult-dominant world. *Jiujiu from the Ghost Mansion* (2010) by Tang Tang explores the relationship between a ghost child and her adoptive human parents and sister. Che Qiqi (literally "Seven seven"), the only daughter of the Che family, finds a baby abandoned on a ruined railway. The family thinks the baby is a normal human child and thus adopts her, giving her the name Jiujiu (literally "Nine nine," which pairs her with the sister, Qiqi). Subsequently, Qiqi finds out that her younger sister is, in fact, an enslaved ghost from the mysterious Ghost Mansion. The central section of this novel deals with the long and difficult process of Jiujiu's integration into the human community as a figure of otherness. Qiqi is more than willing to embrace a ghost sister, whereas her parents have trouble accepting the ghost daughter as a family member. This novel thus embodies an intriguing example of the struggle between adult and child, which might also be represented as a struggle between rationality and sensibility.

In her book on hauntology, Gordon discusses the function a ghost plays for the perceiver: "the ghostly haunt gives notice to that something [which] is missing" (10). The ghost Jiujiu as an adoptive child in the Che family and the warm welcome she receives from her father, mother, and older sister Qiqi signals their longing for the "missing" family member, a member whose existence is denied by the state's one-child policy. It is also intriguing that Tang makes all the ghosts who inhabit the underground Ghost Mansion *xiaogui*, which literally means little ghosts, a nickname for children in the Chinese language. Tang does not explain the origin of these little ghosts, nor their previous life information. But we are left to ask what is signified metaphorically by a Ghost Mansion that is full of children. If the suggestion that the ghosts in Tang's novel are a metaphor for the missing second children in contemporary Chinese families seems too narrow and far-fetched, then the ghosts in Tang's novels are definitely the symbols of children in a more general sense in a world dominated by adult authority. The otherness of Tang's little ghosts is manifested as mischievousness and naughtiness, which are also the iconic features of young children.

Compared to Chen's fairy mother, the ghost Jiujiu in Tang's novel occupies an even more shadowy and marginalized position at both the thematic and discursive levels. Although she is the titular protagonist, the novel is narrated by Qiqi, her human sister. Jiujiu's voice can be heard only in conversation, and readers are therefore given limited access to her feelings through the focalizing narration of Qiqi. In his analysis of the migrant characters in early multicultural Australian children's literature, Stephens has observed that, although these novels "pivot on aspects of difference . . . their narratives are usually focalized by members of the majority culture, and hence the privilege of narrative subjectivity is rarely bestowed upon minority groups" ("Advocating Multiculturalism" 181). Tang's novel is likewise focalized through a mainstream perspective.

Qiqi, like Miaomiao, works as a mediator between the ghost and human realms. Although she shows more sympathy for her ghost sister than her parents do, she exhibits a paradoxical mix of admiration and condescension toward the world of ghosts. When Tang describes a journey to the Ghost Mansion by Qiqi and Jiujiu, her presentation of the underground world is focalized through the tourist gaze of Qiqi, particularly in terms of its exoticism. The terms "mansion," "castle," and "princess" are indicative of a Western Gothic aura, and thus evoke feelings of mystery in Chinese readers. However, the Gothic mansion schema is also blended with an Eastern schema since "the Ghost Mansion is like a dreamlike place stylishly decorated with red lanterns, lotus, and other oriental cultural symbols" (You 97). The blending of Western tropes with Eastern symbols successfully renders the Ghost Mansion a hybrid space, in between both West and East and past and present. Qiqi is amazed by the exoticism of this other world because it represents a departure from her mundane and study-oriented everyday life. Qiqi's first-person narration depicts her as temporarily at a loss for a language through which to express her perception: "How should I describe the Ghost Mansion? I could not find words for a while. For me, everything here was so fresh, so unique, and so incredible" (Tang 82). The red lanterns, the lotus pattern, and the bronze bell in the Ghost Mansion all make the site a pleasurable spectacle, which effectively tames the threat of the underground world. Tang renders the lives of the residents of the mansion in terms of a puppet show, with their every action ordered by a central bell controlled by the princess. The daily routine, the cuisine, and the activities are all strictly regulated, and even a slight violation risks punishment. After the freshness has faded away, Qiqi soon discovers that life there is plain and boring. Mingling amazement and revulsion, Qiqi's paradoxical feelings show that she views this place as attractive but inferior, fascinating but backward. Her attitude shifts from that of a tourist to that of a colonizer. Her determination to save Jiujiu from this mansion reinforces how desirable the human world is made to seem.

In other words, the ghost Jiujiu and her homeland are merely products of the imagination of the human subjects. Jiujiu's double identity continually feeds the fantasy of both Qiqi and her parents. Her masquerade as a docile daughter satisfies the dream of her parents, which is to have an ideal daughter, whereas Jiujiu's ghostly superpower and naughtiness fulfill Qiqi's fantasies about adventure and play. The affection Jiujiu receives from her adoptive parents indicates that her disguised human image fits with their construction of an innocent and obedient child, while her rejection by them, after her true identity as a ghost is exposed, shows that her parents' dismay comes out of the conflict between an idealized, romantic construction of the child and the uncontrollable nature of an actual one. Qiqi, the older child of the Che family, is mediocre in both appearance and intelligence, whereas the adopted Jiujiu fulfills all of the expectations and wishes of her parents. Even as an infant, Jiujiu is cute, smiles, and has a good appetite. When she grows older, the family discovers that she is also highly intelligent—"a genius . . . a gift from heaven" (Tang 16), as her mother sees her; Qiqi's first-person narration recounts how happy the mother is to "have a daughter like Jiujiu" (19). These remarks show that her mother's pleasure is derived from Jiujiu's complicity with an adult's vision of the ideal child: healthy, beautiful, and smart. When her true identity is disclosed to the parents, their failure to accept her otherness reveals the self-absorbed and self-serving nature of their parental love.

Glocalized Intertextuality

The narratives of Chen and Tang were both produced at a time when China demonstrated openness to foreign cultural influences. Familiar with the local and the Western folk- and fairy-tale traditions, Chen and Tang have appropriated and integrated motifs and signs from such traditions to express local concerns, creating a potentially subversive identity through the practice of cultural hybridity. In *Mixed Magic*, Anna Katrina Gutierrez examines the cross-cultural adaptation of Western fairy tales in various Eastern texts. Within the cognitive frame of conceptual blending, she identifies the process of intercultural dialogue and exchange that differentiates Eastern adaptations from the Western-dominant global versions; namely, the process of glocalization. Using non-Western adaptations of Andersen's fairy tales as examples, she aptly demonstrates how local versions and glocal blends transform the original text so that it reflects local ideologies, which, by "enriching global and local imaginaries . . . simultaneously complement and contradict the original" (Gutierrez, "Globalization and Glocalization" 18). In this sense, glocalization endorses no hierarchical power relationship that emphasizes a Western-dominant hegemony over developing countries; rather, it throws light on a process that makes possible intercultural dialogue and exchange, or diversity. Chen's handling of her source materials is an example of this glocalized intertextuality. Tang's novel is less multicultural than Chen's, but it nevertheless demonstrates the zeitgeist of today's booming cultural exchange.

The fantastic part of Chen's fiction shows a tendency toward syncretism, a bricolage of different folkloric scripts, Western and Eastern, foreign and local, historical and contemporary. In the afterword to her novel, Chen provides a detailed description of the resources she has drawn upon:

> In this story, there are many elements borrowed from other stories. A mother that can fly comes from "The Feather Garment," the disappointment about life comes from *The Red Candle and the Mermaid*, and the image of a group of people flying out of a window into the sky comes from *Peter Pan*. The blending of a fantastic story, the realistic setting of Shanghai and fictional characters, comes from *Stuart Little* and *The Cricket in Times Square* and their vivid depiction of New York, the exposure caused by drinking alcohol comes from "The Legend of the White Snake." . . . The final disappearance of the mom comes from *The*

Witches, and the secret behind the cabinet comes from *The Lion, the Witch and the Wardrobe*. (Chen, *Wo de Mama shi Jingling* 221)

In the cited list of titles, classic children's fantasies written by Western authors such as J. M. Barrie, E. B. White, George Selden, Roald Dahl, and C. S. Lewis sit companionably alongside Eastern folk and fairy tales. The folklore "The Feather Garment" ("Hagoromo") is the Japanese version of the Swan Maiden tale, in which a celestial maiden is compelled to become the wife of a fisherman who steals her feather robe. It is also a variant (or analogue) of the Chinese "The Cowherd and the Weaver Girl." *The Red Candle and the Mermaid* is a literary fairy tale written by Japanese author Ogawa Mimei in 1921. In this tale, a pregnant mermaid has left her infant daughter for a childless old couple to raise since she has heard that humans are the most gentle and kindly creatures. However, gradually the old couple's greed overwhelms their love of the adoptive daughter, and they sell her to a merchant as a circus animal. The angry mermaid mother curses the untrustworthy humans with wild storms, and the whole village soon disappears. Chen states that what links her novel with Ogawa's tale is "the disappointment about life" or, to put it more bluntly, the heartbreak caused by betrayal. Ogawa criticizes the human who allows avarice to outweigh love in his tale (Farnell and Noiva 70), while Chen laments that discrimination against the nonhuman finally outweighs the love from the husband.

In additional to literary allusions, historical and cultural landmarks are also engaged in *My Mother Is a Fairy*. Chen chose the Holy Trinity Church in Shanghai as one of the main settings of her novel.[5] The church is described as the temporary settlement of the fairy clan, to which Miaomiao's mother belongs: the building has recently been restored, but when Chen published the novel in 1998 it was dilapidated, and Chen identifies it as "an unoccupied old church of red bricks" (*My Mother Is a Fairy* 33). It is also the location where her mother first met her father and fell in love with

---

5. Consecrated in 1869, the Holy Trinity Church was one of the oldest Anglican cathedrals in China. Colloquially known as "the Red Church" (because it is built with red bricks), it was designed in a Gothic Revival style by British architect Sir George Gilbert Scott. From the second part of the nineteenth century to the first part of the twentieth century, Shanghai retained semicolonial status, occupied by a small population of foreigners who partly controlled the city. Their dominant position shows in the landscape and architecture.

him. In a Western cultural context, there is a certain ideological incompatibility inherent in the combination of fairies and churches, since fairy is a concept that is rooted in pagan cultural traditions. According to Zipes, fairies, sorceresses, and witches all owe their existence to pagan goddesses (*The Irresistible Fairy Tale* 58). However, for Chen, a Chinese writer, fairies and churches share more similarities than differences; they are both representatives of a transcendent sphere of a foreign culture, contrasted with the practical, materialist everyday local world. Leslie Ellen Jones's view is pertinent here because rather than viewing pagan fairies and Christian angels as oppositional concepts, she points out that fairies can be seen as a secular complement to the angels and demons of the religious sphere (298). While her reference point is medieval Europe, several attributes Jones identifies appear in this novel: fairies inhabit a separate realm; there is a region without sunshine; they sometimes venture into the human world; and there they inhabit liminal zones such as places where humans no longer dwell. Such attributes are illustrated by the scene in which Miaomiao's mother recalls her first encounter with the human world:

> After a group of us had arrived, we hid in an unoccupied old church of red bricks. It was very quiet there. *Although the church was not prepared for us, it is to our taste.* The angels in the church were also of our kind. We had to stay there a while to get used to the strong heat of this world. Most of us lost weight. (Chen, *My Mother Is a Fairy* 33)

In Chen's creative world, fairies and angels are kindred spirits, partly because they are both foreign to Chinese culture. The church was built by foreign missionaries, provides religious services for both foreigners and Chinese, and thus acts as a bridge between West and East and global and local. The church is also a remnant of Shanghai's semicolonial history in the early twentieth century, a bridge between the past and now. In the novel, it becomes a fairy settlement and also the place where a romance between a human man and an otherworldly woman can occur, and as such it represents the intersection between the fantastic and the real. The Red Church becomes a "glocal heterotopia," within the world of the novel, created by intersecting and unique elements from East and West, local and global, real and unreal, and past and present (Gutierrez, "Metamorphosis" 30). Her creative use of the Red Church, which is transformed from a religious, colonial, and historical symbol into a spot memorable only because a romance has happened there, means that the narrative turns away from larger cultural symbolism in order to embrace the ordinary, everyday lives of local people.

The novel's rich intertextuality manifests in the image of the fairy mother, who is not a simple replication of the Western idea of fairies. The original Chinese word in Chen's novel would translate as *jingling*, which is a traditional term referring to unreal beings. It has become the corresponding translation for the English word "elf" in the modern era, so that Tolkien's word "elves" is translated as *jingling* (Reinders 6). The word can also refer to Shakespeare's Ariel, leprechauns, djinns, or the Smurfs (*lanjingling*, which literally means "blue fairies"), all of which are imported terms, and thus have become words that implicitly signify Western literature and culture.[6] "Fairy" has multiple literal and conceptual implications, just like the Chinese *jingling*. As Clare Bradford expresses it: "Fairies may be human-like, but they are not human, and their alterity takes on a variety of forms depending on the conventions, the ideological directions and the literary and historical contexts of the texts in which they appear" (117).

Chen's textual depiction of the fairy is one that absorbs many characteristics of earlier literary and cultural traditions:

> Fairies like Mom came from a world without a sun. They wanted to live in a human world, but it was hostile to them in some respects. So they frequently had to drink the coolest blood they could find to maintain their human appearances. (Chen, *My Mother Is a Fairy* 191)

The cold body temperature and need to drink blood shows the fairy mother's affinity with the mythical vampire, whereas the transparent and light physical form of Western fairies is probably inherited from the fragile, elusive creatures found in Victorian paintings:

---

6. Here I follow the practice of the translator, Jiang, in translating *jingling* as "fairy," while Chengcheng You translates the title as "My Mother is a Goblin" (97). However, I think goblin is less accurate than fairy because it connotes beings who are small, ugly, and mischievous, whereas in Chen's description, *jingling* is another kind of being, blue in color, transparent, and fragile, but superior to humans because of her ability to fly.

Mom was another kind of being, just as Dad said. She told me that blue humans could fly, and lived in another space, with fairies and mermaids *from the stories*. She was more fragile than human beings; even a slight wind could blow her away. While we humans could not enter the realm where they lived, they could enter our world only at a given moment in the day. They could walk, and they could fly. In a way, they were superior to us. (Chen, *My Mother Is a Fairy* 24)

Finally, there is the fairies' longing for love and other human feelings, which echo those of "The Little Mermaid" (1837). Andersen's work is explicitly mentioned in the novel. After hearing her mother's account of the encounter between her parents, Miaomiao confesses that:

In her realm, she told me, people never showed emotion because they didn't have feelings. Their hearts were made of light crystals. They never got angry or expressed joy. They never fought or loved. They didn't even talk and had no language. Light as air, they floated about, with the wind as their music. Her people came to our world in search of feelings. Mom said she wanted to glue herself to Dad and me. . . .

Her words reminded me of the princess mermaid in Hans Christian Andersen's fairy tale. The little mermaid wanted to be a human being. Mom told me once she dived into the depths of the sea and saw the princess mermaid there. But she was an unhappy mermaid because no human had fallen in love with her. *Compared to her, I think mom was much happier.* (Chen, *My Mother Is a Fairy* 33–35)

The mention of her mother's meeting with the little mermaid consolidates the mother's fictional status and blurs the boundary between fiction and reality. Chen's novel is connected with Andersen's fairy tale through a shared theme. However, she removes Andersen's Christian notion of an eternal soul and, instead, places more emphasis on the secular emotional interconnections that arise between people. By explicitly stating that the little mermaid is far from happy when she encounters the mother, Chen questions Andersen's relatively optimistic Christian ending. *My Mother Is a Fairy* thus localizes its fairy narrative in an attempt to secularize the Christian message as well as the implicitly patriarchal paradigm in which a male Christian God oversees the destinies of characters. Chen's fairy mother is a softer, more domesticated character who does not want to part with her human husband and daughter. She is "much happier" than Andersen's little mermaid, since she successfully marries her prince and becomes temporarily incorporated into the human world. However, no matter how hard she tries to be a good wife and mother, to be the ideal "angel in the house," she is fundamentally branded by her otherness and, in the end, is evicted. In its innovative adaptation of Western and Eastern tales of interspecies marriage, Chen's novel exposes the competing forces that women experience in the family and their vulnerability in the face of the normative discourse of patriarchy.

Apart from Andersen's "The Little Mermaid," the local tale of "The Legend of the White Snake" is also alluded to in Chen's narrative. Whereas the fairy and the mermaid are Western concepts that may be unfamiliar to some young Chinese readers, the White Snake is a recognizably local character, and Miaomiao's understanding, as well as that of the reader, needs to be constructed from the active blending of foreign and local scripts. At the beginning of the story, Miaomiao accidentally pours her father's wine into her mother's drink, which leads to the latter being exposed as a nonhuman since she has an acute intolerance to alcohol. For readers who are familiar with the White Snake script, this event immediately evokes a well-known plot in which Xu Xian, the husband of the White Snake, following the monk Fa Hai's advice, makes his wife drink wine, which results in her true animal identity being revealed. The link to this specific pre-text is made explicit early on:

> Ah! Suddenly it all became clear. Mom was just like the White Snake, who always shied away from alcohol. Once touched by alcohol, it would show its original shape. So, the things that happen in fairy tales can also happen in real life. Was Mom as kind and capable as the White Snake? Could she become invisible? Could she fly? Could she create things she wanted out of the air? *But Mom always seemed to be afraid of Dad. What Dad said, she followed him. . . . Mom had never been as perky as the White Snake.* (Chen, *My Mother Is a Fairy* 20)

Miaomiao and her father interpret this folktale differently. Miaomiao, with a child's imagination and the assistance of folklore, tries to make sense of the fantastic thing that has been disclosed in her family. Here Miaomiao's practice affirms what Marek Oziewicz calls "the cognitive scripting of acts in fictional worlds" and their capacity to comment on real world issues (34). She uses stored folkloric knowledge to understand the revelation of her mother's identity, which is one of the key components of the interspecies marriage script, as described earlier. Her interpretation is filled with wonder and excitement about the powers that her mother might possess as a nonhuman creature; in contrast, for her adult father, it is fundamentally a sad romance. Miaomiao's father reveals that he is afraid that he will end up like Xu Xian. In the folktale, when Xu Xian is confronted with his wife's true shape as a serpent, he is terrified, and the couple inevitably part because the monk has imprisoned the White Snake below Leifeng Pagoda. Her father informs Miaomiao that, like the folkloric hero, he is afraid of his nonhuman wife. However, Miaomiao's narrated inner thoughts indicate that, from her perspective, "Mom always seemed to be afraid of Dad" (Chen 20). The contrast between Miaomiao's observation and the father's words lay bare the socially and culturally constructed discourse of femininity and otherness. He may be frightened by the otherness of female sexuality, but the truly intimidating power comes from the normative male principle of dominance and rationality. Through this multivoiced dialogical discourse juxtaposing, on the one hand, folklore and Miaomiao's family story and, on the other, the conflicting messages of the father and daughter, Chen's first-person narrative prompts its implied reader to align with the young protagonist and thus encourages a resistant reading position that challenges and interrogates patriarchal discourses both in traditional stories and in everyday social practices.

Tang's novel draws on Chinese traditional stories, especially on the long and rich history of ghost stories, of which Pu Songling's *Strange Tales from Liaozhai* is the epitome. As discussed in the previous chapter, Pu's ghost tales are notorious for their anthropocentric and male-centric depiction of a worldview. Such a worldview "places value on quasi-human qualities, as exemplified in the ghost's willingness to forsake her ghostly but mobile existence, and embraces a limited and risky human identity" (Hui Luo 132). Similarly, Jiujiu in Tang's novel willingly gives up her unique identity as a ghost in order to be accepted by her adoptive family. Jiujiu insists that she will not use her magic power to win back the heart of her adoptive parents after her true identity is exposed, nor will she use her supernatural power anymore under any circumstances. Jiujiu's self-denial of her previous, ghostly identity is also manifest in the name Jiujiu, which is given by her human parents to pair her with her sister. Although she has an original ghost name, Man Xiaoyi, she is very happy to have a new human name and prefers being called by the latter. When her parents refuse to accept her otherness and try to get rid of her, they call her Man Xiaoyi, which hurts Jiujiu's feelings: "I'd like to be called Jiujiu," she insists (Tang 148). In this sense, although Tang's novel ends happily with the ghost daughter successfully integrated into the human family, Jiujiu's acceptance is nevertheless achieved only after she has willingly discarded her particularity. Chengcheng You contends that the closure of this novel "creates the fictional space in which affectionate ghosts and humans are allowed to cohabit harmoniously" (97), but such an interpretation focuses on the ostensibly happy ending and ignores the physical and emotional suffering Jiujiu must endure to escape the Ghost Mansion and win back the love of her indifferent adoptive parents. In her longing for humanity and mortality, Jiujiu, just like Pu's female ghosts, would rather give up her uniqueness and supernatural power in exchange for a normative life. She ultimately turns herself into the ideal daughter dreamed of by her parents.

The disempowerment and marginalization of the ghost/child character in *Jiujiu from the Ghost Mansion* are achieved by erasing the liminality of the ghostly other and by depriving the ghost figure of her rich cultural meanings and implications. The potentially horrific aspect of the ghost has been significantly downplayed by the author, whereas the cuteness is emphasized, which might be a recent global trend, especially in children's literature. Children have taken a particular liking to the chilling stories about ghosts. As Jessica R. McCort remarks, "young readers and viewers, like many adults, find delight and pleasure in that which makes them frightened" (10). But ghost stories for children are usually diluted versions of safe horror, achieved through "transforming what once was utterly horrifying into safe, funny, and delightful novels and films" for the young (McCort 28). Noriko T. Reider has explored this phenomenon, noting, in her analysis of the Japanese demon, *oni*, how "the frightening and diabolical *oni* in Medieval culture was transformed into a new type of kind and benevolent being in the modern era, and this transformation was initiated by writers of children's stories" (145). Similarly, Alison Waller observes how, in the fantastic realist novels of Margaret Mahy, which draw on Western witchcraft history, "the magic is sharply undercut by a return to domesticity that refuses to allow a darker side to the witchcraft" (85). A counter example may be found in Neil Gaiman's *Coraline* (2002), in which a sense of true horror is aroused by the image of the other mother. It is interesting that the titles of Gaiman's novel and Henry Selick's animation adaptation (2009) are both translated as *gui mama* (ghost mother) in China. Within Gaiman's text, there is no reference to the word *ghost* when addressing the other mother, though her monstrous and grotesque features do resemble ghosts as demons rather than as spirits of dead people. The translation strategy demonstrates that the ghost is a cross-cultural symbol of the repressed and the darker side of humanity. But Tang's novel skews away from any depiction that might disturb and scare her young readers. Her little ghost is innocent, kind, and sympathetic, desiring to build a sincere bond with her sister and parents without any menacing purpose.

Considering the rigid censorship the state exerts upon evil ghosts in cultural representations (see chapter 5), as well as the conservative nature of most children's literature works in China, the cute ghost is a compromising strategy for a novel targeting young audiences. But such an endearing construction of the ghost character is not unproblematic. For Chengcheng You, these cute, cheerful, and docile specters fail to invoke a "positive psychic function of the Gothic that young readers can embrace," since their images are "rarely nightmarishly configured to reflect the nature of children's fear" (99). More generally, as Fiona Yuk-wa Law argues in her eco-critical analysis of two Chinese commercial films that feature monsters and mermaids, the cuteness of nonhuman creatures, not limited to ghosts, "is often a self-deception imposed by the human believers of absolute innocence, purity, obedience and eternal infancy performed by nonhuman others" (78). Innocence, purity, and obedience are, of course, also the major features of the romantic construction of childhood, which still predominates in Chinese culture. Thus, Jiujiu's transformation from a ghostly other at the beginning of Tang's novel to a human child at the end is comparable with Chinese children's coming-of-age in real life, during which time, conforming to the expectations of parents and society results in the children having to abandon and sacrifice their particularity and uniqueness. The struggle Jiujiu has endured in order to be accepted by the human community points out some fundamental social and political problems inherent in the contemporary Chinese family, which problems are especially manifested in the unbalanced power relationship between parents and children. Therefore, this novel is more likely to confirm and amplify the prevailing "authority and control adults wield over children" in contemporary China (Lifang Li 88), rather than to challenge them.

Conclusion

One common characteristic of the two novels is that they are both focalized though the eyes of female children, which shapes the way the reader understands the narratives. As human children, Miaomiao and Qiqi work as mediators, facilitating negotiation and communication between alien and mortal members of their families. In contrast to the alien family members (mother and sister, respectively), the children, as human beings, belong to the majority culture, and hence the focalization in each novel derives from the mainstream. However, being both female and young, they are also in a more marginal position than adults, and particularly the authoritative father figures. As such, the focalized narrations of Miaomiao and Qiqi are not straightforward. Moreover, the reader, by aligning with the subject position of these narrators, should also adopt a more interrogative stance, questioning conventional ways of being and experiencing the artificiality of that divide between the normal and abnormal (Stephens and McCallum, "Discourses of Femininity" 141).

Both Chen's and Tang's children's fantasies deal with a family crisis caused by an alien member within the kinship unit, and the alien members inside the family are inveterately female. This chapter has therefore employed a feminist perspective to examine these two narratives with particular attention being paid to their intertextual and discursive aspects. Moreover, as argued, these two narratives also foreground a thematic dimension beyond gender politics, in that the Chinese family is structured according to traditional Confucian principles that require not only the subordination of wives to husbands but also of children to parents. These "two dimensions of authority," one based on gender and the other on seniority (Zuo 542), continue to influence post-socialist China. In contemporary China, the means by which the dominant power functions are analogous to the way that adult and, particularly, male power represses both the female and the child. It does this in two linked ways: by deterring the imaginative and the fantastic and by privileging the rational.

Thus, fantasy as a literary mode may submit to the ideological status quo characterized by a patriarchal family structure, but it also has the potential to be subversive. As Sanna Lehtonen argues in her study of invisibility in British children's fantasy, such motifs suggest different kinds of connections between femininity and power, in which it "can be either a form of power or a state of powerlessness, or indeed both at the same time" (223). Such an argument could also be applied to the alien woman schema in Chinese children's fantasy. Neither Chen's nor Tang's narratives provide a satisfying answer to the plight of the alien characters in their imaginary scenarios: the fairy mother in Chen's novel retreats to her own world, and the ghost girl, Jiujiu, becomes purely human without any trace of difference or uniqueness. These depictions may give the impression that the human and nonhuman worlds are irreconcilable, that alternative subjectivities are unwelcome, and that the normalizing powers of society are irresistible. However, the characterization of both Miaomiao and Qiqi also indicates certain space for hope. As first-person narrators, they are human girls who exhibit acceptance and sympathy toward their otherworldly family members. They are also active, brave, and not afraid to interrogate their narrow-minded parents; furthermore, their questioning voices can at least be heard. Finally, they demonstrate that it is possible, as hybrid characters, to transgress the binary opposition between the female-fantastic-child and the male-rational-adult, as they interact and connect these two realms. Their coming-of-age through their intersubjective relations with these otherworldly figures entails a kind of subjectivity that is based on understanding and acceptance, rather than on rejection and dominance.

Conclusion

Fantasy narratives in contemporary China are stamped with distinct social and cultural traits. They are influenced by Western and Japanese fantasy works, and draw upon traditional Chinese literature with fantastic elements for inspiration. They are fundamentally focused on current issues faced by Chinese people, and on the negotiation between traditional and modern value. Although any literary text might be inherently intertextual, fantasy is more densely intertextual than realist fiction, for a significant component of tropes of fantasy comes from previous texts, while realism claims originality based on the empirical experience of humanity. The book has thus far provided a balanced and critical appraisal of discrete fantasy narratives that rewrite and adapt old stories, and attempts to point out if, where, and how some adaptations fail to live up to their full potential of interrogating the implicit social and gender norms inherent in old materials. After the preceding chapters' text-focused discussions, the lens will now be pulled back for a more synchronic view of trends in contemporary fantasy adaptations, and their thematic and ideological implications. Upon recognizing these trends and tendencies, and summarizing the main findings of the study, this concluding section will suggest directions that future research could pursue as regards adaptation, fantasy narratives, and gender in contemporary China.

Chinese family structure informed by traditional Confucian principles requires not only the subordination of wives to husbands but also children to fathers. Similarly, women and children are sometimes put in a similar situation of subordination, as Maria Tatar (96) observes from European folktales:

> Moving from the culture of childhood to the world of women and their marriages does not require a giant step. Fairy tales with children as heroes and heroines often culminate in marriage, and the gap between the behavior expected from children and the conduct demanded of wives is not, as we shall see, as great

as one might expect. Like children, women—by nature volatile and unruly—were positioned as targets of disciplinary intervention that would mold them for subservient roles, making more visible forms of coercion superfluous.

The intersection of gender and age affirms the pervasiveness of the authoritarian structure within the family, and the ways in which authority over the other is achieved in the name of protecting the weak. In some fantastic texts, the dichotomy between the irrational, feminine, and childish and rational, masculine, and mature is established. Some narratives, nevertheless, question the repression of female sexuality and the heteronormative framework. Novels and novellas from Larissa Lai, Li Bihua, Yan Geling, and Bai Yushi queer the interspecies romance script either by using female companionship to overshadow heterosexual romance or by replacing a heterosexual relationship with lesbian desire. Online novels such as *Flowers of Four Seasons* and *Story of the Golden Bowl*, despite being censored, express female sexual desires boldly through meticulous pornographic depictions.

The female characters in the main chapters—the snake sisters, the fox spirits, the female ghost, the fairy mother, and the hybrid daughter—and their arduous quest to be integrated into the human realm mirror the status and the lived experience of women and children in a society primarily dominated by male authority. They also present a kind of posthumanism that has transcended a need for human/male centeredness and revel in their alterity. Fantasy has a paradoxical relationship with gender. On the one hand, stereotyped and sexist female characters abound in commercial fantasy novels; on the other hand, due to the cultural assumption of the affinity between nature and female sex, women are often viewed as prone to magic, superstition, and other forms of spiritual activities (Gvili 7 n.8). If we see subordinate female characters in some popular fantasy fiction as in a state of invisibility, and women empowered by supernatural abilities as visible, then the entanglement of invisibility and visibility renders women both versatile and precarious. Invisibility means being denied existence, being erased, and being silenced. Visibility brings power, agency, and respect, but being visible can also be dangerous, and generates discrimination, stigma, and persecution.

My investigations of four groups of contemporary Chinese fantasy narratives that transform traditional stories demonstrate that tensions and frictions arise from ideological opposition between new concepts of subjectivities grounded in independence and autonomy and the traditional demand for obedience and conformity. Gordon Chan's *Painted Skin*, the cinematic adaptation of Pu's tale of the same name, reflects the paradoxical condition women have faced in contemporary China, in that their rising economic independence cannot protect them from the traditional patriarchal paradigm. Chen Danyan's fairy mother in her novel, like Xiao Wei the fox spirit in *Painted Skin*, also embodies such a dilemma. Both narratives end with the expulsion of the alien women intruders from the human realm, indicating the anxiety a male-dominated society has felt toward rising female autonomy. The endings that feature the retreat from the human realm back into their alien worlds of otherworldly figures like the fairy mother and the fox spirit signal the restoring of normality and conventional orders; however, the closures have been depicted as full of sorrow and sadness, which implicitly undermine the thematic implications of returning to normality. Unlike *Painted Skin* and *My Mother Is a Fairy*, which end in sorrowful separation, the animation *Xiaoqian* presents a narrative closure full of joyful laughter of reunion. Both delight and grief leave emotional trances on readers and viewers, and the potentials signified by affect provide different and transformative ways of living for readers and reviewers to imagine.

The role emotion plays In the process of adaptation is especially significant. For Hogan, the sequence of a story and a certain genre is "inseparable from the operation of our emotion systems," and "the structures of stories and works are largely incomprehensible without reference to those systems" (124). Readers' engagement with adapted works are inseparable from their affect toward the original work, and professional adapters may be driven by the same affective impulse to retell their favorite story. The application of affective narratology into adaptations works to enrich the understanding of "adaptation as a more subjective, fannish process" (Louttit 181). Being affective does not necessarily mean being uncritical and unreflective; instead, the process of the production and reception of adaptation works entails the interaction between an incisive critical reading and a subjective and affective appreciation of both the adapters and the audiences.

The close textual analyses conducted in the four chapters suggest a primary argument, that the patriarchal ideology is seldom subverted thoroughly in contemporary adaptations. But these works are capable of reflecting social issues as well as questioning ideological attitudes, even in a limited way. The adaptation strategies deployed to update old stories include role reversal, parody, and the endeavor to retrieve a buried and marginalized voice.

Cognitive literary criticism provides heuristic tools to examine adaptation in a deeper and more nuanced way. Theories of scripts and schemas are effective because they capture the amorphous and multiple forms of a particular traditional story and compress them into a recognizable action sequence. A change in the script functions as a purposeful play with readers' cognitive recognition, and meaning is born out of readers' negotiation between old and new inputs. In the comprehension of adaptations whose narrative discourses are explicitly distinguished from their source materials, readers' "intertextual expectations about certain medium and genre, as well as about this specific work, are brought to the forefront of our attention" (Hutcheon, *A Theory of Adaptation* 22). This is in no way passive reading and reception. Instead, readers are cognitively active in their comparison and making sense of a new narrative that both resembles and departs from the narrative they know and are familiar with. The deviation from an expected sequence has the potential to unmask the familiar script's hidden normative force, and thus "the ability of master narratives to occlude the contingency and variability of norms for conduct" will be exposed (Herman et al. 173). Deviation instead suggests new possibilities: if not necessarily progressive in ideology, it will nevertheless bring to light the capacity of the human mind to "imagine other possibilities for action" (Herman et al. 173).

Conceptual blending in general and glocalization in particular prove to be helpful because the modern and contemporary reincarnations of fantastic narratives in China are nevertheless prompted by the imported and highly popular works produced in the Western and Japanese fantasy tradition, as Chen's *My Mother Is a Fairy* illustrates. Therefore, the examination of adaptations of ancient classical literature entails a negotiation between not only literary inheritance and contemporary concerns but also indigenous tradition and global influence. Blended and hybrid texts result from such an interaction of different cultures and traditions. Blending is also a primary means of script refreshment and update. Adaptations as revisions do not usually entail a fullscale changeover of the old story; rather, they are inclined to blend old and new scripts to produce narratives both familiar and defamiliarized.

A crucial aspect this book fails to address is the reinvention of certain masculine genres (*wuxia* and *xiuzhen*) by female authors. Female characters in martial arts novels occupy a paradoxical position. Whereas in the overall masculine world of European chivalric romance female characters are merely rewards for the hero's martial prowess, female knights-errant are an indispensable component of the martial arts genre, from the Tang tales to modern works such as Ang Lee's award-winning film *Crouching Tiger, Hidden Dragon* (2000). However, the fictional world of martial arts, both inside (characters, plots) and outside (authors, readers, critics), is by and large a masculine one whose codes, disciplines, and paradigms are suffused with a male perspective. Female characters in novels by male martial arts authors are either idealized romantic partners or villainesses who embody the fear and anxiety of males confronted with female autonomy. Not until recently have female authors started to appropriate this masculine genre. By revolting against the generic conventions and thematic implications set up by male authors, such as sexism, cultural nationalism, historicism, and a good/evil dichotomy, female martial arts writers have set out to reform and recreate the genre in a new era to express the concerns from contemporary society. How contemporary female authors subvert this male authorial mode deserves scholarly attention. Moreover, the scope of adaptation can also be broadened by including fan-produced online fiction and thus promoting the interaction between subcultural studies and adaptation studies, like Xiaofei Tian's research on the online slashing of *Romance of the Three Kingdoms* by female writers shows.

All in all, this book proposes a critical reception and interpretation of adaptation works in the contemporary Chinese context. A sensitively nuanced comprehension of adaptation processes and products must take into consideration the close intertextual relationship with their pre-texts (and perhaps many other adaptations based on a common script) as well as their inextricable correlation with the social and cultural context from which they have been produced. This book has sought to foreground two facts: first, no story is retold without a purpose, and no adaptation is produced in a vacuum; and second, a retold and adapted story, no matter how hard its author has tried to remain close and faithful to their source, has inevitably changed in the process. Instead of proposing telling a different story in the same way, this study celebrates works that tell the same story differently, which effectively frees readers from passive positions and opens up multiple interpretations.

Glossary

Abe no Seimei . . . . . . 安倍晴明

Akutagawa
　　Ryunosuke . . . . . 芥川龍之介

Alisi zhongguo
　　youji . . . . . 阿丽思中国游记

Andrew Chan . . . . 陈伟文

Ayanami Rei . . . . . . 綾波レイ

Bai niangzi yongzhen
　　leifeng ta . . 白娘子永镇雷峰塔

Bai Suzhen . . . . 白素贞

Bai Yushi . . . . 白羽石

Baishe . . . . 白蛇

Baishe chuanshuo . . . . 白蛇传说

Baishe zhuan . . . . . . 白蛇传

Ban Ma . . . . 班马

Biancheng . . . . 边城

Bianji . . . . 辩机

Biji xiaoshuo . . . . . . 笔记小说

Bu . . . . 补

Cang Yue . . . . 沧月

Chan wei shui ming . . . 蝉为谁鸣

Che Jiujiu . . . . 车九九

Che Qiqi . . . . 车七七

Cheang Pou-soi . . . . . 郑保瑞

Chen Danyan . . . . . . 陈丹燕

Chen Kaige . . . . 陈凯歌

Chen Kun . . . . 陈坤

Ching Siu-Tung . . . . . 程小东

Chuanqi . . . . 传奇

Chuanyue . . . . 穿越

Chusheng . . . . 褚生

Dahua xiyou . . . . . . 大话西游

Daji . . . . 妲己

Danmei . . . . 耽美

Daocao ren . . . . 稻草人

Daomu . . . . 盗墓

Datang Sanzang qujing
　　shihua . . . 大唐三藏取经诗话

Datang xiyu ji . . . . 大唐西域记

Derek Kwok . . . . 郭子健

Di . . . . 帝

Dingdong . . . . 丁冬

Dong Yong . . . . 董永

Dong Zhongshu . . . . . 董仲舒

Du Mu . . . . 杜牧

Duo (Jiugong) (characters
　　from *Jing Hua Yuan*) . . 多(九公)

Duyi zhi . . . . 独异志

Eileen Chang . . . . . . 张爱玲

Fa Hai . . . . 法海

Fang . . . . 仿

Fei·Qihuan shijie . . . 飞·奇幻世界

Feng Lingxue . . . . . . 风凌雪

Feng Menglong . . . . . 冯梦龙

Fengkuang lü ciwei . . 疯狂绿刺猬

Fengshen chuanqi . . . 封神传奇

Fengshen yanyi . . . . 封神演义

Fengsu Tongyi . . . . 风俗通义

Fuxi . . . . 伏羲

Gai . . . . 改

Ling . . . . 灵

Liuyi zhuan . . . . 柳毅传

Lu Xun. . . . . 鲁迅

Luotuo xiangzi . . . . . 骆驼祥子

Ma Xiaotiao . . . . 马小跳

Man Xiaoyi. . . . . 满小意

Mao cheng ji . . . . . . 猫城记

Maodun . . . . .矛盾

Mei Niang . . . . 梅娘

Mei Sanniang . . . . . . 梅三娘

Meng Chao . . . . 孟超

Miaomiao . . . . 淼淼

Mili. . . . . 米粒

Mishima Yukio. . . . 三島由紀夫

Mizuki Shigeru. . . 水木しげる

Mo . . . . 魔

Mo Yan. . . . . 莫言

Moe . . . . 萌

Mogui . . . . 魔鬼

Mohuan . . . . 魔幻

Mohuluojia. . . . . . 摩呼洛伽

Mougong. . . . . 某公

Nan shengzi . . . . 男生子

Nei . . . . .内

Ni Huanzhi . . . . 倪焕之

Nie Xiaoqian . . . . . . 聂小倩

Ning Caichen . . . . . . 宁采臣

Niugui sheshen. . . . . 牛鬼蛇神

Niulang zhinü . . . . . . 牛郎织女

Nü jie. . . . . 女诫

Nüer guo . . . . 女儿国

Nüer qing . . . . 女儿情

Nüwa . . . . 女娲

Nüwa shi . . . . 女娲石

Nüzun . . . . 女尊

Ogawa Mimei . . . . . . 小川未明

Oni. . . . . 鬼

Onmyōji . . . . 陰陽師

Otaku . . . . 御宅 / おたく

Pan Gu. . . . . 盘古

Pang Yong . . . . 庞勇

Pei Rong . . . . 佩蓉

Peng Xuejun . . . . 彭学军

Peng Yi. . . . . 彭懿

Pu Songling . . . . 蒲松龄

Qian nü you hun . . . . .倩女幽魂

Qianzi wen . . . . 千字文

Qidian . . . . 起点

Qihuan . . . . 奇幻

Qin Wenjun . . . . 秦文君

Qingchun wenxue . . . 青春文学

Qingmei . . . . 青梅

Qingqing. . . . . 青青

Qingshe . . . . 青蛇

Qiongguo . . . . 琼果

Raman Hui. . . . . 许诚毅

Renshi zhuan. . . . . . . 任氏传

Riben guizi . . . . 日本鬼子

Ruizhu . . . . 瑞珠

Sangang . . . . 三纲

Sanguo yanyi . . . . . . 三国演义

Sansheng. . . . . .三生

Sanzi jing. . . . . 三字经

Sha Wujing. . . . . 沙悟净

Shanhai jing . . . . 山海经

Shan He Fu . . . . 山河赋

Shanshan. . . . . 珊珊

Shen . . . . .神

Shen Congwen . . . . . 沈从文

Shen Yingying . . . . . 沈璎璎

Shenmo xiaoshuo . . . 神魔小说

Shibian . . . . .尸变

Shiji . . . . 史记

Shuihu zhuan . . . . . . 水浒传

Shuiying . . . . 水影

Sima Qian . . . . 司马迁

Sishi Huakai zhi Huanhun Nüer
    Guo . . 四时花开之还魂女儿国

Sou shen ji . . . . 搜神记

Śramaṇa Kūkai . . . . . 沙门空海

Stephen Chow . . . . . . 周星驰
Su Mian . . . . 苏眠
Su Tong . . . . 苏童
Sun Likun . . . . 孙丽坤
Sun Wukong . . . . . . 孙悟空
Tai Ping . . . . 太平
Taishigong . . . . 太史公
Takahashi Rumiko . . . 高桥留美子
Tanaka Yoshiki . . . . . . 田中芳树
Tang (Ao) (characters
    from *Jing Hua Yuan*) . . . 唐(敖)
Tang Hongying . . . . . 汤宏英
Tang Tang . . . . 汤汤
Tian Han . . . . 田汉
Tianxia bachang . . . . 天下霸唱
Tianxia mingjiang . . . . 天下名将
Tianxian pei . . . . 天仙配
Toriyama Sekien . . . . 鸟山石燕
Tsui Hark . . . . 徐克
Tu long . . . . 屠龙
Wai . . . . 外
Wang Anyi . . . . 王安忆
Wang Xifeng . . . . . . 王熙凤
Wen . . . . 文
Wilson Yip . . . . 叶伟信
Wo de mama shi
    jingling . . . . 我的妈妈是精灵
Wu Cheng'en . . . . 吴承恩
Wu Ershan . . . . 乌尔善
Wuxia xiaoshuo . . . . 武侠小说
Wuxing . . . . 五行
Xi Xuanzan . . . . 奚宣赞
Xia (Ying) (characters from
    Fengkuang lü ciwei) . . . 夏(瀛)
Xia Bing . . . . 夏冰
Xian . . . . 仙
Xiang yichi . . . . 向异翅
Xiao Wei . . . . 小唯
Xiaogui . . . . 小鬼
Xiaoqian . . . . 小倩

Xiaoqing . . . . 小青
Xiaoshuo . . . . 小说
Xihu santa ji . . . . 西湖三塔记
Xin bainiangzi
    chuanqi . . . . 新白娘子传奇
Xiongnu . . . . 匈奴
Xiuzhen . . . . 修真
Xiyou fuyao pian . . . 西游伏妖篇
Xiyou Ji . . . . 西游记
Xiyou Ji Zaju . . . . . 西游记杂剧
Xiyou Ji zhi danao
    tiangong . . . 西游记之大闹天宫
Xiyou Ji zhi
    nüer guo . . . . 西游记之女儿国
Xiyou Ji zhi sun wukong
    sanda baigujing
    . . . 西游记之孙悟空三打白骨精
Xiyou xiangmo pian . . . 西游降魔篇
Xu . . . . 续
Xu Qunshan . . . 徐群山/徐群珊
Xu Shilin . . . . 许仕林
Xu Xian . . . . 许仙
Xu Xuan . . . . 许宣
Xuanhuan . . . . 玄幻
Xuanzang . . . . 玄奘
Xueqing . . . . 雪晴
Xueying (characters from
    Fengkuang lü ciwei) . . . 雪莹
Xushu . . . . 续书
Yan Chixia . . . . 燕赤霞
Yan Geling . . . . 严歌苓
Yang guizi . . . . 洋鬼子
Yang Hongying . . . . . 杨红樱
Yao . . . . 妖
Yaomao zhuan . . . . . 妖猫传
Ye Shengtao . . . . . . 叶圣陶
Ye Xian . . . . 叶限
Yi faming shendao
    zhi buwu . . . 以发明神道之不诬
Yin Jianling . . . . 殷健灵

Yin-Yang . . . . 阴阳
Yishishi . . . . 异史氏
Yiyin . . . . 意淫
Yiyuan . . . . 异苑
Yōkai . . . . 妖怪
Yu . . . . 禹
Yu Hua . . . . 余华
Yuan Mei . . . . 袁枚
Yumemakura Baku . . . . . 夢枕獏
Yunhuang . . . . 云荒
Zhang Zhilu . . . . 张之路
Zhao . . . . 昭
Zhenhun . . . . 镇魂
Zhiguai . . . . 志怪

Zhong buduan de
   qinsheng . . . . 终不断的琴声
Zhou (King of Shang) . . . . . . 纣
Zhu Bajie . . . . 猪八戒
Zhu Xueheng . . . . 朱学恒
Zhu Yingtai . . . . 祝英台
Zhu Ziqiang . . . . 朱自强
Zhuangshen nonggui . . . 装神弄鬼
Zhuangzi . . . . 庄子
Zhucheng moujia . . . . 诸城某甲
Zhuoyao ji . . . . 捉妖记
Zi bu yu . . . . 子不语
Zi bu yu guai li luan
   shen . . . . . . 子不语怪力乱神

Major Chinese Dynasties Timeline

Xia 夏	ca. 2100—ca. 1600 BC
Shang 商	ca. 1600—1046 BC
Zhou 周	1046—771 BC
Spring and Autumn period 春秋	770—476 BC
Warring States period 战国	475—221 BC
Qin 秦	221—207 BC
Han 汉	202 BC—220 AD
Three Kingdoms 三国	220–265
Jin 晋	265–420
Southern and Northern Dynasties 南北朝	420–589
Sui 隋	581–618
Tang 唐	618–907
Five Dynasties and Ten Kingdoms 五代十国	907–979
Song 宋	960–1279
Liao 辽	907–1125
Yuan 元	1271–1368
Ming 明	1368–1644
Qing 清	1644–1911
Republic of China 中华民国	1912–1949

Primary Sources

Bai Yushi. *Jinbo Ji* [*Story of the Golden Bowl*]. www.sto.cx/book-91326-1.html. Accessed 11 Aug. 2021.

Birrell, Anne, translator. *The Classic of Mountains and Seas*. Penguin, 1999.

Cao, Xueqing. *Honglou meng* [*Dream of the Red Chamber*]. Beijing: Renmin wenxue chubanshe, 2012.

Chang, Eileen. *Red Rose, White Rose*. Translated by Karen S. Kingsbury, Penguin, 2007.

Chen, Danyan. *Wo de Mama shi Jingling* [*My Mother Is a Fairy*]. Shenyang: Chunfeng wenyi chubanshe, 1998.

Chen, Danyan. *My Mother Is a Fairy*. Translated by J. J. Jiang, Better Link Press, 2006.

Chen, Jun, editor. *Xiyou Ji Zaju Pingzhu Ben* [*Annotated Edition of Variety Drama of Journey to the West*]. Guiyang: Guizhou jiaoyu chubanshe, 2018.

A Chinese Ghost Story. Directed by Siu-Tung Ching, produced by Hark Tsui. Cinema City Film Productions, 1987.

A Chinese Ghost Story: The Tsui Hark Animation. Directed by Andrew Chan, written and produced by Hark Tsui, Film Workshop, 1997.

A Chinese Ghost Story. Directed by Wilson Yip, Asia Bright Investment, 2011.

A Chinese Odyssey. Directed by Jeffrey Lau. Xi'an Film Studio and Choi Sing Film Company, 1995.

Coraline. Directed by Henry Selick. Focus Features, 2009.

Fakeyang. *Mohuluojia* [*Mahoraga*]. https://www.sto.cx/book-45008-1.html. Accessed 10 Mar. 2023.

Feng, Menglong. "Bai niangziyongzhen leifeng ta" ["Madam White Is Kept Forever under the Thunder Peak Tower"]. *Jingshi tongyan* [*Stories to Caution the World*]. Beijing: Renmin wenxue chubanshe, 1995, pp. 435–64.

Gaiman, Neil. *Coraline*. HarperCollins, 2002.

Gan, Bao. *Sou shen ji* [*In Search of the Supernatural*]. Beijing: Zhonghua shuju, 2012.

Gao, Ming. *Pipa ji* [*Tale of the Pipa*]. Beijing: Huaxia chubanshe, 2000.

Gilman, Charlotte Perkins. *The Yellow Wall-Paper, Herland, and Selected Writings*. Penguin Books, 2019.

Gongteng Shenxiu. *Sishi Huakai zhi Huanhun Nüer Guo* [*Flowers of Four Seasons: Reborn in the Kingdom of Women*]. www.sto.cx/book-163950-1.html. Accessed 11 Aug. 2021.

Green Snake. Directed by Hark Tsui. Film Workshop, 1993.

Jiang Nan. *Jiuzhou: Piaomiao lu vol. 3, Tianxia mingjiang* [*Novaland: Eagle Flag III World Famous Generals*]. Beijing: Xinshijie chubanshe, 2007.

Jin Hezai. *Jiuzhou: Yu chuanshuo* [*Novaland: The Legend of Feathers*]. Beijing: Xinshijie chubanshe, 2005.

Journey to the West. Directed by Yang Jie. CCTV, 41 episodes, 1986.

Journey to the West: Conquering the Demons. Directed by Stephen Chow and Derek Kwok, Bingo Move Development, 2013.

Kingston, Maxine Hong. *The Woman Warrior: Memoirs of a Girlhood among Ghosts*. Picador, 1976.

Lai, Larissa. *When Fox Is a Thousand*. Press Gang, 1995.

———. *Salt Fish Girl*. Thomas Allen Publishers, 2002.

Lao, She. *Mao cheng ji* [*Cat Country*]. 1933. Beijing: Renmin wenxue chubanshe, 2008.

———. *Luotuo xiangzi* [*Rickshaw Boy*]. 1939. Beijing: Renmin wenxue chubanshe, 2000.

The Land of Many Perfumes. Directed by Ho Menghua. Shaw Brothers Studio, 1968.

Legge, James, translator. *Confucian Analects. The Chinese Classics, vol. 1*. Taipei: Southern Materials Centre, 1985.

Li, Bihua. *Qingshe* [*Green Snake*]. 1986. Beijing: Xinxing chubanshe, 2013.

Li Duan. "Hu Yao" ["Fox Medicine"]. *Zhongguo qihuan shiren xuan—Yunhuang Nüshen Li Duan* [*Ten Key Authors of Chinese Fantasy—The Volume of Li Duan*]. Nanjing: Jiangsu wenyi chubanshe, 2007, pp. 1–46.

Li, Ruzhen. *Jing Hua Yuan* [*Flowers in the Mirror*]. Beijing: Renmin wenxue chubanshe, 2014.

Louie, Ai-Ling, and Ed Young. *Yeh-Shen: A Cinderella Story From China*. Philomel Books, 1982.

Louie, Kam, and Louise Edwards, translators and editors. *Censored by Confucius: Ghost Stories by Yuan Mei*. M.E. Sharpe, 1996.

Luo, Guanzhong. *Sanguo yanyi* [*Romance of the Three Kingdoms*]. Beijing: Renmin wenxue chubanshe, 1997.

Lu, Xun. "A Madman's Diary" ["Kuangren riji"]. 1918. *Nahan* [*Call to Arms*]. Beijing: Renmin wenxue chubanshe, 1979, pp. 1–13.

———. *Gushi xinbian* [*Old Tales Retold*]. 1936. Beijing: Renmin wenxue chubanshe, 2006.

The Monkey King 3: Kingdom of Women. Directed by Pou-soi Cheang, Filmko Entertainment, 2018.

Monster Hunt. Directed by Raman Hui. Edko Films, 2015.

The New Legend of Madame White Snake. Directed by Xia Zuhui and He Lin, produced by Cao Jingde, Taiwan Television, 50 episodes, 1992.

Painted Skin. Directed by Bao Fang. Feng Huang Motion Pictures, 1966.

Painted Skin. Directed by King Hu. New Treasurer Film Company, 1992.

Painted Skin. Directed by Gordon Chan. Mediacorp Raintree Pictures, 2008.

Painted Skin: Resurrection. Directed by Wuershan, Kylin Pictures, 2012.

Peng, Xuejun. *Zhong buduan de qinsheng* [*Endless Piano Sound*]. Nanchang: 21 shiji chubanshe, 1998.

Peng, Yi. *Fengkuang lü ciwei* [*The Crazy Green Hedgehog*]. Nanjing: Jiangsu shaonian ertong chubanshe. 1996.

Pu, Songling. *Liaozhai Zhiyi* [*Strange Tales from Liaozhai*]. Beijing: Renmin wenxue chubanshe, 1989.

———. *Strange Stories from a Chinese Studio.* Translated by Herbert Giles. London: Thos. de la Rue, 1880.

———. *Strange Tales from a Chinese Studio.* Translated by John Minford. Penguin Books, 2006.

———. *Strange Tales from Liaozhai.* Translated by Sidney L. Sondergard. Jain Publishing Company, 2008–14. 6 vols.

Shen, Congwen. *Alisi zhongguo youji* [*Alice's Adventures in China*]. 1928. Beijing: Renmin wenxue chubanshe, 2009.

———. *Biancheng* [*Border Town*]. 1934. Beijing: Renmin wenxue chubanshe, 2000.

Shen, Yingying. "Tu Long" ["Slaying Dragons"]. *Xiaoshuo Yuebao Zengkan: Xin Xiaoshuo* [*Fiction Monthly Plus: New Fiction*], vol. 1, 2008, pp. 103–11.

Shu Xianting. *Tai Ping.* www.jjwxc.net/onebook.php?novelid=100134. Accessed 11 Aug. 2021.

Sima, Qian. *Shiji* [*Records of the Grand Historian*]. Beijing: Zhonghua shuju, 2006.

Song of the Sea. Directed by Tomm Moore, Cartoon Saloon, 2014.

Spirited Away. Directed by Miyazaki Hayao. Studio Ghibli, 2001.

Strange Tales from Liaozhai. Directed by Wu Jinyuan, Huang Weiming, and Wei Hantao. Tangren Media. 36 episodes, 2005.

Strassberg, Richard, translator and editor. *A Chinese Bestiary: Strange Creatures from the Guideways through Mountains and Seas*. University of California Press, 2002.

Tan, Amy. *The Hundred Secret Senses*. G.P. Putnam's Sons, 1995.

———. *The Bonesetter's Daughter*. G.P. Putnam's Sons, 2001.

Tang Tang. *Laizi gui zhuangyuan de Jiujiu* [*Jijiu from the Ghost Mansion*]. Beijing: Zhongguo shaonian ertong chubanshe, 2010.

Tchana, Katrin Hyman, and Trina Schart Hyman. *The Serpent Slayer: And Other Stories of Strong Women*. Little, Brown and Co., 2000.

Wang, Anyi. "Match Made in Heaven." Translated by Todd Foley. *Frontiers of Literary Studies in China*, vol. 12, no. 1, 2018, pp. 20–42.

Wu, Cheng'en. *Xiyou Ji* [*Journey to the West*]. Beijing: Renmin wenxue chubanshe, 2005.

Wolf Children. Directed by Mamoru Hosoda, Studio Chizu, 2012.

Xu, Zhonglin. *Fengshen yanyi* [*Investiture of the Gods*]. Beijing: Renmin wenxue chubanshe, 1997.

Yan, Geling. *Baishe* [*White Snake*]. Guangzhou: Huacheng chubanshe, 2005.

Yan, Geling. *White Snake and Other Stories*. Translated by Lawrence A. Walker. Aunt Lute Books, 1999.

Ye, Shengtao. *Scarecrow* [*Daocao ren*]. 1923. Beijing: Renmin wenxue chubanshe, 2000.

———. *Ni Huanzhi*. 1929. Beijing: Renmin wenxue chubanshe, 2000.

Yin, Jianling. *Kuqi Jingling* [*The Crying Fairy*]. Nanchang: 21 shiji chubanshe, 1999.

Yuan, Mei. *Zi bu yu* [*What the Master Would Not Discuss*]. Shanghai: Shanghai guji chubanshe, 2016.

Yumemakura, Baku. *Onmyōji*. Tokyo: Bungeishunjū, 1988.

———. *Śramaṇa Kūkai*. Tokyo: Tokuma, 2004.

Zhang, Youhe, editor. *Tang Song Chuanqi Xuan* [*Selected Tales of the Marvelous from Tang and Song*]. Beijing: Renmin wenxue chubanshe, 1997.

Zhang, Zhilu. *Chan wei shui ming* [*For Whom the Cicada Sings*]. Nanchang: 21 shiji chubanshe, 1999.

Zhao Tongying. *Shan He Fu* [*A Song of Mountains and Rivers*]. www.jjwxc.net/onebook.php?novelid=139056. Accessed 11 Aug. 2021.

Secondary Sources

Abel, Elizabeth, Marianne Hirsch, and Elizabeth Langland. *The Voyage In: Fictions of Female Development*. University Press of New England, 1983.

Allen, Graham. *Intertextuality*. Routledge, 2011.

Anderson, Marston. *The Limits of Realism: Chinese Fiction in the Revolutionary Period*. University of California Press, 1990.

Armitt, Lucy. *Contemporary Women's Fiction and the Fantastic*. Palgrave Macmillan, 2000.

Attebery, Brian. *Strategies of Fantasy*. Indiana University Press, 1992.

———. *Stories about Stories: Fantasy and the Remaking of Myth*. Oxford University Press, 2014.

Azuma, Hiroki. *Otaku: Japan's Database Animals*. Translated by Jonathan Abel and Shion Kono. University of Minnesota Press, 2009.

Bacchilega, Cristina. *Fairy Tales Transformed? Twenty-First-Century Adaptation and the Politics of Wonder*. Wayne State University Press, 2013.

Bacchilega, Cristina, and John Rieder. "Mixing It Up: Generic Complexity and Gender Ideology in Early Twenty-First Century Fairy Tale Films." *Fairy Tale Films: Visions of Ambiguity*, edited by Pauline Greenhill and Sidney Eve Matrix, Utah State University Press, 2010, pp. 23–41.

Bachofen, Johann Jakob. *An English Translation of Backhofen's Mutterrecht (Mother Right) (1861): A Study of the Religious and Juridical Aspects of Gynecocracy in the Ancient World*. Translated by David Partenheimer, The Edwin Mellen Press, 2007.

Bakhtin, Mikhail. *The Dialogic Imagination: Four Essays*. Translated by Caryl Emerson and Michael Holquist, edited by Michael Holquist, University of Texas Press, 1981.

———. *Rabelais and His World*. Translated by Helene Iswolsky, Indiana University Press, 1984.

Barthes, Roland. *Image-Music-Text*. Translated by Stephen Heath, Fontana, 1977.

Beauchamp, Fay. "Asian Origins of Cinderella: The Zhuang Storyteller of Guangxi." *Oral Tradition*, vol. 25, no. 2, 2010, pp. 447–96.

Bennett, Andrew, and Nicholas Royle. *An introduction to Literature, Criticism and Theory*. Pearson/Longman, 2009.

Bi, Lijun, Xiangshu Fang, and Clare Bradford. "Parent, Child and State in Chinese Children's Books." *Papers: Explorations into Children's Literature*, vol. 23, no. 1, 2015, pp. 34-52.

Birrell, Anne. *Chinese Mythology: An Introduction*, with a foreword by Yuan Ke. Johns Hopkins University Press, 1993.

———. "Myth." *The Columbia History of Chinese Literature*, edited by Victor H. Mair, Columbia University Press, 2001, pp. 58–69.

Blanco, María del Pilar, and Esther Peeren. "Introduction: Conceptualizing Spectralities." *The Spectralities Reader: Ghosts and Haunting in Contemporary Cultural Theory*, edited by María del Pilar Blanco and Esther Peeren, Bloomsbury Academic & Professional, 2014, pp. 1–27.

Bowers, Maggie Ann. *Magic(al) Realism*. Routledge, 2004.

Bradford, Clare. "The Return of the Fairy: Australian Medievalist Fantasy for the Young." *Australian Literary Studies*, vol. 26, no. 3–4, 2011, pp. 115–32.

Bradford, Clare, Kerry Mallan, John Stephens, and Robyn McCallum. *New World Orders in Contemporary Children's Literature: Utopian Transformations*. Palgrave Macmillan, 2011.

Butler, Judith. "The Force of Fantasy: Feminism, Mapplethorpe, and Discursive Excess." *differences: A Journal of Feminist Cultural Studies*, vol. 2, no. 2, 1990, pp. 105–25.

Campany, Robert F. "The Culture of Ghosts in Six Dynasties Zhiguai." *Chinese Literature: Essays, Articles, Reviews (CLEAR)*, vol. 13, 1999, pp. 15–34.

Cartmell, Deborah, and Imelda Whelehan, editors. *Adaptations: From Text to Screen, Screen to Text*. Routledge, 1999.

Cartmell, Deborah, and Imelda Whelehan. *Screen Adaptation: Impure Cinema*. Palgrave MacMillan, 2010.

Chan, Kenneth. *Remake in Hollywood: The Global Chinese Presence in Transnational Cinemas*. Hong Kong University Press, 2009.

Chang, Chia-Ju. "The Chinese Snake Woman: Mythology, Culture and Female Expression." Dissertation. State University of New Jersey, 2004.

Chao, Shih-Chen. "Desire and Fantasy On-line: A Sociological and Psychoanalytical Approach to the Prosumption of Chinese Internet Fiction." Dissertation. University of Manchester, 2012.

Chen, Danyan. "Rang shenghuo pujin tonghua—Xifang xiandai tonghua chuangzuo de yige xin qingxiang" ["Let the Life Rush into the Fairy Tale: The New Tendency of Western Modern Fairy Tales"]. *Weilai* [*The Future*], vol. 5, 1983, pp. 199–205.

Chen, Shunxin. "Nüxing zhuyi dui minzu zhuyi de jieru." ["Feminist Intervention of Nationalism"]. *Funü, Minzu yu Nüxing Zhuyi* [*Women, Nation, and Feminism*], edited by Chen Shunxin and Dai Jinhua, Beijing: Zhongyang bianyi chubanshe, 2002, 1–26.

Chiang, Lydia Sin-Chen. *Collecting the Self: Body and Identity in Strange Tale Collections of Late Imperial China*. Brill, 2005.

Cho, Sookja. *Transforming Gender and Emotion: The Butterfly Lovers Story in China and Korea*. University of Michigan Press, 2018.

Chow, Rey. "A Souvenir of Love." *Modern Chinese Literature*, vol. 7, no. 2, 1993, pp. 59–78.

Chung, Yu-Ling. *Translation and Fantasy Literature in Taiwan: Translators as Cultural Brokers and Social Networkers*. Palgrave Macmillan, 2013.

Clute, John. "Taproot Texts." *The Encyclopedia of Fantasy*, edited by John Clute and John Grant, Orbit, 1997, pp. 921–22.

Cohen, Jeffrey Jerome. "Monster Culture (Seven Theses)." *Monster Theory: Reading Culture*, edited by Jeffrey Jerome Cohen, University of Minnesota Press, 1996, pp. 3–26.

Cole, Nicki Lisa. "Definition of Intersectionality: On the Intersecting Nature of Privileges and Oppression." *ThoughtCo.* 2019. www.thoughtco.com/intersectionality -definition-3026353. Accessed 3 July 2019.

Collins, Patricia Hill. "It's All in the Family: Intersections of Gender, Race, and Nation." *Hypatia*, vol. 13, no. 3, 1998, pp. 62–82.

Corrigan, Timothy. "Defining Adaptation." *The Oxford Handbook of Adaptation Studies*, edited by Thomas Leitch, Oxford University Press, 2017, pp. 23–35.

Cranny-Francis, Anne. "Feminist Fantasy." *Feminist Fiction: Feminist Uses of Generic Fiction*. St Martin's Press, 1990, pp. 75–106.

Crenshaw, Kimberle. "Mapping the Margins: Intersectionality, Identity Politics, and Violence Against Women of Color." *Stanford Law Review*, vol. 43, no. 6, 1991, pp. 1241–99.

Deppman, Hsui-Chuang. *Adapted for the Screen: The Cultural Politics of Modern Chinese Fiction and Film*. University of Hawai'i Press, 2010.

Derecho, Abigail. "Archontic Literature: A Definition, a History, and Several Theories of Fan Fiction." *Fan Fiction and Fan Communities in the Age of the Internet:*

New Essays, edited by Karen Hellekson and Kristina Busse, McFarland, 2006, pp. 61–78.

DeWoskin, Kenneth J. "The Six Dynasties Chih-Kuai and the Birth of Fiction." *Chinese Narrative: Critical and Theoretical Essays*, edited by Andrew H. Plaks, Princeton University Press, 1977, pp. 21–52.

———. "Gan Bao (fl. 315) In Search of Spirits: Twelve Tales." *Classical Chinese Literature: An Anthology of Translations. Vol. 1: From Antiquity to the Tang Dynasty*, edited by John Minford and Joseph S. M. Lau, Columbia University Press, 2000, pp. 652–65.

Dong, Lan. *Mulan's Legend and Legacy in China and the United States*. Temple University Press, 2011.

Dooling, Amy D. *Women's Literary Feminism in Twentieth-Century China*. Palgrave Macmillan, 2005.

Duan, Guozhong. "Chinese Internet Literature: Digital Literary Genres and New Writing Subjects." *Routledge Handbook of Modern Chinese Literature*, edited by Ming Dong Gu, Routledge, 2019, pp. 669–81.

Dudbridge, Glen. *The Hsi-Yu Chi: A Study of Antecedents to the Sixteenth-Century Chinese Novel*. Cambridge University Press, 1970.

Duh, Ming Cherng. "The Hegemony of Western Categorisation and the Underdevelopment of Children's Literature in 'Other' Words." *Papers: Explorations into Children's Literature*, vol. 17, no. 2, 2007, pp. 7–15.

Edwards, Louise. *Men and Women in Qing China: Gender in the Red Chamber Dream*. University of Hawai'i Press, 2001.

———. "Transformations of the Woman Warrior Hua Mulan: From Defender of the Family to Servant of the State." *Nan Nü: Men, Women and Gender in China*, vol. 12, 2010, pp. 175–214.

Eller, Cynthia. *The Myth of Matriarchal Prehistory: Why an Invented Past Won't Give Women a Future*. Beacon Press, 2000.

———. *Gentlemen and Amazons: The Myth of Matriarchal Prehistory, 1861–1900*. University of California Press, 2011.

Eoyang, Eugene. *The Promise and Premise of Creativity: Why Comparative Literature Matters*. Continuum, 2012.

Epstein, Maram. *Competing Discourses: Orthodoxy, Authenticity, and Engendered Meanings in Late Imperial Chinese Fiction*. Harvard University Press, 2001.

Erni, John Nguyet. "Enchanted: Harry Potter and Magical Capitalism in Urban China." *Chinese Journal of Communication*, vol. 1, no. 2, 2008, pp. 138–55.

Farnell, David, and Rute Noiva. "Monstrous Beauty, Monstrous Strength: The Case of the Mermaid." *Re-visiting Female Evil: Power, Purity and Desire*, edited by Melissa Dearey, Susana Nicolás and Roger Davis, Brill, 2017, pp. 53–81.

Farquhar, Mary Ann. *Children's Literature in China: From Lu Xun to Mao Zedong*. M.E. Sharpe, 1999.

Feng, Jin. *Romancing the Internet: Producing the Consuming Chinese Web Romance*. Brill, 2013.

Feng, Yiqing. "Nüerguo de xingshuai yanbian: wangluo nüzun xiaoshuo tanxi." ["The Rise and Fall of 'The Women's Kingdom': A Study on Internet Women-Superior Fiction"]. *Shanghai wenhua* [*Shanghai Culture*], no. 8, 2017, pp. 34–43.

Foster, Michael Dylan. *Pandemonium and Parade: Japanese Monsters and the Culture of Yōkai*. University of California Press, 2009.

Fraser, Lucy. *The Pleasures of Metamorphosis: Japanese and English Fairy-Tale Transformations of "The Little Mermaid."* Wayne State University Press, 2017.

Freedman, Estelle B., editor. *The Essential Feminist Reader*. The Modern Library, 2007.

Freeman, Matthew, and William Proctor. "Introduction: Conceptualizing National and Cultural Transmediality." *Global Convergence Cultures: Transmedia Earth*, edited by Matthew Freeman and William Proctor, Routledge, 2018, pp. 1–16.

Freud, Sigmund. "The Uncanny." *The Standard Edition of the Complete Psychological Works of Sigmund Freud*. Vol. 17, translated by James Strachey, Alix Strachey, and Alan Tyson. Hogarth, 1955, pp. 219–52.

Frus, Phyllis, and Christy Williams. *Beyond Adaptation: Essays on Radical Transformations of Original Works*. McFarland, 2010.

Gamble, Sarah. "Editor's Introduction." *The Routledge Companion to Feminism and Postfeminism*, edited by Sarah Gamble, Routledge, 2006, pp. vii–ix.

Gan, Min. "The Phantom Returns: On Lilian Lee's Three Supernatural Stories." Master's thesis. University of Iowa, 2010.

García, Patricia, and Teresa López-Pellisa, editors. *Fantastic Short Stories by Women Authors from Spain and Latin America: A Critical Anthology*. University of Wales Press, 2019.

Gates, Pamela S, Susan B. Steffel, and Francis J. Molson. *Fantasy Literature for Children and Young Adults*. Scarecrow, 2003.

Genette, Gérard. *Palimpsests: Literature in the Second Degree*. Translated by Channa Newman and Claude Doubinsky, University of Nebraska Press, 1997.

Gilbert, Sandra M., and Susan Gubar. *The Madwoman in the Attic: The Woman Writer and the Nineteenth-Century Literary Imagination*. 2nd ed. Yale University Press, 2000.

Gilead, Sarah. "Magic Abjured: Closure in Children's Fantasy Fiction." *PMLA*, vol. 106, no. 2, 1991, pp. 277–93.

Giskin, Howard. "Chinese Folktales and the Family." *An Introduction to Chinese Culture through the Family*, edited by Howard Giskin and Bettye S. Walsh, State University of New York Press, 2001, pp. 123–39.

Gordon, Avery. *Ghostly Matters: Haunting and the Sociological Imagination*. University of Minnesota Press, 1997.

Greene, Maggie. *Resisting Spirits: Drama Reform and Cultural Transformation in the People's Republic of China*. University of Michigan Press, 2019.

Gu, Ming Dong. "Theory of Fiction: A Non-Western Narrative Tradition." *Narrative*, vol. 14, no. 3, 2006, pp. 311–38.

Guo, Yingjie. *Cultural Nationalism in Contemporary China: The Search for National Identity under Reform*. Routledge, 2003.

Gutierrez, Anna Katrina. "Metamorphosis: The Emergence of Glocal Subjectivities in the Blend of Global, Local, East, and West." *Subjectivity in Asian Children's Literature and Film: Global Theories and Implications*, edited by John Stephens, Routledge, 2013, pp. 19–42.

———. "Globalization and Glocalization." *The Routledge Companion to International Children's Literature*, edited by John Stephens, Celia Abicalil Belmiro, Alice Curry, Lifang Li, and Yasmine S. Motawy, Routledge, 2017, pp. 11–21.

———. *Mixed Magic: Global-Local Dialogues in Fairy Tales for Young Readers*. John Benjamins, 2017.

Gvili, Gal. "Gender and Superstition in Modern Chinese Literature." *Religious*, vol. 10, no. 10, 2019, pp. 1–17.

Haase, Donald, editor. *Fairy Tales and Feminism: New Approaches*. Wayne State University Press, 2004.

———. "Hypertextual Gutenberg: The Textual and Hypertextual Life of Folktales and Fairy Tales in English-Language Popular Print Editions." *Fabula*, vol. 47, no. 3–4, 2006, pp. 222–30.

Hartman, Charles. "Literary Chinese." *The Indiana Companion to Traditional Chinese Literature*, vol. 2, edited by William H. Nienhauser Jr., Indiana University Press, 1998, pp. 92–97.

Harvey, Colin. *Fantastic Transmedia: Narrative, Play and Memory Across Science Fiction and Fantasy Storyworlds*. Palgrave Macmillan, 2015.

Hassler-Forest, Dan. *Science Fiction, Fantasy, and Politics: Transmedia World-Building Beyond Capitalism*. Rowman & Littlefield International, 2016.

Hayward, Philip, and Pan Wang. "Millennial Měirényú: Mermaids in 21st Century Chinese Culture." *Scaled for Success: The Internationalisation of the Mermaid*, edited by Philip Hayward, Indiana University Press, John Libbey Publishing, 2018, pp. 129–47.

Henningsen, Lena. "Harry Potter with Chinese Characteristics: Plagiarism between Orientalism and Occidentalism." *China Information*, vol. 20, no. 2, 2006, pp. 275–311.

Herman, David. *Story Logic: Problems and Possibilities of Narrative*. University of Nebraska Press, 2002.

———. "Cognitive Narratology." *Handbook of Narratology*, 2nd ed., edited by Peter Hühn, Jan Christoph Meister, John Pier, and Wolf Schmid, Berlin: Walter de Gruyter, 2014, 46–64.

Herman, David, James Phelan, Peter J. Rabinowitz, Brian Richardson, and Robyn Warhol. *Narrative Theory: Core Concepts and Critical Debates*. The Ohio State University Press, 2012.

Hipkins, Danielle. *Contemporary Italian Women Writers and Traces of the Fantastic: The Creation of Literary Space*. Legenda, 2007.

Ho, Aaron K. H. "The Lack of Chinese Lesbians: Double Crossing in *Blue Gate Crossing*." *Genders*, no. 49, 2009. www.colorado.edu/gendersarchive1998-2013/2009/02/01/lack-chinese-lesbians-double-crossing-blue-gate-crossing. Accessed 11 Aug. 2021.

Hodgkins, John. *The Drift: Affect, Adaptation, and New Perspectives on Fidelity*. Bloomsbury Academic, 2014.

Hogan, Patrick Colm. *Affective Narratology: The Emotional Structure of Stories*. University of Nebraska Press, 2011.

Hsu, Jen-Hao. "Queering Chineseness: The Queer Sphere of Feelings in *Farewell My Concubine* and *Green Snake*." *Asian Studies Review*, vol. 36, no. 1, 2012, pp. 1–17.

Hu, Tingting. *Victims, Perpetrators, and Professionals: The Representation of Women in Chinese Crime Films*. Sussex Academic Press, 2021.

Huang, Dahong. *Tangdai xiaoshuo chongxie yanjiu* [*Studies on Rewriting of Tang Tales*]. Chongqing: Chongqing Press, 2004.

Huang, Martin Weizong. "Dehistoricization and Intertexualization: The Anxiety of Precedents in the Evolution of the Traditional Chinese Novel." *Chinese Literature: Essays, Articles, Reviews (CLEAR)*, vol. 12, 1990, pp. 45–68.

———. "Introduction." *Snakes' Legs: Sequels, Continuations, Rewritings, and Chinese Fiction*, edited by Martin W. Huang, University of Hawai'i Press, 2004, pp. 1–18.

Huang, Michelle N. "Creative Evolution: Narrative Symbiogenesis in Larissa Lai's *Salt Fish Girl*." *Amerasia Journal*, vol. 42, no. 2, 2016, pp. 118–38.

Huang, Peter I-min. "Material Feminism and Ecocriticism: Nu Wa, White Snake, and Mazu." *Neohelicon*, vol. 44, no. 2, 2017, pp. 361–73.

Hughes, Henry J. "Familiarity of the Strange: Japan's Gothic Tradition." *Criticism: A Quarterly for Literature and the Arts*, vol. 42, no. 1, 2000, pp. 59–89.

Hume, Kathryn. *Fantasy and Mimesis: Response to Reality in Western Literature.* Methuen, 1984.

Hunt, Peter, and Millicent Lenz. *Alternative Worlds in Fantasy Fiction.* Continuum, 2001.

Huntington, Rania. "The Supernatural." *The Columbia History of Chinese Literature*, edited by Victor H. Mair, Columbia University Press, 2001, pp. 110–31.

———. *Alien Kind: Foxes and Late Imperial Chinese Narrative.* Harvard University Press, 2003.

Huss, Ann Louise. "Old Tales Retold: Contemporary Chinese Fiction and the Classical Tradition." Dissertation. Columbia University, 2000.

Hutcheon, Linda. *A Theory of Adaptation.* Routledge, 2006.

———. "Harry Potter and the Novice's Confession." *The Lion and the Unicorn*, vol. 32, no. 2, 2008, pp. 169–79.

Idema, Wilt L. *The White Snake and Her Son, a Translation of the Precious Scroll of Thunder Peak, With Related Texts.* Hackett Publishing Company, 2009.

———. "Old Tales for New Times: Some Comments on the Cultural Translation of China's Four Great Folktales in the Twentieth Century." *Taiwan Journal of East Asian Studies*, vol. 9, no. 1, 2012, pp. 25–46.

Inwood, Heather. "Internet Literature: From YY to MOOC." *The Columbia Companion to Modern Chinese Literature*, edited by Kirk A. Denton, Columbia University Press, 2016, pp. 436–40.

Iwabuchi, Koichi. "East Asian Popular Culture and Inter-Asian Referencing." *Routledge Handbook of East Asian Popular Culture*, edited by Koichi Iwabuchi, Eva Tsai, and Chris Berry, Routledge, 2017, pp. 24–33.

Jackson, Rosemary. *Fantasy: The Literature of Subversion.* Methuen, 1981.

Jackson, Stevi, Jieyu Liu, and Juhyun Woo. "Introduction: Reflections on Gender, Modernity and East Asian Sexualities." *East Asian Sexualities: Modernity, Gender and New Sexual Cultures*, edited by Stevi Jackson, Jieyu Liu, and Juhyun Woo, Zed Books, 2013, pp. 1–30.

Jacobs, Katrien. *The Afterglow of Women's Pornography in Post-Digital China.* Palgrave Macmillan. 2015.

James, Edward, and Farah Mendlesohn. Introduction. *The Cambridge Companion to Fantasy Literature*, edited by Edward James and Farah Mendlesohn, Cambridge University Press, 2012, pp. 1–4.

Jay, Jennifer W. "Imagining Matriarchy: 'Kingdoms of Women' in Tang China." *Journal of the American Oriental Society*, vol. 116, no. 2, 1996, pp. 220–29.

Jenkins, Henry. *Convergence Culture: Where Old and New Media Collide.* New York University Press, 2008.

———. "Adaptation, Extension, Transmedia." *Literature/Film Quarterly*, vol. 45, no. 2. 2017.

Johnson, Barbara. "Taking Fidelity Philosophically." *Difference in Translation*, edited by Joseph F. Graham, Cornell University Press, 1985, pp. 142–48.

Jones, Leslie Ellen. "Fairies." *Medieval Folklore: A Guide to Myths, Legends, Tales, Beliefs, and Customs*, vol. 1, edited by Carl Lindahl, John McNamara, and John Lindow, ABC-CLIO, 2000, pp. 298–303.

Joo, Hee-Jung Serenity. "Reproduction, Reincarnation, and Human Cloning: Literary and Racial Forms in Larissa Lai's *Salt Fish Girl*." *Critique: Studies in Contemporary Fiction*, vol. 55, no. 1, 2014, pp. 46–59.

Kao, Karl S. Y. *Classical Chinese Tales of the Supernatural and the Fantastic: Selections from the Third to the Tenth Century.* Indiana University Press, 1985.

King, Ambrose Yeo-chi. "Kuan-his and Network Building: A Sociological Interpretation." *Daedalus*, vol. 120, no. 2, 1991, pp. 63–84.

Kinkley, Jeffrey C. *Visions of Dystopia in China's New Historical Novels.* Columbia University Press, 2015.

Ko, Dorothy. *Teachers of the Inner Chambers: Women and Culture in Seventeenth-Century China.* Stanford University Press, 1994.

Koehler, Julie, Shandi Lynne Wagner, Anne E. Duggan, and Adrion Dula, editors and translators. *Women Writing Wonder: An Anthology of Subversive Nineteenth-Century British, French, and German Fairy Tales.* Wayne State University Press, 2021.

Lai, Paul. "Stinking Bodies: Mythological Futures and the Olfactory Sense in Larissa Lai's Salt Fish Girl." *MELUS*, vol. 33, no. 4, 2008, pp. 167–87.

Lai, Whalen. "Unpacking 'Madame White Snake.'" *Asian Folklore Studies*, vol. 51, no. 1, 1992, pp. 51–66.

Law, Fiona Yuk-wa. "Fabulating Animals–Human Affinity: Towards an Ethics of Care in *Monster Hunt* and *Mermaid*." *Journal of Chinese Cinemas*, vol. 11, no. 1, 2017, pp. 69–95.

Leavy, Barbara Fass. *In Search of the Swan Maiden: A Narrative on Folklore and Gender*. New York University Press, 1994.

Lee, Haiyan. *The Stranger and the Chinese Moral Imagination*. Stanford University Press, 2014.

Lee, Ken-fang. "Cultural Translation and the Exorcist: A Reading of Kingston's and Tan's Ghost Stories." *MELUS*, vol. 29, no. 2, 2004, pp. 105–27.

Lee, Sung-Ae. "The Fairy-Tale Film in Korea." *Fairy-Tale Films Beyond Disney: International Perspectives*, edited by Jack Zipes, Pauline Greenhill, and Kendra Magnus-Johnston, Routledge, 2015, pp. 207–21.

———. "Lost in Liminal Space: Amnesiac and Incognizant Ghosts in Korean Drama." *Mosaic: a journal for the interdisciplinary study of literature*, vol. 48, no. 3, 2015, pp. 125–40.

Lefebvre, Benjamin. "Introduction: Reconsidering Textual Transformations in Children's Literature." *Textual Transformations in Children's Literature: Adaptations, Translations, Reconsiderations*, edited by Benjamin Lefebvre, Routledge, 2013, pp. 1–6.

Lehtonen, Sanna. "Invisible Girls: Discourses of Femininity and Power in Children's Fantasy." *International Research in Children's Literature*, vol. 1, no. 2, 2008, 213–26.

Levy, Michael, and Farah Mendlesohn. *Children's Fantasy Literature: An Introduction*. Cambridge University Press, 2016.

Li, Fengmao. *Shenhua yu bianyi: yige "chang yu feichang" de wenhua siwei* [*Deification and Variation: The Culture of Thinking Between Normal and Abnormal*]. Beijing: Zhonghua shuju. 2010.

Li, Jing. "Chinese Tales." *The Greenwood Encyclopedia of Folktales and Fairy Tales*, edited by Donald Haase, Greenwood Press, 2008, pp. 194–200.

Li, Lifang. "Subjectivity and Culture Consciousness in Chinese Children's Literature." *Subjectivity in Asian Children's Literature and Film: Global Theories and Implications*, edited by John Stephens, Routledge, 2012, pp.79–95.

Liang, Yan. "A Myth about the Present: The Shaw Brothers' *The Monkey Goes West* Series in the 1960s." *The Journal of Popular Culture*, vol. 45, no. 6, 2012, pp. 1289–1309.

Lin, Chen. *Shenguai xiaoshuo shi* [*The History of Novels about Gods and Strange*]. Hangzhou: Zhejiang Guji Press, 1998.

Loock, Kathleen, and Constantine Verevis. "Introduction: Remake/Remodel." *Film Remakes, Adaptations and Fan Productions: Remake/Remodel*, edited by Kathleen Loock and Constantine Verevis, Palgrave Macmillan, 2012, pp. 1–15.

Lorde, Audre. *Sister Outsider: Essays and Speeches*. Crossing Press, 1984.

Louttit, Chris. "Remixing Period Drama: The Fan Video and the Classic Novel Adaptation." *Adaptation*, vol. 6, no. 2, 2013, pp. 172–86.

Lu, Xun. *A Brief History of Chinese Fiction*. Foreign Language Press, 1976.

Lugg, Alexander. "Chinese Online Fiction: Taste publics, Entertainment, and Candle in the Tomb." *Chinese Journal of Communication*, vol. 4, no. 2, 2011, pp. 121–36.

Luo, Hui. "The Ghost of *Liaozhai*: Pu Songling's Ghostlore and Its History of Reception." Dissertation. University of Toronto, 2009.

Luo, Liang "The White Snake as the New Woman of Modern China." *New Modern Chinese Women and Gender Politics: The Centennial of the End of the Qing Dynasty*, edited by Chen Ya-chen, Routledge, 2014, pp. 86–103.

———. "Writing Green Snake, Dancing White Snake, and the Cultural Revolution as Memory and Imagination—Centered on Yan Geling's *Baishe*." *Frontiers of Literary Studies in China*, vol. 11, no. 1, 2017, pp. 7–37.

———. *The Global White Snake*. University of Michigan Press, 2021.

———, editor. *Retelling Fantastic Tales in the East Asian and Global Contexts*. Brill, forthcoming.

Macdonald, Sean. *Animation in China: History, Aesthetics, Media*. Routledge, 2016.

———. "Notes on the Fantastic in Chinese Literature and Film." *Frontiers of Literary Studies in China*, vol. 13, no. 1, 2019, pp. 1–24.

Madsen, Deborah Lea. "'Mo No Boy': The Negative Rhetoric of Nation in the Work of Wayson Choy." *West Coast Line*, vol. 42, no. 3, 2008, pp. 100–11.

———. "The Rhetoric of Double Allegiance: Imagined Communities in North American Diasporic Chinese Literatures." *Recherches anglaises et nord américaines*, vol. 46, 2013, pp. 29–44.

Martin, Fran. *Backward Glances: Contemporary Chinese Cultures and the Female Homoerotic Imaginary*. Duke University Press, 2010.

McCall, Leslie. "The Complexity of Intersectionality." *Signs*, vol. 30, no. 3, 2005, pp. 1771–1800.

McCallum, Robyn. *Screen Adaptations and the Politics of Childhood: Transforming Children's Literature into Film*. Palgrave Macmillan, 2018.

McCort, Jessica R. "Introduction: Why Horror? (Or, The Importance of Being Frightened)." *Reading in the Dark: Horror in Children's Literature and Culture*, edited by Jessica R. McCort, University Press of Mississippi, 2016, pp. 3–36.

Meissner, Werner. "New Intellectual Currents in the People's Republic of China." *China in Transition: Issues and Policies*, edited by David C. B. Teather and Herbert S. Yee, Macmillan Press, 1999, 3–24.

Mendlesohn, Farah and Edward James. *A Short History of Fantasy*. Libri Publishing, 2012.

Miller, Alan L. "The Swan-Maiden Revisited: Religious Significance of 'Divine-Wife' Folktales with Special Reference to Japan." *Asian Folklore Studies*, vol. 46, no. 1, 1987, pp. 55–86.

Monaghan, Whitney. *Queer Girls, Temporality and Screen Media: Not 'Just a Phase.'* Palgrave Macmillan, 2016.

Moraru, Christian. "Intertextuality." *Routledge Encyclopedia of Narrative Theory*, edited by David Herman, Manfred Jahn, and Marie-Laure Ryan, Routledge, 2005, pp. 256–61.

Morris, Robyn L. "What does it mean to be human?: Racing Monsters, Clones and Replicants." *Foundation: The International Review of Science Fiction*, vol. 33, no. 91, 2004, pp. 81–96.

Moskowitz, Marc. "Yang-Sucking She-Demons: Penetration, Fear of Castration, and Other Freudian Angst in Modern Chinese Cinema." *The Minor Arts of Daily Life: Popular Culture in Taiwan*, edited by David K. Jordan, Andrew D. Morris, and Marc L. Moskowitz, University of Hawai'i Press, 2004, pp. 204–18.

Murai, Mayako. *From Dog Bridegroom to Wolf Girl: Contemporary Japanese Fairy-Tale Adaptations in Conversation with the West*. Wayne State University Press, 2015.

Murray, Simone. *The Adaptation Industry: The Cultural Economy of Contemporary Literary Adaptation*. Routledge, 2012.

Nash, Jennifer C. "Re-thinking Intersectionality." *Feminist Review*, no. 89, 2008, pp. 1–15.

Ni, Zhange. "Xiuzhen (Immortality Cultivation) Fantasy: Science, Religion, and the Novels of Magic/Superstition in Contemporary China." *Religions*, vol. 11, no. 1, 2020, pp. 1–24.

———. "Fantasy / Magical Experiences and Postsecular Fiction." *Literature and Religious Experience*, edited by Matthew J. Smith and Caleb D. Spencer, Bloomsbury, 2022, pp. 241–58.

Nienhauser, William H. Jr. *Tang Dynasty Tales: A Guided Reader*. World Scientific, 2010.

Ong, Walter. *Orality and Literary: The Technologizing of the Word*. Methuen, 1982.

Ostriker, Alicia. "The Thieves of Language: Women Poets and Revisionist Mythmaking." *Signs*, vol. 8, no. 1, 1982, pp. 68–90.

———. *Feminist Revision and the Bible*. Blackwell, 1993.

Ou, Li-Chuan. "A New Interpretation of the Myths in The Dream of the Red Chamber—Rethinking from the Perspective of Feminist Critique." *Journal of Chinese Literature of National Cheng Kung University*, vol. 30, 2010, pp. 101–40.

Oziewicz, Marek C. "Restorative Justice Scripts in Ursula K. Le Guin's *Voices.*" *Children's Literature in Education*, vol. 42, no. 1, 2011, pp. 33–43.

Palo, Annbritt, and Lena Manderstedt. "Beyond the Characters and the Reader? Digital Discussions on Intersectionality in *The Murderer's Ape.*" *Children's Literature in Education*, vol. 50, no. 2, 2019, pp. 125–41.

Pang, Laikwan. "The State Against Ghosts: A Genealogy of China's Film Censorship Policy." *Screen*, vol. 52, no. 4, 2011, pp. 461–76.

Plaks, Andrew. *Archetype and Allegory in the Dream of the Red Chamber*. Princeton University Press, 1976.

Plate, Liedeke. *Transforming Memories in Contemporary Women's Rewriting*. Palgrave Macmillan, 2011.

Prusek, Jaroslev. "History and Epics in China and in the West." *Diogenes*, vol. 11, no. 42, 1963, pp. 20–43.

Pugsley, Peter C. *Exploring Morality and Sexuality in Asia Cinema: Cinematic Boundaries*. Routledge, 2015.

Purkiss, Diane. "Women's Rewriting of Myth." *The Woman's Companion to Mythology*, edited by Carolyne Larrington, Pandora, 1992, pp. 441–57.

Qiao, Yigang and Wang, Shuainai. "Zhongguo Ertong Wenxue de Xingbie Yanjiu Shijian jiqi Fansi." ["Gender Studies of Chinese Children's Literature: Practices and Reflections"]. *Zhongguo Xiandai Wenxue Yanjiu Congkan* [*Modern Chinese Literature Studies*] no. 5, 2017, pp. 17–29.

Qin, Liyan. "Trans-media Strategies of Appropriation, Narrativization, and Visualization: Adaptations of Literature in a Century of Chinese Cinema." Dissertation. University of California, San Diego, 2007.

———. "The Intertwinement of Chinese Film and Literature: Choices and Strategies in Adaptations." *A Companion to Chinese Cinema*, edited by Zhang Yingjin, Blackwell, 2012, pp. 361–76.

Reider, Noriko T. "Transformation of the Oni: From the Frightening and Diabolical to the Cute and Sexy." *Asian Folklore Studies*, vol. 62. 2003, pp. 133–57.

Reinders, Eric. "Reading Tolkien in Chinese." *Journal of the Fantastic in the Arts*, vol. 25, no. 1, 2014, pp. 3–27.

Rich, Adrienne. "When We Dead Awaken: Writing as Re-vision." *College English*, vol. 34, no. 1, 1972, pp. 18–30.

Roas, David. "The Female Fantastic vs. The Feminist Fantastic: Gender and the Transgression of the Real." *CLCWeb: Comparative Literature and Culture*, vol. 22, no. 4, 2020, pp. 1–10.

Roberts, Jude, and Esther MacCallum-Stewart, editors. *Gender and Sexuality in Contemporary Popular Fantasy*. Routledge, 2016.

Rogers, Brett M., and Benjamin Eldon Stevens, editors. *Classical Traditions in Modern Fantasy*. Oxford University Press, 2017.

Rojas, Carlos. "Queering Time: Disjunctive Temporalities in Modern China." *Frontiers of Literary Studies in China*, vol. 10, no. 1, 2015, pp. 1–8.

Rosenlee, Li-Hsiang Lisa. *Confucianism and Women: A Philosophical Interpretation*. State University of New York Press, 2006.

Rehling, Petra. "Harry Potter, Wuxia and the Transcultural Flow of Fantasy Texts in Taiwan." *Inter-Asia Cultural Studies*, vol. 13, no. 1, 2012, pp. 69–87.

Salmonson, Jessica Amanda. *The Encyclopedia of Amazons: Women Warriors from Antiquity to the Modern Era*. Open Road Media, 2015.

Sanders, Julie. *Adaptation and Appropriation*. Routledge, 2006.

Schafer, Edward H. *The Divine Woman: Dragon Ladies and Rain Maidens in Tang Literature*. University of California Press, 1973.

Schanoes, Veronica L. *Fairy Tales, Myth, and Psychoanalytic Theory: Feminism and Retelling the Tale*. Ashgate, 2014.

Schleep, Elisabeth. "'Steady Updating Is the Kingly Way': The VIP System and Its Impact on the Creation of Online Novels." *Chinese Literature Today*, vol. 5, no. 1, 2015, pp. 65–73.

Sellers, Susan. *Myth and Fairy Tale in Contemporary Women's Fiction*. Palgrave, 2001.

Shahar, Meir. "Vernacular Fiction and the Transmission of Gods' Cults in Late Imperial China." *Unruly Gods: Divinity and Society in China*, edited by Meir Shahar and Robert Weller, University of Hawai'i Press, 1996, pp. 184–211.

Shamoon, Deborah. *Passionate Friendship: The Aesthetics of Girl's Culture in Japan*. University of Hawai'i Press, 2012.

———. "The Yōkai in the Database: Supernatural Creatures and Folklore in Manga and Anime." *The Fairy Tale in Japan*, special issue of *Marvels & Tales*, vol. 27, no. 2, 2013, pp. 276–89.

Shang, Wei. "The Literati Era and Its Demise (1723–1840)." *The Cambridge History of Chinese Literature, Volume II From 1375*, edited by Kang-I Sun Chang. Cambridge University Press, 2010, pp. 245–342.

Shen, Lisa Chu. "Femininity and Gender in Contemporary Chinese School Stories: The Case of *Tomboy Dai An*." *Children's Literature in Education*, vol. 50, no. 3, 2019, pp. 278–96.

———. "The Effeminate Boy and Queer Boyhood in Contemporary Chinese Adolescent Novels." *Children's Literature in Education*, vol. 51, no. 1, 2020, pp. 63–81.

Simon, Sherry. *Gender in Translation*. Routledge, 1996.

Smith, Steve. "Talking Toads and Chinless Ghosts: The Politics of 'Superstitious' Rumors in the People's Republic of China, 1961–1965." *American Historical Review*, vol. 111, no. 2, 2006, pp. 405–27.

Song, Mingwei. "Popular Genre Fiction: Science Fiction and Fantasy." *The Columbia Companion to Modern Chinese Literature*, edited by Kirk A. Denton, Columbia University Press, 2016, pp. 394–99.

Song, Xianlin. "Reconstructing the Confucian Ideal in 1980s China: The 'Cultural Craze' and New Confucianism." *New Confucianism: A Critical Examination*, edited by John Makeham, Palgrave Macmillan, 2003, pp. 81–104.

Sontag, Susan. *On Photography*. Farrar, Straus and Giroux, 1977.

Spengler, Birgit. *Literary Spinoffs: Rewriting the Classics—Re-Imagining the Community*. Campus Verlag, 2015.

Stam, Robert. *Subversive Pleasure: Bakhtin, Cultural Criticism and Film*. Johns Hopkins University Press, 1989.

Stam, Robert, and Alessandra Raengo, editors. *Literature and Film: A Guide to the Theory and Practice of Adaptation*. Blackwell, 2005.

Stephens, John. "Advocating Multiculturalism: Migrants in Australian Children's Literature after 1972." *Children's Literature Association Quarterly*, vol. 15, no. 4, 1990, pp. 180–85.

———. *Language and Ideology in Children's Fiction*. Longman. 1992.

———. "Witch-Figures in Recent Children's Fiction: The Subaltern and the Subversive." *The Presence of the Past in Children's Literature*, edited by Ann Lawson Lucas, Praeger Publishers, 2003, pp.195–202.

———. "Retelling Stories across Time and Cultures." *The Cambridge Companion to Children's Literature*, edited by M. O. Grenby and Andrea Immel, Cambridge University Press, 2009, pp. 91–107.

———. "Narratology." *The Routledge Companion to Children's Literature*, edited by David Rudd, Routledge, 2010, pp. 51–62.

Stephens, John, and Robyn McCallum. *Retelling Stories, Framing Culture: Traditional Story and Metanarratives in Children's Literature.* Garland, 1998.

———. "Discourses of Femininity and the Intertextual Construction of Feminist Reading Positions." *Girls, Boys, Books, Toys: Gender in Children's Literature and Culture,* edited by Beverly Lyon Clark and Margaret R. Higonnet, The John Hopkins University Press, 1999, pp. 130–41.

Stockwell, Peter. *Cognitive Poetics: An Introduction.* Routledge, 2002.

Tang, Simin. "Chuanju baishezhuan tanwei." ["A Preliminary Discussion of the Sichuan Opera White Snake"]. *Zhongguo Xiju* [*Chinese Theatre*], no. 4, 2013, pp. 56–58.

Tao, Dongfeng. "Zhongguo wenxue yi jinru zhuangshen nonggui de shidai? You 'xuanhuan' xiaoshuo yinfa de yidian lianxiang." ["Has Chinese Literature Entered an Era of Being Deliberately Mystifying? A Few Thoughts on 'Fantasy Fiction'"]. *Dangdai wentan* [*Contemporary Literary Criticism*], vol. 5, 2006, pp. 8–11.

Tatar, Maria. *Off With Their Heads! Fairytales and the Culture of Childhood.* Princeton University Press, 1992.

Teverson, Andrew. *Fairy Tale.* Routledge, 2013.

Thornham, Sue, and Pengpeng Feng. "'Just a Slogan': Individualism, Post-Feminism, and Female Subjectivity in Consumerist China." *Feminist Media Studies,* vol. 10, no. 2, 2010, pp. 195–211.

Tian, Xiaofei. "Slashing the Three Kingdoms: A Case Study of Fan Production on the Chinese Web." *Modern Chinese Literature and Culture,* vol. 27, no. 1, 2015, pp. 224–77.

Tian, Xiaoli, and Michael Adorjan. "Fandom and Coercive Empowerment: The Commissioned Production of Chinese Online Literature." *Media, Culture & Society,* vol. 38, no. 6, 2016, pp. 881–900.

Ting, Nai Tung. *The Cinderella Cycle in China and Indo-China.* Helsinki: Suomalainen Tiedeakatemia, 1974.

———. *A Type Index of Chinese Folktales: In the Oral Tradition and Major Works of Non-Religious Classical Literature.* Helsinki: Suomalainen Tiedeakatemia, 1978.

Todorov, Tzvetan. *The Fantastic: A Structural Approach to a Literary Genre.* Translated by Richard Howard, Cornell University Press, 1975.

Tolkien, J. R. R. "On Fairy-Stories." *Tree and Leaf.* Unwin, 1964, pp. 3–83.

Tong, Rosemary, and Tina Fernandes Botts. *Feminist Thought: A More Comprehensive Introduction.* Fifth Edition. Routledge, 2018.

Trites, Roberta Seelinger. "Introduction: The Uncanny in Children's Literature." *Children's Literature Association Quarterly,* vol. 26, no. 4, 2001, p. 162.

Tsai, Hsiu-chih. "Female Sexuality: Its Allurement and Repression in Geling Yan's 'White Snake.'" *American Journal of Semiotics*, vol. 23, no. 1–4, 2007, pp. 123–46.

Tse, Michael S. C., and Maleen Z. Gong. "Online Communities and Commercialization of Chinese Internet Literature." *Journal of Internet Commerce*, vol. 11, no. 2, 2012, pp. 100–116.

Turner, Mark. "The Cognitive Study of Art, Language, and Literature." *Poetics Today*, vol. 23, no. 1, 2002, pp. 9–20.

Tuttle, Lisa. "Gender." *The Encyclopedia of Fantasy*, edited by John Clute and John Grant, Orbit, 1997, pp. 393–95.

Van Gulik, Robert. *Sexual Life in Ancient China: A Preliminary Survey of Chinese Sex and Society from ca. 1500 B.C. till 1644 A.D.* Brill, 1974.

Venuti, Lawrence. "Adaptation, Translation, Critique." *Journal of Visual Culture*, vol. 6, no. 1, 2007, pp. 25–43.

Villegas-López, Sonia. "Body Technologies: Posthuman Figurations in Larissa Lai's *Salt Fish Girl* and Jeanette Winterson's *The Stone Gods*." *Critique: Studies in Contemporary Fiction*, vol. 56, no. 1, 2015, pp. 26–41.

Wagner, Geoffrey. *The Novel and the Cinema*. Fairleigh Dickinson University Press, 1975.

Waller, Alison. "'Solid All the Way Through': Margaret Mahy's Ordinary Witches." *Children's Literature in Education*, vol. 35, no. 1, 2004, pp. 77–86.

Wan, Margaret B. *Green Peony and the Rise of the Chinese Martial Arts Novel*. State University of New York Press, 2009.

Wang, Ban. "History in a Mythical Key: Temporality, Memory, and Tradition in Wang Anyi's Fiction." *Journal of Contemporary China*, vol. 12, no. 37, 2003, pp. 607–21.

Wang, Cathy Yue. "Officially Sanctioned Adaptation and Affective Fan Resistance: The Transmedia Convergence of the Online Drama *Guardian* in China." *Series: International Journal of TV Serial Narratives*, vol. 5, no. 2, 2019, pp. 45–58.

———. "'You Two Seem to Be the Same Person': Death, Sexuality and Female Doubles in Chinese Young Adult Fiction and Film." *Sexuality in Literature for Children and Young Adults*, edited by Paul Venzo and Kristine Moruzi, Routledge, 2021, pp. 127–39.

Wang, Cathy Yue, and Maria Alberto, editors. *Catching Chen Qing Ling: The Untamed and Adaptation, Production, and Reception in Transcultural Contexts*. Peter Lang, 2023, forthcoming.

Wang, Cathy Yue, and Tingting Hu. "Transmedia Storytelling in Mainland China: Interaction between TV Drama and Fan Narratives in *The Disguiser*."

Transmedia in Asia and the Pacific: Industry, Practice and Transcultural Dialogues, edited by Filippo Gilardi and Celia Lam, Palgrave Macmillan, 2021, pp. 107–26.

Wang, David Der-wei. "Second Haunting." *The Monster that is History: History, Violence, and Fictional Writing in Twentieth-Century China*. University of California Press, 2004, pp. 262–91.

Wang, Hongjian. "*A Chinese Ghost Story*: A Hong Kong Comedy Film's Cult Following in Mainland China." *Journal of Chinese Cinemas*, vol. 12, no. 2, 2018, pp. 142–57.

Wang, Jing. *The Story of Stone: Intertextuality, Ancient Chinese Stone Lore, and the Stone Symbolism in Dream of the Red Chamber, Water Margin, and The Journey to the West*. Duke University Press, 1992.

Wang, Yiman. *Remaking Chinese Cinema: Through the Prism of Shanghai, Hong Kong, and Hollywood*. University of Hawai'i Press, 2013.

Wang, Yuxi. "Globalization of Chinese Online Literature: Understanding Transnational Reading of Chinese *Xuanhuan* Novels Among English Readers." *Inquiries Journal*, vol. 9, no. 12, 2017, pp. 1–16.

Wilcox, Emily. *Revolutionary Bodies: Chinese Dance and the Socialist Legacy*. University of California Press, 2019.

Wilkie, Christine. "Relating Texts: Intertextuality." *Understanding Children's Literature*, edited by Peter Hunt, Routledge, 1999, pp. 130–37.

Williamson, Jamie. *The Evolution of Modern Fantasy: From Antiquarianism to the Ballantine Adult Fantasy Series*. Palgrave Macmillan, 2015.

Willis, Andy. "Painted Skin: Negotiating Mainland China's Fear of the Supernatural." *Asian Cinema*, vol. 22, no. 1, 2011, pp. 20–30.

Wong, Alvin Ka Hin. "Transgenderism as a Heuristic Device: On the Cross-historical and Transnational Adaptations of the Legend of the White Snake." *Transgender China*, edited by Howard Chiang, Palgrave Macmillan, 2012, pp. 127–58.

Woodland, Sarah. *Remaking Gender and the Family: Perspectives on Contemporary Chinese-Language Film Remakes*. Brill, 2018.

Wu, Angela Xiao, and Yige Dong. "What Is Made-in-China Feminism(s)? Gender Discontent and Class Friction in Post-Socialist China." *Critical Asian Studies*, vol. 51, no. 4, 2019, pp. 471–92.

Wu, Laura H. "Through the Prism of Male Writing: Representation of Lesbian Love in Ming-Qing Literature." *Nan Nü: Men, Women and Gender in China*, vol. 4, no. 1, 2002, pp. 1–34.

Wu, Qingyun. *Female Rule in Chinese and English Literary Utopias.* Syracuse University Press, 1995.

Xiao, Faye Hui. *Youth Economy, Crisis, and Reinvention in Twenty-First-Century China: Morning Sun in the Tiny Times.* Routledge, 2020.

Xu, Lanjun. "Constructing Girlhood: Female Adolescence, Depression and the Making of a Female Tradition in Modern Chinese Literature." *Frontiers of Literary Studies in China*, vol. 5, no. 3, 2011, pp. 321–49.

Xu, Yanrui, and Ling Yang. "Forbidden Love: Incest, Generational Conflict, and the Erotics of Power in Chinese BL fiction." *Journal of Graphic Novels and Comics*, vol. 4, no. 1, 2013, pp. 30–43.

Yang, Baoyun. "The Relevance of Confucianism Today." *Asian Values: An Encounter with Diversity*, edited by Josiane Cauquelin, Paul Lim, and Birgit Mayer-Konig, Routledge, 1998, pp. 70–94.

Yang, Lihui. *Nüwa shenhua yu xinyang* [*Nüwa Myth and Belief*]. Beijing: Zhongguo Shehui Kexue Press, 1997.

Yang, Lihui, and Deming An. *Handbook of Chinese Mythology.* ABC-CLIO, 2005.

Yang, Ling, and Hongwei Bao. "Queerly Intimate: Friends, Fans and Affective Communication in a Super Girl Fan Fiction Community." *Cultural Studies*, vol. 26, no. 6, 2012, pp. 842–71.

Yang, Ling, and Yanrui Xu. "Queer Texts, Gendered Imagination, and Popular Feminism in Chinese Web Literature." *Queer/Tongzhi China: New Perspectives on Research, Activism and Media Cultures*, edited by Elisabeth L. Engebretsen, William F. Schroeder, and Hongwei Bao, NIAS Press, 2015, pp. 131–52.

———. "'The Love that Dare Not Speak Its Name': The Fate of Chinese Danmei Communities in the 2014 Anti-Porn Campaign." *The End of Cool Japan: Ethical, Legal, and Cultural Challenges to Japanese Popular Culture*, edited by Mark McLelland, Routledge, 2017, pp. 163–83.

Yang, Yi. *Zhongguo xushi xue* [*Chinese Narratology*]. Beijing: Renmin Press, 1997.

Yao, Xinzhong, and Yanxia Zhao. *Chinese Religion: A Contextual Approach.* Continuum, 2010.

Ye, Shuxian. "Myth in China: The Case of Ancient Goddess Studies." *Religion Compass*, vol. 3, no. 2, 2009, pp. 288–302.

Ye, Shuxian, and Kangyi Sun. "Zhongguo shanggu de nüshen" ["Chinese Primeval Goddesses"]. *Lingnan Xuebao* [*Lingnan Journal of Chinese Studies*], no. 2, 2000, pp. 1–16.

You, Chengcheng. "Ghostly Vestiges of Strange Tales: Horror, History and the Haunted Chinese Child." *New Directions in Children's Gothic: Debatable Lands*, edited by Anna Jackson, Routledge, 2017, pp. 81–101.

Yu, Anthony C. "'Rest, Rest, Perturbed Spirit!' Ghosts in Traditional Chinese Fiction." *Harvard Journal of Asiatic Studies*, vol. 47, no. 2, 1987, pp. 397–434.

Yuan, Ke. Foreword. *Chinese Mythology: An Introduction*, by Anne Birrell, Johns Hopkins University Press, 1993, pp. xi–xii.

Zeitlin, Judith T. *Historian of the Strange: Pu Songling and the Chinese Classical Tale*. Stanford University Press, 1993.

———. "Xiaoshuo." *The Novel. Vol. 1, History, Geography, and Culture*, edited by Franco Moretti, Princeton University Press, 2006, pp. 249–61.

———. *The Phantom Heroine: Ghosts and Gender in Seventeenth-Century Chinese Literature*. University of Hawai'i Press, 2007.

Zeng, Li. "Horror Returns to Chinese Cinema: An Aesthetic of Restraint and the Space of Horror." *Jump Cut: A Review of Contemporary Media*, vol. 51, 2009, n.p.

———. "Adaptation as an Open Process: Dahua Fandom and the Reception of *A Chinese Odyssey*." *Adaptation*, vol. 6, no. 2, 2012, pp. 187–201.

———. "*Painted Skin*: Romance with the Ghostly Femme Fatale in Contemporary Chinese Cinema." *Cinematic Ghosts: Haunting and Spectrality from Silent Cinema to the Digital Era*, edited by Murray Leeder, Bloomsbury Academic & Professional, 2015, pp. 219–33.

Zhang, Jiahua. "Gendered Imaginaries of Childhood in Qin Wenjun's Jia Li and Jia Mei Stories." *Bookbird: A Journal of International Children's Literature*, vol. 44, no. 3, 2006, pp. 48–55.

Zhang, Ying. "Big Heroine Dramas in Contemporary China: Costume, Authenticity and an Alternative History of Women of Power." *Studies in Costume & Performance*, vol. 5, no. 2, 2020, pp. 211–38.

Zhao, Henry Y. H. "Historiography and Fiction in Chinese Culture." *The Novel. Vol. 1, History, Geography, and Culture*, edited by Franco Moretti, Princeton University Press, 2006, pp. 69–93.

Zhao, Xiaohuan. *Classical Chinese Supernatural Fiction: A Morphological History*. Edwin Mellen Press, 2005.

Zhao, Zifeng. "Metamorphoses of Snake Women: Melusine and Madam White." *Melusine's Footprint: Tracing the Legacy of a Medieval Myth*, edited by Misty Urban, Deva Kemmis, and Melissa Ridley Elmes, Brill, 2017, pp. 282–300.

Zheng, Xiqing. "Borderless Fandom and Contemporary Popular Cultural Scene in Chinese Cyberspace." Dissertation. University of Washington, 2016.

Zhu, Ping, and Hui Faye Xiao. "Feminism with Chinese Characteristics: An Introduction." *Feminism with Chinese Characteristics*, edited by Ping Zhu and Hui Faye Xiao, Syracuse University Press, 2021, pp. 1–34.

Zhu, Ziqiang, "Xiaoshuo tonghua: yizhong xinde wenxue ticai" ["Novelized Fairy Tale: A New Literature Genre"]. *Dongbei shida xuebao zhexue shehui ban* [*Journal of Northeast Normal University, Philosophy and Social Sciences*], no. 4, 1992, pp. 63–68.

Zhu, Ziqiang, and He Weiqin. *Zhongguo huanxiang xiaoshuo lun* [*On Chinese Fantasy Fiction*]. Shanghai: Shaonian ertong Press, 2006.

Zimmerman, Bonnie. "Perverse Readings." *Sexual Practice, Textual Theory: Lesbian Cultural Criticism*, edited by Susan J. Wolfe and Julia Penelope, Blackwell, 1993, pp. 135–49.

Zipes, Jack. editor. *Don't Bet on the Prince: Contemporary Feminist Fairy Tales in North America and England*. Routledge, 1986.

———. *Breaking the Magic Spell: Radical Theories of Folk and Fairy Tales*, University Press of Kentucky, 2002.

———. *The Enchanted Screen: The Unknown History of Fairy-Tale Films*. Routledge, 2011.

———. *The Irresistible Fairy Tale: The Cultural and Social History of a Genre*. Princeton University Press, 2012.

Ziv, Amalia. *Explicit Utopias: Rewriting the Sexual in Women's Pornography*. State University of New York Press, 2015.

Zuo, Jiping. "Rethinking Family Patriarchy and Women's Positions in Presocialist China." *Journal of Marriage and Family*, vol. 71, no. 3, 2009, pp. 542–57.

Index